Other Dell Books by Nan Ryan:

NAN RYAN

WRITTEN IN THE STARS

A DELL BOOK

Published by
Dell Publishing
a division of
Bantam Doubleday Dell Publishing Group, Inc.
666 Fifth Avenue
New York, New York 10103

The trademark Dell® is registered in the U.S. Patent and Trademark Office.

ISBN: 0-440-21072-0

Printed in the United States of America

Published simultaneously in Canada

FOR

Kathleen Patricia Ryan Du Quette—Laguna Beach

Kimberly Ann Ryan Morris—Costa Mesa

Sally Jernigan Ryan Allen—Phoenix

The Strong Western Contingent

The Prophet said:
"And lo, the beast looked upon the face of Beauty.
And it stayed its hand from killing. And from
that day, it was as one dead."

An old Arabian Proverb

Prologue

The Nevada Territory
July 1860

➤➤➤ The summer night was warm and clear. A gentle breeze stirred from out of the east. The hour was late. Bright stars winked in the heavens, and a full white moon shone down on Nevada's soaring Sun Mountain. At the mountain's southern base, nestled in its giant shadow, a small, newly built frame house sat alone on the banks of the Carson River.

Inside the darkened house a young prospector and his wife were asleep in their canopied bed. The tired man lay sprawled on his back, a long arm flung up above his dark head. He snored softly. His young, exhausted wife lay on her side, facing away from her husband, the fingers of her pale right hand loosely curled over the mattress's edge, as if poised expectantly, ready to reach out instantly at the slightest sound. Directly beside the bed, less than two feet from its slumbering mother, a week-old infant slept in a hand-carved crib of pungent cedar.

All was quiet and peaceful in the small darkened house and in the vast moon-splashed basin. But as the young parents and their firstborn slept, an unseen danger was silently, steadily stalking them.

Around a fluted slope of the towering mountain, lightning flashed less than a mile from the new frame house, and a brittle twig suddenly snapped and burst into flame. In seconds the rain-starved plain was ablaze. Aided by the rising night wind, the deadly fire swiftly spread.

The blazing inferno raced directly toward the small frame house, a hungry beast greedily devouring everything in its path.

As the fire moved ever closer, the pristine white dwelling, which had dozed so serenely in the shadows, now stood out in bold relief against Sun Mountain, its shape and size distinct, its hue an eerie orange. The hungry beast soon licked at the house's pane glass windows, its hot breath upon the wooden walls, flinging handfuls of bright red sparks upon its cedar roof, angrily demanding entrance.

Inside, the family slept on, oblivious of the uninvited guest pounding on the door. A deadly guest determined to get in, to suck the very breaths from their bodies, to burn the flesh from their bones.

High above the house, on the timbered slopes of the towering Sun Mountain, a small band of Shoshoni Indians—the nomads of the American desert—rode out into a clearing and spotted the blaze below. Their solemn leader, the powerful Chief Red Fox, abruptly pulled up on his prancing mustang. The horse snorted and danced in place. Chief Red Fox's black eyes narrowed with horror as he caught sight of the small frame house about to be enveloped in the leaping, lethal flames.

The chief swiftly raised his right hand, then brought it down and dug his moccasined heels into his big mustang's belly. The horse shot forward down the mountain. Following their chief's signal, six Shoshoni braves, mounted astride fleet-footed horses, raced obediently after him.

Leaping deep ravines, evading huge boulders, the chief and his warriors plunged down the steep, treacherous mountainside. Within minutes they had reached the house on the bank of the river, but already the frame building was engulfed in flames. The heat was fierce. The roar of the blaze, the breaking of glass, and the creaking of burning timber were almost deafening.

Chief Red Fox, patting his terrified mount's sleek neck to calm him, kneed the reluctant mustang closer to the fire. His black eyes staring, his bare chest constricting, Chief Red Fox felt drawn to the blaze, as if a powerful voice from the spirit world were calling to him. Telling him to go inside.

The half dozen braves shook their dark heads and remained mounted. While the worried warriors shouted to their chief to turn back, he moved closer. So close he could feel the intense heat blistering his face, making his eyes sting. Still, he did not turn away. Could not turn away.

Then he heard it.

Faint at first, barely audible above the fire's roar. The chief turned his head, listened, his big body taut with tension. He heard it again. A baby's cry.

Chief Red Fox leaped from his horse and dashed into the burning building. As if guided by an unseen force, his long, powerful legs carried him through the dense, choking smoke straight to the bedroom. Flames danced up the walls and made a funeral pyre of the big canopied bed.

One quick glance, and the chief knew it was too late for the man and woman. But beside the burning bed an infant squalled its outrage from a crib yet untouched by the flames. Chief Red Fox snatched the baby from its crib, grabbed up the bedding, threw the blanket over the screaming infant, and crossed the smoke-filled room.

Cradling the infant to his chest, with one big hand resting protectively on its blanketed tiny head, Chief Red Fox crashed through a window and dropped agilely to the ground, the scent of his own singed hair heavy in his nostrils.

A shout of relief went up from his braves as the chief sprinted to safety. Behind him the house's roof collapsed with a mighty rumble, and the flames shot higher in the night sky. A shower of orange sparks rained down on the chief's bare bronzed back, burning the smooth flesh in a dozen places.

But he never felt it.

He wouldn't realize that he had been burned until hours later. For now the thirty-five-year-old Shoshoni chief was totally focused on the precious human cargo he carried beneath the covering white blanket.

When he reached the cool safety of the rushing Carson River, the chief dropped to his knees beside the water. Gently he placed the crying baby on the bank and swept the smothering covers away from its face and body.

For the first time since his great personal tragedy Chief Red Fox smiled.

Screaming at the top of its lungs, its face beet red, the tiny baby squirmed, its fists flailing, legs kicking. Not one dark hair on its head had been touched by the deadly fire.

As any new father might behave, the fierce, feared Shoshoni chieftain patted awkwardly at the baby's jerking tiny stomach and murmured unintelligible words.

The baby cried on.

The chief smiled on. Then he whistled for his mustang and picked up the screaming infant. He rose and stood in the moonlight beside the river, jostling the child in his arms, bouncing the unhappy baby up and down and gurgling foolishly.

While his warriors watched from a respectful distance, the chief, speaking in his own native tongue, told the baby "not to be afraid, I will not harm you. Nor will I ever allow anyone else to harm you.

"There is"—the chief spoke in a low, soft voice against the baby's downy head—"someone who will love you nearly as much as your own mother loved you."

His faithful mustang mount nuzzled the chief's bare shoulder to announce his ready presence. The chief lifted his head and nodded. Then, with the crying baby held in the crook of his arm, the chief picked up the trailing reins and swung up onto the mustang's bare back.

The horse pricked up his ears when his master said, "Now take us home, Nightwind."

And so it was done.

The mustang whinnied, shook his great head up and down, and turned away from the Carson River. He went at once into a comfortable, ground-eating lope, heading straight toward the looming Sun Mountain. In seconds man, baby, and horse disappeared into the trees blanketing the southern slopes. The Shoshoni braves followed.

Chief Red Fox was eager to be home. His heart was almost free of the pain that had weighed so heavily on him of late. He was sure it was all the work of Appe, creator of the universe. Appe had caused him to come with his braves on this night ride. He hadn't wanted to. They had insisted, had almost dragged him away.

A week had passed since his wife, the beautiful Wind River Shoshoni princess Daughter-of-the-Stars, had given birth to their first child. A boy. Their son had lived for only a few hours. Daughter-of-the-Stars had not stopped grieving since, was near death herself. He had not left her bedside since the baby's death. He worshiped her. He would not wish to live if he lost Daughter-of-the-Stars. And she did not wish to live without their dead son.

Chief Red Fox lowered his eyes to the tiny baby resting trustingly in the crook of his arm. If anyone could save Daughter-of-the-Stars, it was this white man's child.

The full, bright moon had gone down when the chief and his precious cargo reached the High Sierra hideout of his Shoshoni Bannock band. He knee-reined his mustang through the sleeping camp toward his tipi at camp's outer edge. As it had been when he had ridden away, a gathering of the tribe's women remained around his lodge. A fire burned brightly just outside the big tipi; a kettle boiled over the flame.

The women turned sad eyes on him when they saw him nearing. They appeared the same: solemn, resigned, defeated. Fearing he might be too late, Chief Red Fox, still mounted, inquired of the nearest woman, "Daughter-of-the-Stars still lives?"

"She lives, but not much longer," came the reply.

Relieved, the chief slipped from his horse and rushed into his lodge. Ordering the women inside to leave them, he crossed the dim tipi to where Daughter-of-the-Stars lay weak and barely conscious on their bed of furs. Kneeling beside her, Chief Red Fox gently placed the blanket-wrapped baby beside his distraught wife.

He held his breath.

For a moment nothing happened. Daughter-of-the-Stars continued to lie unmoving on her back, her sightless black eyes staring straight up, seeing nothing.

But then the infant squirmed and fretted. Daughter-of-the-Stars felt a welcome warmth against her chilled left arm. Slowly the grieving young woman's dark head turned.

Quickly, carefully the chief swept the white blanket away from the baby's face and looked hopefully at his stirring wife. Puzzled, Daughter-of-the-Stars turned her head more fully and saw the baby lying beside her. At once her dulled dark eyes glimmered with light.

The chief hurried to explain what had happened. But Daughter-of-the-Stars wasn't listening to her husband. Her undivided attention was on the baby at her side. Strength began to flow back into Daughter-of-the-Stars' slender, weakened body. She sat up.

Never taking her eyes off the infant, the frail young woman fully unwrapped its white blankets. She then slipped the long white nightshirt up over its dark head and off. Carefully she removed the baby's diaper.

And for the first time since losing her child, the beautiful Wind River Shoshoni Indian princess smiled.

"My son?" she said in her native tongue, lifted the tiny naked boy up into her arms, and hugged him so tightly his squalling started anew.

The chief was quick to shake his head. "No. The child is of the white man's blood."

Daughter-of-the-Stars's head snapped around. She turned wild, angry eyes on her husband. "This white man's son lives while mine dies!"

She placed the baby back on the soft bed of furs. Then, taking the chief by surprise, she swiftly drew the sharp hunting knife from his waist scabbard.

"No!" pleaded the horrified chief as the blade glittered in the dancing firelight.

Daughter-of-the-Stars grabbed the baby's tiny fist. The infant stopped crying, looked straight up into her wild dark eyes. She quickly slashed an X on the tender inside of his right wrist, bent, and sucked the blood away. She then pricked her finger with the knife's sharp point. When a dark red droplet of blood appeared, she stuck the tip of her finger into the toothless mouth of the baby boy. Starving, he greedily sucked on her finger.

Daughter-of-the-Stars smiled triumphantly, dropped the knife, picked up the baby boy, and said defiantly, "*Now* we are same blood! *My* son. *Mine!*" Her fierce black eyes dared her husband to deny it. Chief Red Fox merely nodded.

Daughter-of-the-Stars touched her husband's bronzed cheek lovingly. Then quickly unlaced her soft doeskin dress to feed her crying, hungry son.

Part One

Part One

Chapter 1

San Francisco, California
August 1895

At a gala dinner party in a luxurious Nob Hill mansion, a dark, lean man in an impeccably tailored suit of slate gray linen lazed comfortably on a Louis XV patterned brocade chair. The legs of the gentleman's stylish trousers were narrow in cut and sharply creased. The cuffs and collar of his pristine white shirt were stiffly starched. His neckpiece was a pale lavender silk four-in-hand with a large, flat knot. His shoes were of the softest English leather and polished to a high gleam.

His slightly too-long jet black hair, raked by dramatic silver streaks at the temples, was clean and carefully brushed. That thick raven hair shone with healthy luster in the light cast by electric chandeliers which party decorators had swagged with silver lamé. The gentleman's tanned face was not handsome in the classical sense. It was a lean, hard-set face with dark, brooding eyes which remained constantly half hidden by lazy lids. Those lids, plus a small white scar beneath his dark left eyebrow, a nose that had been broken and imperfectly set, a mouth that was full enough to suggest sensuality, yet amazingly looked cruel, added up to a slightly sinister appearance.

His name was Benjamin Star, and his manners were polished, his intellect was keen. He had a quick, self-deprecating sense of humor. He was tall, slim, and graceful. He moved with stylish masculine ease. His lean brown hands were nothing short of beautiful, the fingers long with clean, short clipped nails. Those attractive hands never gestured nervously as he spoke. He didn't fidget about on the brocade chair or twist and crane his neck to catch a glimpse of late-arriving guests. He never laughed too loudly or drank to excess or purposely attracted attention to himself.

Benjamin Star was, in every sense of the word, a gentleman. Educated. Cultured. Urbane.

And yet . . .

The expensively dressed ladies in their elegant gowns and glittering diamonds were not drawn to the maddeningly elusive Ben Star because he was the consummate gentleman. Every female present at the summertime Nob Hill party was helplessly attracted to the wild, animalistic side of his nature which they were certain lurked dangerously close to the surface. Was there any doubt that beneath that smooth, imperturbable veneer and those perfectly tailored clothes there was an abundance of such frightening untamed masculinity that no female would be safe alone with him?

Ben Star lifted a sparkling fluted glass to his lips and drank of the fine French champagne. He was casually aware of a trio of very rich, very pretty young socialites staring hungrily at him as if he were a part of the tempting buffet laid out in the mansion's dining room.

A tiny muscle twitched in his tanned jaw. Their twittering reaction to his nearness was nothing new or unique. Ben Star was used to causing a stir. Had been used to it for the past fifteen years.

But at this particular party on this particular night, it seemed to Ben Star that he had lived through just such an annoying moment a hundred times before. Struck with a strong sense of déjà vu, he suddenly longed to bolt and run. To head for the nearest exit this very minute. To seek out the sweet solitude awaiting him far from this crowded room.

He didn't do it.

Rudeness was intolerable. In himself as well as in others. He had been invited to this gathering, and he had accepted. He would stay for a decent length of time, endure the tiresome chatter, the uncomfortable feeling of being trapped. Observed. Caged.

Then tomorrow . . .

"Your attention, everyone!" His beautiful hostess clapped her delicate hands, pulling Ben Star from his reverie. "Your attention please, ladies and gentlemen."

Ben Star's dark eyes lazily lifted, came to rest on the slender blonde in a stunning, frothy gown of midnight blue chiffon. She stood on the marble steps leading down into the sunken drawing room. Widowed for less than a year, the thirty-four-year-old Mrs. Richard Barnes Crocker was one of the Bay City's wealthiest, most respected citizens.

San Francisco's Old Guard adored and admired the glamorous Maribelle Crocker. The manner in which she had conducted herself since the loss of her doting husband was commendable beyond belief. Grief-stricken though she was, Maribelle had continued to discharge her charitable and social duties with a stiff upper lip.

Though desperately lonely she surely must be, the well-brought-up young widow was never seen alone in the company of a gentleman. Never. Maribelle wouldn't consider allowing another man to take her dear departed Richard's place for years. Perhaps never.

Or so they thought.

". . . a lovely surprise for your enjoyment," Maribelle was telling the attentive gathering. "You're all to take your drinks and go out into the garden. I've arranged for the most spectacular pyrotechnic display this city's ever seen!" She flashed a charming smile, her upswept white-blond hair shimmering like moonbeams. "Shall we?" She lifted the swirling skirts of her blue chiffon gown and gracefully descended the marble steps, a bare slender arm extended toward the open French doors across the room.

Laughter and chatter filled the air as the crush of guests excitedly exited the spacious beige and white drawing room, eagerly rushing outdoors to pick a choice spot for watching the fireworks. Waiting politely, Ben Star set his wineglass aside and came to his feet. He unhurriedly started toward the tall French doors to join the guests as they made their way down to the manicured garden.

But the blond, beautiful Maribelle Crocker, authoritatively ushering everyone quickly outdoors, spun about as the last ones spilled out onto the stone terrace. She anxiously pulled the doors shut behind her, leaned back, and smiled at the tall, imposing Ben Star.

Ben smiled back. "Are you shutting them out or us in?" he asked, his voice an intriguing low, deep monotone.

"Both." Maribelle's smile became flirtatious. "Them outdoors in the garden. You inside with me."

"And here I thought you enjoyed fireworks," said Ben, the corners of his cruel-looking mouth lifting in an engaging half-smile.

"Oh, I do," Maribelle said, slowly advancing on him. "You know I do, Ben." She stopped directly before him, lifted a pale, bejeweled hand up to toy with his silk lavender tie. "I thought perhaps while the others watch the burst of fireworks over the bay, you and I could launch skyrockets upstairs in my bed." She smiled up at him and added, "Think I can ignite your fuse, darling?"

Ben Star was not particularly shocked. Despite the spotless reputation enjoyed by the blue-blooded widow, he had shared Maribelle Crocker's bed more than once in the past few weeks. But always they had been totally discreet. He was slightly taken aback that she would suggest such a tryst with a house full of guests.

"Sounds delightful." He was gracious. "But isn't it a bit dangerous?"

"Yes . . . dangerous," Maribelle replied breathlessly, her large emerald eyes already glittering with anticipation. She took his tanned right hand in both her hands and led him toward the marble steps. "We'll have to hurry so we won't get caught." Laughter bubbled from her berry red lips.

Ben Star grinned and allowed the foolish, spoiled woman to lead him up the grand staircase toward the opulent master suite. He had no objection to giving her the physical satisfaction she so brashly sought. Maribelle was a most desirable woman and a delightfully insatiable one as well. He and the beautiful blond widow had spent precious little time in conversation. He knew almost nothing about her, other than the fact that she was like dozens of other pale beauties he'd known over the years.

She desired him because he represented the forbidden, the wild, the dangerous. She was thrilled by the notion of breaking long-lasting taboos. Titillated by the idea of giving herself to a man prohibited by the mores dictated by polite society. Aroused by the savage touch of his dark hands on her pale, perfect flesh. Guilty pleasures.

It mattered little to Ben.

In his arms Maribelle Crocker was a warm, responsive lover, willing to do anything that pleased him. She never failed to provide exquisite sexual pleasure, so he had no call for complaint.

As for Maribelle Crocker, she certainly had no complaints. To her delight, the tall, dark Ben was male enough to make love on demand, and that was all Maribelle cared about. It never for a moment occurred to her that her handsome lover might also be sensitive enough to long secretly for a kind of lovemaking that went beyond the physical.

When the pair stepped inside Maribelle's shadowy bedroom, she dropped Ben's hand and rushed across the room to throw the tall French doors open to the wide balcony.

"There," she said, turning back to him. Smiling, she reached up to release her long blond hair from its diamond-studded restraints so that it spilled about her shoulders the way Ben liked it. "We can watch fireworks while we make some ourselves. Won't that be exciting?"

"Out of this world," said Ben. He moved toward her. She stood framed in the open doors, the suffused glow of the city lights behind her. "Shall I help you with your dress?"

Tingling with excitement, Maribelle eagerly nodded and pushed her shimmering white-blond hair behind her small, perfect ears.

"Would you, darling? Your fingers are so deft at that sort of thing." She looked up into his dark, smoldering eyes, strangely compelling eyes which at odd moments she could almost swear were a deep navy blue instead of black. "I love the feel of your hands on me," she added in a throaty whisper.

Star leaned down, placed a soft, lingering kiss on the left corner of her brightly painted mouth, and teasingly bit her full bottom lip. Then he lifted his hands, cupped her bare shoulders, and gently turned her about so that her back was to him. The first of the fireworks display began as he started unfastening the tiny hooks going down the center back of Maribelle's blue chiffon dress.

Shouts of delight went up from the gay party crowd in the gardens below as great showers of multicolored light filled the night sky. At the same time gasps of delight filled the shadowy bedroom as Ben Star skillfully peeled his hostess's gown and satin chemise down to her waist, then filled his dark hands with her bare ivory breasts.

For a long, enjoyable moment the pair stayed as they were, standing before the open French doors, watching the splendid spectacle. As the blues and reds and golds exploded against the black velvet San Francisco sky, Maribelle Crocker sighed and pressed her head back against Ben's hard chest while his hands caressed and lifted her heavy, swelling breasts, his lean, dexterous fingers teasing and toying with the large, aching nipples.

Squirming happily against his tall, ungiving frame, Maribelle wasn't certain which was the more pleasing sight: the magnificent fireworks in the distance or the dark, skilled hands of her lover covering her pale, naked breasts.

Suddenly dying to get Ben Star into her bed before the wondrous fireworks display ended, Maribelle drew his hands away, turned them up to her face, kissed each palm gratefully, then spun quickly to face him.

"Ben, make love to me. Now, darling, right now. Let's hurry . . . hurry, before it's too late."

Not waiting for his reply, she pushed the frothy blue skirts of her gown down over her generous hips, squirming to be free of them. Watching her with a half-smile curving his lips, Ben Star leisurely shrugged wide shoulders out of his gray linen suit coat. As he pulled the jacket off, a folded paper fell out of an inside pocket. It fluttered to the deep beige carpet. Curious, Maribelle kicked her lovely gown aside, bent, and picked up the fallen paper.

"What's this?" she said, and withheld it when Ben reached for it. Lips parted questioningly, she unfolded the slim document and saw that it was the current Union Pacific train schedule. "Denver, Colorado," had been circled in red ink. Her emerald eyes frantically met his. "Darling, you're not planning to—"

Before she could finish her question, Ben Star silenced her with a commanding kiss. Pulling her close, he thrust a lean brown hand into her flowing white-blond tresses.

In the shadowy light a wide silver bracelet flashed on Star's dark right wrist. Concealed beneath that silver bracelet was a white, satiny scar.

The scar was a perfectly shaped X.

Chapter 2

On that same August evening, three thousand miles across
America, a young woman stood alone on the balcony of a
Washington, D.C., town house. She was an exotic-looking creature. Her
hair was as black as the darkest midnight, and it reached to her waist
when unbound. Her skin was as pale and flawless as porcelain.

A tall, slender woman, she wore a cool pastel gown which was the
exact same color as her large, expressive eyes, an enchanting pale violet. Shaded by a double row of black, spiky lashes, those violet eyes
darkened to purple when she was angry or aroused. Directly above
those magnificent violet-hued eyes were perfectly winged black brows,
which shot up with inquiry when something interested her, lifted impishly when she was in a teasing mood, and knitted together ferociously
when she was annoyed or upset.

Her small nose was decidedly patrician, but her lush, lovely mouth
suggested an undeniable earthiness. With her firm chin and finely
boned face, she appeared haughty and unattainable. At the same time
there was about her a sense of arousal beneath the gentility, a hint of
the passion that lurked below the cool exterior.

Her name was Diane Buchannan. *Miss* Diane Howard Buchannan.
She was unmarried, and she had just passed a very important birthday.
A milestone in the life of any female. One quarter of a century.

Diane Howard Buchannan was twenty-five years old and not the
least bit nervous or apologetic about the fact that she was neither married nor engaged to be married. While society considered any woman

still single upon reaching the ripe age of twenty-five sadly destined to be an old maid, Diane Howard Buchannan didn't give a fig about such foolish concerns.

She was perfectly content to be single, independent, her own boss. "I am the master of my fate;/I am the captain of my soul," she was fond of quoting to doubters and worrisome would-be matchmakers. Including her well-meaning aunt Lydia, with whom she lived. Grudgingly her friends were forced to admit that the spirited, self-reliant Diane was maddeningly successful at running her own life, captaining her own ship.

It had always been so.

Orphaned when a carriage accident claimed the lives of her parents when Diane was only two, she was reared by her paternal grandparents, the fiery Colonel Buck Buchannan and the calm, unshakable Granny Ruth Buchannan. From the devoted, strong-willed pair Diane had learned a great deal about life and love and loyalty.

And independence.

So Diane Howard Buchannan stood alone in the moonlight because she chose to do so. She looked dreamily down at the silver ribbon of the Potomac as it wound its sure, slow way eastward to Chesapeake Bay and on out to the great Atlantic Ocean. From behind her, inside the roomy, well-lighted town house, the sounds of music and laughter and chatter drifted out on the still, muggy air.

A party, with dozens of guests, was in progress. The party was for her, given in her honor. Diane knew she should go back inside, knew her behavior bordered on rudeness. But, Lord, she was bored and restless and anxious to leave. She had long since tired of Washington's endless parties, where the conversation predictably centered on politics.

An educated woman, the raven-haired, violet-eyed Diane was bright and sophisticated. At twenty-one she had come to the nation's capital, her mother's birthplace and still home to her only living Howard relative. The Howard name was an old and highly respected one in Washington. Her aunt, Lydia Howard Dansby, enjoyed a great deal of influence with the city's powerful.

Lydia Howard Dansby had invited her only niece, Diane, to share the imposing Howard ancestral home, with a promise to help Diane find just the correct position in the nation's capital, if she insisted on being employed. Diane had quickly accepted, and Aunt Lydia had been as good as her word.

For the past four years Diane had held the envied position of well-paid stenographer and trusted aide to one of the country's most dynamic young senators. At first it had been a challenge. Now she was anxious for a different kind of challenge.

Despite Montana Senator Clay Dodson's urging her to stay on, Diane was leaving, and she could hardly wait to be gone. Her mind was made up. She couldn't be swayed. Either by her aunt Lydia or the handsome senator.

"But, my dear Diane," the young senator had entreated when first she told him of her plans, "you can't desert me. You can't. Diane, I need you."

"I'm sorry, Clay, truly I am," she had replied, touched by the tenderness and disappointment in his warm brown eyes, "but someone else needs me more."

It was the truth.

She was badly needed by those whom she most loved, the Colonel and Granny Buchannan.

From the time she was five years old, Diane's paternal grandparents had owned and operated the *Colonel Buck Buchannan's Wild West Show.* When she was a child, the touring extravaganza had played to sold-out houses all over America and Europe. In its heyday the show had been so successful the troupe crisscrossed the country in shiny custom-made rail cars, sailed to the Continent on the Cunard Line's finest ships, booked the most opulent hotel rooms at home and abroad.

Sadly that was no longer the case.

Colonel Buck Buchannan's Wild West Show was in deep financial trouble. Had been in trouble for the past few years. There were numerous reasons for the show's steady decline. First, the bloom was off the rose. What had been a new, exciting spectacle twenty years ago was now familiar. The paying customers had become jaded. They had seen, dozens of times, the Rough Riders and the Mexican charros and the buffalo herds and the reenactment of the stagecoach ambushed by hostiles.

There were no surprises to the program. No new daring acts to make the crowds cheer or gasp with excitement.

Then, too, other forms of entertainment had become increasingly popular. The theater. The opera. The colorful P. T. Barnum's Circus. Thomas Edison's new kinetoscope shows.

Most damaging of all was the proliferation of other wild west shows. When *Colonel Buck Buchannan's Wild West Show* began, it was the first and only traveling extravaganza of its kind. Every performance was sold out weeks in advance, and crowds were awed and amazed by what they saw in the arena. Now there were more than two dozen similar shows, most with far better acts and more original programs than the Colonel's.

Worse, Diane had been hearing rumors that Pawnee Bill—owner of the moneymaking *Pawnee Bill's Wild West Show* and the archenemy of her grandfather—was planning a takeover of the Colonel's ailing show. Diane couldn't let that happen. She *wouldn't* let that happen!

She would do what she had been considering for the past year. She'd give up her position in Washington, D.C., and join her grandfather's troubled troupe. She'd add her own name and act to the bill in an attempt to beef up the take. She'd install modern business procedures. Using her D.C. connections, she'd help the Colonel search out a bank willing to lend the much-needed operating capital.

Her violet eyes flashing with fierce determination, Diane forcefully slapped the palm of her right hand down atop the balcony railing and murmured aloud, "Yes, sirree, I'll be there to meet that show train when it pulls into—"

"Diane? Are you out here, Diane?" Senator Clay Dodson's voice interrupted her reveries. "Are you with someone?" The slim blond man looked around, searching for the person or persons with whom she'd been conversing.

Diane took a deep breath and turned to face him.

She smiled. "No, Clay. I'm alone. I suppose I must have been thinking out loud."

"Well, that's allowed," he said, advancing on her. "However, hiding out at your own party is not." His smile was warm, forgiving.

"I know," she said apologetically. "It's so stuffy inside. I just came out for a breath of fresh air." She gave him her brightest smile, took his arm, and added, "Let's go back in."

Clay Dodson didn't move. Just kept looking at her. Finally he said, "It *is* nice out here. Just the two of us. Why don't we . . ."

"Now who's hiding out?" she said, seeing that look in his eyes that she wished weren't there. "Come. I'm dying to make another trip to the buffet."

Reluctantly Senator Dodson accompanied her back inside. The party lasted for another hour. Finally the gathered group raised champagne toasts to their smiling guest of honor, and it was Clay Dodson who led them in a rousing rendition of "For She's a Jolly Good Fellow."

Properly pleased, Diane blushed and smiled and made a short, parting speech. And, surprisingly, found herself near tears as she looked around at all the familiar faces she wouldn't be seeing again.

Then everyone was hugging her and telling her to stay in touch, and at last Clay was guiding her down the steps and out into the humid Washington night.

The young senator from Billings walked Diane slowly back to the Howard home, three blocks away. It was quite late. The street was nearly deserted. Crickets croaked in the silence, and somewhere on the river a steamer tug gave a short blast on its whistle.

The couple leisurely strolling down the sidewalk said little. There was really nothing left to say. The senator—his brown eyes sweeping over Diane's pale, beautiful face, that upswept midnight hair—was in a decidedly somber mood. Diane, not looking at him, was feeling just the opposite.

She was so excited about tomorrow's departure she could hardly keep her feet on the sidewalk, but she was considerate enough to hide it.

At last they reached the imposing three-story brownstone that was the old Howard mansion. Dreading this final good-bye, eager to have it over with, Diane turned to Clay Dodson as soon as they reached her fanlighted front door.

"Clay, dear Clay," she said softly, "it's been a wonderful four years. Thanks for everything."

"Diane," came his strangled reply. "Diane . . ."

Impulsively he grabbed her hand to draw her closer. Diane's mouth flew open in startled surprise, and a folded piece of paper slipped from her grasp. It fluttered down to the stone steps at their feet. The senator's eyes followed it. He picked up the fallen paper, unfolded it, and held it to the faint light of an electric streetlamp.

A current Union Pacific train schedule with "Denver, Colorado," circled in bright blue ink.

"Diane, I wish you'd reconsider leaving—"

Her lips stopped him from further pleading. She kissed him quickly, said good-bye, then hurried eagerly inside to pack for her long trip.

Chapter 3

➡➡➡ It was about two o'clock in the afternoon several days later that a long westbound train snaked its way across Colorado's flat eastern plains. Its journey from Kansas City, Missouri, was nearing an end. Just ahead and looming steadily closer on the near western horizon, the forbidding Front Range of the awesome Rocky Mountains rose to meet a cloudless August sky.

Steaming directly toward those soaring peaks, the train boasted an impressive procession of thirty-four rail cars. On each and every one of those cars, with the exception of the locomotive's powerful steam engine, prominent gold lettering decorated the shiny black sides. "Colonel Buck Buchannan's Wild West Show," the gold letters proudly proclaimed.

At the very front of that long show train, in the big steam engine's sweltering cab, Boz Whitman, the engineer, jumped down off his stool. Grinning from ear to ear, Boz reached up and gave a firm tug on an overhead rope. The train's whistle instantly sounded a long, loud blast, startling a small herd of white-faced cattle grazing near the tracks.

The aging engineer laughed, then moved his big wad of chewing tobacco from right cheek to left, and spit a string of brown juice over the side of the train. Boz wore his regulation striped railroad cap with a bright red bandanna, a red shirt, striped overalls, and a pair of goggles to protect his sensitive sixty-two-year-old eyes from cinders as he leaned out the window.

Continuing to laugh, Boz gave the whistle cord another yank, eased off on the throttle, and slammed on the brakes. A great grinding sound was almost deafening. Orange sparks flew from beneath the heavy steel wheels. Finally the train began to slow. Curious show people poked their heads out the windows, wondering why they were stopping when Denver was still a couple of miles west.

When the locomotive had come to a complete stop on the tracks, a pair of loading doors slid open on an animal car at the train's rear. A wooden ramp was lowered into place. Then a broad-shouldered, powerfully built young man with dark blond hair appeared in the car's opening.

Billed on the program as the Cherokee Kid, the big suntanned man coaxed a nervous chestnut stallion, heavily packed with weapons and camping gear, down the wooden ramp and off the train.

Following the Cherokee Kid were a pair of the show's brawny equipment handlers, the Leatherwood brothers, Danny and Davey. The playful, loudmouthed Leatherwoods yanked brutally on their mounts' reins, unmindful and uncaring of the steel bits punishing the horses' tender mouths.

On their heels came a short middle-aged cowboy. William "Shorty" Jones was a leathery-faced little man who was so painfully thin he had trouble keeping his faded denim pants up. A silver whistle hung from a chain around Shorty's neck and a cigarette dangled from his lips. Hitching his breeches with one hand, leading a roan gelding with the other, he squinted through the smoke curling up into his eyes. Never taking the handmade cigarette from his mouth, Shorty warned the thoughtless, overgrown Leatherwood pair, "Take it easy, boys. Take it easy!"

Shorty was the troupe's animal wrangler and he couldn't stand to see any kind of animal abused. A very quiet, very shy little man, Shorty was consistently gentle with all God's creatures—man and beast—and it sorely rankled him to see the bullying Leatherwoods mistreat frightened horses.

Sharing Shorty's concern, a white-haired old Indian, his bronzed, stony face deeply creased and sun-weathered, led a big paint pony down the ramp after Shorty. He was called Ancient Eyes, and he had once been a powerful subchief of Colorado's Uncompahgre Utes. Those days had long since passed. Ancient Eyes had seen seventy-five winters come and go. The last twenty had been spent with *Colonel Buck Buchannan's Wild West Show*. Ancient Eyes realized his value to the Colonel was not so great as it once had been. He was far too old to be the daring fierce warrior, which had been his role in the beginning. Still, he knew that so long as the troubled show kept operating, he had a place with the troupe, with the Colonel, his old and valued friend.

Drawing the long leather reins up over his paint's lowered head, Ancient Eyes groaned a little as he climbed up into the saddle. Then, seated astride the paint, the old Ute suddenly shuddered involuntarily. Shorty, mounting his roan near Ancient Eyes, saw the tremor go through the Ute's thick, squat body.

"Chief, you okay?" Shorty spoke in low tones so the others couldn't hear. "You feeling sick?"

Ancient Eyes shrugged and shook his head no, sending his coarse shoulder-length white hair swinging around his dark, wrinkled face. He looked Shorty in the eye and admitted, "For one split second it was as if"—he lifted a broad hand and gestured toward the clear blue sky—"as if old friends from spirit world were warning me this trip not be good. Something bad happen."

Shorty neither laughed nor made light of the old chief's superstitions. He asked gently, "You mean the show's upcoming engagement in Denver?"

Ancient Eyes again shook his head. "No. Mean this hunt we go on up in Shining Mountains."

Before Shorty could respond, the loading doors slammed shut behind them, the signal was given, and Boz, the engineer, pumped up the train's engine again. And the eager Cherokee Kid, standing in the stirrups atop his chestnut stallion, shouted loudly, "What are we waitin' for? Let's go get us a big cat!"

He lowered himself into the silver-trimmed saddle, dug his sharp roweled spurs into his mount's belly, and the responsive chestnut shot away. The train slowly began to pick up speed. The rowdy Leatherwoods galloped after the Cherokee Kid, whooping and hollering. Shorty and Ancient Eyes exchanged looks of disgust, then set out after the younger riders.

In the lead the Cherokee Kid raced across the plain, his horse's hooves kicking up dust and flinging clumps of grass. He rode directly toward the towering Rockies.

The riders would not be stopping in the city. It was three days until the show's first scheduled Denver performance. While the troupe spent that time pitching the tents and erecting the grandstands and doing a dress run-through, the five who had left the train early were to spend those days camped in the high country west of Denver. Their mission: to find a mountain lion for the show. Always eager to gain the Colonel's approval, the Cherokee Kid had promised the old showman that they wouldn't come down from the hills until they had trapped a prize specimen.

He meant to keep that promise.

So the horsemen thundered swiftly toward the foothills as the much slower show train steamed steadily toward the outskirts of Denver.

On the platform outside Denver's newly refurbished Union Depot, Diane Buchannan squinted into the brilliant sunlight on that warm August afternoon. She was both comfortable and striking in a crisp white piqué frock and wide-brimmed straw hat, a violet silk scarf tied around its crown, the ends fluttering in the slight breeze stirring from the north. On her slender hands were violet cotton gloves, and above her head to shade her face and pale white shoulders from the fierce alpine sun was a dainty silk parasol of the same hue. Diane anxiously looked down the tracks for the train, which was due at the station any minute. She had been looking down those tracks for the past half hour.

That, and pacing restlessly back and forth on the nearly deserted depot platform. She could hardly wait to see the Colonel and Granny Buchannan. Could hardly wait to see the look on the Colonel's face when he stepped down from the train and found her waiting.

Diane smiled, anticipating the moment.

She hadn't wired her grandparents that she was meeting them in Denver, hadn't informed them that she was joining the troupe. It was to be a total surprise and she wasn't at all certain how the Colonel would take the news. The fiery old man might be downright furious that his upstart granddaughter would deign to think he needed *her* to help bail him out of his financial woes.

The Colonel was and always had been an extremely proud man. His adventurous life had been one of which legends are made. An Arizona native, Buck Buchannan had been an Indian fighter, a scout for the Army, a Civil War soldier with medals of bravery decorating his blue uniform blouse.

Numerous scars of which he was proud were left from his glorious youth. An Apache's arrow had pierced his left shoulder; a Reb's bullet had wounded his right hip. His broad chest was scarred from an encounter with a grizzly, and a run-in with a jealous husband had put character into his youthful, perfect face.

At age fifty, as he was breaking a wild mustang for the show, the angered thousand-pound beast fell on his left leg, leaving him with a permanent limp.

The Colonel had fully enjoyed every day of his life. It had all been a lark, and none of it more satisfying than being the owner of the traveling wild west show. And so it was painful for the fearless old scout even to admit that his beloved wild west show was in serious trouble.

The short, loud blast of a train's whistle made Diane look up and again squint down the tracks. And her heart skipped a beat.

Steaming down those vibrating tracks directly toward her—old Boz, the engineer, leaning out the window and waving his striped cap—was that long, very special train she was waiting for.

Suddenly there were crowds of excited, chattering people swirling around her. She realized—and was delighted by the knowledge—that they, too, had come to meet the troupe's train. At the sight of all those eager faces, Diane felt a great sense of relief. She had been so afraid that the crowd would be embarrassingly sparse, that only a handful of people would turn out. And that the Colonel would be miserably disappointed.

A smile of pleasure curving her lips, Diane quickly lowered her violet parasol, tucked it under her arm, and hurried toward the train, jostled and pushed by the swelling crowd. She tried, but couldn't break through the mass of humanity gathered around the very first of the passenger cars, the lead passenger car with big gold letters shining in the sun: "Colonel Buck Buchannan's Wild West Show."

At last the train came to a complete stop.

A uniformed conductor opened the car's door. In his gloved hand he held a set of portable steps, which he placed on the ground directly beneath the door. He straightened, tugged his black jacket back down into place, lifted then lowered his black-billed cap, folded his hands behind him, then nodded to someone unseen on the train.

All eyes were riveted to that train door. Reporters from the *Rocky Mountain News* and the *Denver Post* were poised with pads, pens, and flash cameras, ready to conduct interviews.

Minutes passed. Anticipation grew. Diane grinned.

She knew the Colonel. The crafty old showman knew exactly how to play crowds. Likely as not, he was standing just inside, concealed in shadow, purposely making his audience wait, allowing the excitement to build.

Then, sure enough, after several long minutes, the very first passenger to step down to the platform was a stately figure in velvet-soft buckskins with fringed collar and leg seams, rust suede gauntlets, hand-tooled cowboy boots, a white Stetson, and a butter yellow silk bandanna tied at his throat. Ruddy-cheeked, blue eyes eager, teeth flashing in a broad smile, the Colonel gallantly doffed his Stetson to the cheering, whistling crowd, revealing a full head of long white hair pulled back and secured in a ponytail.

"Colonel!" Diane happily shouted, addressing her grandfather by the title he most favored. "Colonel Buchannan!"

He didn't hear her.

Frustrated, manners totally forgotten, she pushed and elbowed her way through the crowd, rushing toward the noticeably lame, aging man who was already posing happily for the Denver newspaper photographer.

"Colonel!" Diane shouted again, and a pair of bright blue twinkling eyes cut quickly to her.

Total shock flared for a brief second in those expressive blue eyes, but the surprised, quick-witted Colonel never missed a beat. He was instantly overjoyed. Instinctively he knew why Diane had come. And in a flash he realized that she would be sure to draw audiences with her delicate good looks and her fancy trick roping and riding, skills he himself had taught her when she was a child.

As if it all had been planned, the Colonel swiftly swept his slender, raven-haired granddaughter into his massive arms, placed a quick kiss on her cheek, and proudly announced to the press, "Boys, meet *Colonel Buck Buchannan's Wild West Show*'s newest star attraction, Miss Diane Buchannan!"

Chapter 4

❦❦❦❦ Colonel Buck Buchannan and *Rocky Mountain News* reporter
Robert Mitchell stood with their arms draped over the tall
fence at the West Denver Fairgrounds.

The eyes of the old Colonel and the young reporter were riveted on a
lone horse and rider in the center of the dusty arena. They studied the
silhouette, framed against the azure sky, moving as if the two were one.
The horse was a shimmering, saddleless black stallion with one white-
stockinged foot. The rider was tall and slender, had black hair, and
wore tight buckskin pants, a white cotton shirt, and soft, beaded moccasins.

Robert Mitchell, the reporter, gasped and gripped the wooden fence
when the daredevil rider, galloping the big black at full speed, recklessly rose to a standing position atop his bare back. Knees slightly
bent, back perfectly straight, toes and heels hugging the steed to ensure
good balance, the fearless rider shifted the long leather reins to one
hand, reached up with the other, and withdrew an unseen silver restraint from a mass of lustrous curls.

A shimmering curtain of long hair, the exact shade of the black's
sleek coat, fell for a brief second around a high-cheekboned, delicate
face and white-shirted shoulders, then quickly caught the wind and
streamed out like a beautiful banner of black silk, much like the stallion's long, billowing mane and tail.

For a long moment the reporter was too awed to speak. When he could find his voice, he said, "Colonel, how does it feel to be the grandfather of a legend?"

"Diane," replied the Colonel, putting his hand on the shoulder of the youthful reporter, "is a top star trick rider and lariat artist. *I* am the legend!" He applauded and further boasted, "Son, I taught that girl everything she knows." Then, cupping his hands to his mouth, he called out, "Diane, that's enough for now. Bring him on in. I don't want you gettin' too sore to ride in tomorrow's parade."

It was noon Wednesday.

The troupe had been in Denver for less than forty-eight hours, but Diane had wasted no time. That first evening, a few hours after the train's arrival, she had handpicked the show-trained horse she would use in her act. She knew the minute she laid eyes on the magnificent black that she had to have him. A half hour after choosing him, she'd taken him out into the arena and put him through some tests. He passed with flying colors. She was more than pleased. She and the big brute would make a striking pair.

Since then Diane had been at the arena every free minute, working up a daring routine. She was not alone. The fairgrounds was a beehive of activity from early morning to setting sun.

Handbills advertising the show had been passed out by local schoolboys. Giant posters decorated telephone poles and were prominently displayed in store windows throughout the city. Excitement was in the air, and the male citizens of Denver with time on their hands wandered down to the exhibition grounds. They watched as the troupe's strong-backed laborers hauled in lumber, hammered and sawed under the hot August sun, hurriedly constructing grandstands.

Shorty's boys were busy with the show's many animals. On the arena's north side the unloading of the stock into the holding pens was in progress. Once in the pens, the animals had to be tended constantly, fed and watered, bathed and brushed, doctored and guarded.

Most of the performers hung around the fairgrounds. Many practiced their acts; others watched or played poker or gossiped or simply relaxed, saving their energy for the show. A string of the troupe's rail cars were parked on a spur less than a hundred yards away. The show's performers were quartered in the private rail cars.

And so fellow entertainers, milling about the grounds that sunny August morning, stopped what they were doing and came over to watch along with the curious townsfolk. The slender black-haired rider astride the big black horse had effortlessly caught the attention of every male within sight, a fact which didn't go unnoticed by the crafty old Colonel.

As Diane waved a hand high in the air, bent her knees, and sat back down astride the black, a growing male gathering was at the rail watching, several with field glasses raised. Diane was aware of their presence. And of their interest. She didn't mind their being there. She hoped they were impressed enough by what they saw to come back and pay hard cash to get into the show.

One hand riding her thigh, Diane wheeled the stallion about, cantered over to the fence, leaned down, and spoke into the black's pricked ear.

"Come on, boy. Let's take a bow." She pressed her fingers firmly to his neck, just behind his left jaw, and commanded, "Now, Champ."

The black responded just as she knew he would. The well-trained thousand-pound stallion dropped his right knee to the dirt, then crossed his left white-stockinged foot over it and dramatically lowered his great head.

The uninvited gallery whistled and cheered.

"Bravo, bravo," shouted the pleased Colonel.

"Amazing!" enthused the young reporter.

"Good boy," murmured Diane, patting the black's neck. She softly commanded him to remain as he was, head lowered. Then agilely she slid forward from his bare back, down along his curved neck, over his bowed head, and off.

She threw her arms triumphantly in the air, went up on her moccasined toes, flashed a million-dollar smile, turned immediately back to the black, and snapped her fingers. The stallion instantly rose to his full-imposing height and shook his great head about, sending the long black mane dancing. Diane laughed, stuck two fingers down into the pocket of her snug buckskins and produced a lump of sugar.

Champ eagerly gobbled it up, swallowed, then nudged her gently, whickering softly. Pleading for more.

Diane refused. She grabbed a handful of his coarse mane and gave it a playful yank. She shook her head and told him, "Beggars never get anywhere with me, big boy. The sooner you learn that lesson, the better we'll get along." But she affectionately clamped an arm around his head, pressed it to her chest, and laid her cheek against his. Then she swiftly slapped him away when he sniffed and nuzzled her breasts, searching for the hidden sugar.

One of the animal handlers hurried forward. Diane tossed him the reins, thanked him, and gave the black's rump a swat, sending him on his way. The sun was behind her, making a halo of her dark hair, when she stepped up to the tall fence where her grandfather and the young reporter waited.

The Colonel made the introductions. Robert Mitchell eagerly reached through the fence to shake Diane's hand.

"Miss Buchannan," he said admiringly, "you were wonderful!"

"Not really." She was modest. "It's the horse who is wonderful." She withdrew her hand and shifted her attention to her grandfather. "Colonel, soon as Shorty gets back, I don't want anyone but him around Champ."

"I'll tell him," assured the Colonel. The reporter cleared his throat. The Colonel glanced at the younger man. Robert Mitchell was making faces. "What is it, son? Oh . . . oh, yes." The Colonel turned back to Diane. "This young man has invited me to have lunch with him at the Metropolitan and he thought you might like to join us."

"Sorry, I've already promised Texas Kate I'd have lunch with her." Diane smiled at the reporter. "Some other time perhaps."

His face immediately registering his disappointment, Robert Mitchell nodded. "Yes. Sure, maybe tomorrow we—"

But Diane had already turned and walked away.

Texas Kate sat playing Klondike solitaire. With a deck of fifty-one. It was her favorite way to pass the time. She bragged that she had beat the old joker twice as many times as he had beaten her. She had worn out at least a hundred decks of cards since joining *Colonel Buck Buchannan's Wild West Show.*

Texas Kate was a big, rawboned native Texan with warm brown eyes, a surprisingly dainty nose, and a wide mouth which was filled with teeth. Her face was broad, plain, and as suntanned as a man's. She never wore a hat. Her bobbed brown hair was shot with gray and there were permanent laugh lines fanning out from her brown eyes.

Texas Kate was loud, loyal, and lovable. She enjoyed a good joke, even if it was on her. She never carried tales, or gave unwanted advice, or whined and complained when things didn't go to suit her. She was dependable, good-hearted, and even-tempered.

Kate had been the show's crowd-pleasing female sharpshooter since 1878, the summer she turned thirty-three. She was visiting some distant cousins in Chicago. *Colonel Buck Buchannan's Wild West Show* was in town, and her relatives took her to the Friday night closing performance.

Katherine Louise Worthington was enthralled with the pageantry, the costumes, and the fine horsemanship. But when the portion of the show came wherein a marksman took the arena to show his stuff, she was not impressed.

"I could outshoot that fellow with my eyes closed," she told her cousins.

And then got the chance to prove it.

The cocky sharpshooter called for "any *man* in the audience who thinks he can to come on down. Try and best me." A half dozen equally cocky men quickly rose and hurried from their seats. Katherine Louise Worthington patiently waited. When all six had been easily put away and sent with their tails between their legs back to the grandstands, she stood up.

While the smiling sharpshooter, down in the arena, lifted a pair of matching pearl-handled revolvers in salute to the crowd's appreciative cheers, Katherine Louise Worthington shouted loudly in an unmistakable Texas twang, "How about giving a lady a chance, mister?"

The crowd guffawed. So did the show's sharpshooter. But not for long.

Katherine Louise Worthington didn't wait for his answer. She scrambled down from her seat, reached the tall arena fence, and scaled over it as easily as an acrobat, her skirts and petticoats flying around her knees. The marksman confidently stood there waiting, watching, a superior smile on his smooth, handsome face. Katherine Louise Worthington ignored his arrogance. Her stride long and determined, she headed for the center of the big arena.

And in less than five minutes the Texas woman had claimed it for her own.

Colonel Buck Buchannan was watching that night from the wings. In forty-eight years of living he had never seen such amazing shooting. When the remarkable woman had easily and effectively put his highly paid performer to rest, the Colonel hurried to intercept her before she could go back to her seat.

He offered Katherine Louise Worthington a salary to match that which he was currently paying the man she had beaten. Katherine Louise Worthington refused him. Said she was mighty tempted but she and her husband owned a ranch down in South Texas. She was just in Chicago on a visit.

Thinking fast, the Colonel suggested that her husband become one of his famed Rough Riders. It was then Katherine Louise Worthington explained that her husband wasn't exactly available at the moment to travel with the show.

"You see, Colonel Buchannan," the smiling, stocky woman from Texas explained, running fingers through her light brown curls, "Teddy Ray—that's my sweet husband's name—Teddy Ray hasn't come back yet from the war."

"The war? What war? I know of no war that—"

"Why, the War Between the States!" Kate looked at him as if he didn't have good sense. "Teddy Ray left me behind in Texas and joined up with the Rebs when I was still a bride, sixteen years old. He was no more than nineteen himself, but we had a little spread we worked together, a few head of cattle. I'm still working the place. I expect Teddy Ray will come home one of these days." She smiled, thinking fondly of her husband. "I feel half guilty just being here in Chicago."

Gently the Colonel said, "But, my dear, the war's been over now for thirteen years."

"Lordy, I know that. You think I'm thickheaded?" Katherine Louise Worthington's fists lifted to rest on broadening hips. "I told Teddy Ray I would wait, and I'm waitin'. I never got word he was dead. They said he was missin' after that big battle at Rosy Ridge. Missin' ain't dead, Colonel. No, sir. My sweet Teddy Ray may just show up one of these days, and when he does—"

"Tell you what, Mrs. Worthington." The Colonel interrupted. "You leave word down in Texas where you are, what you're doing. Come with the show. Then, when Teddy Ray gets back, you quit and go home to the ranch. How does that sound?"

Katherine Louise Worthington narrowed her brown eyes and mulled it over. "Mind you now, it could only be temporary," she said thoughtfully, obviously interested in his offer. "The minute my Teddy Ray—"

"Why, certainly, certainly. Just sign on with the show until Teddy Ray's return."

That had been seventeen years ago, and Texas Kate still traveled with the show, dazzling audiences with her incredible shooting talents, endearing herself to her fellow performers with her unflappable nature and sincere friendliness. And still religiously pointing out to the Colonel and everyone else in the troupe that her traveling with *Colonel Buck Buchannan's Wild West Show* was only temporary. Soon as her Teddy Ray returned, she'd be going back home to Texas to help him work the ranch.

Texas Kate slapped a black king—the last card in her hand—atop one of the four stacks of cards on the table and laughed out loud. Diane heard the laughter and knew Texas Kate had beaten the joker again.

Diane knocked, gripped either side of the open door, and stuck her head inside. Texas Kate waved and motioned for her to come in.

Diane was about to do just that when a commotion from across the arena made her turn to look. Texas Kate heard it as well, shoved back her chair, got up, and hurried to the door.

The two women stared as a small band of mounted men approached from the west. In the lead was a big, muscular man with dark blond hair who was calling excitedly to the Colonel.

"Who is that?" asked Diane, a hand lifted to shade her eyes.

"He's the Cherokee Kid," said Texas Kate, squinting as the contingent drew closer. "Come on in. There's nothing to see. Just the boys back down from the mountains. Heck, I'll bet they didn't even manage to catch a big cat." She laughed and turned away.

"Mmm," murmured Diane, still staring. She saw her grandfather, the reporter close on his heels, limping hurriedly toward the arriving riders and secretly wished she could stroll over and see what all the excitement was about.

Inwardly sighing, she dragged her gaze away and stepped up into the cozy rail car she shared with Texas Kate.

The Colonel was out of breath when he reached the western perimeter of the exhibition grounds. The Cherokee Kid swung down out of his saddle, a wide grin on his unshaven face, and stepped up to the older man.

"Well, son, you get us a big cat?" asked the Colonel.

"Sure did," said the Cherokee Kid, stripping off his kidskin gloves and shoving them into his hip pocket. "But forget about the cougar for now. I've brought you a *real* prize, Colonel." Over his shoulder he called out, "Davey, bring him on up here."

Fierce scuffling, grunts, moans, and the sound of clanking chains caused the Colonel's eyes to widen speculatively and blink in the bright noonday sun. The brawny Leatherwoods forcefully dragged their stubborn prey forward.

Ironed hand and foot, a heavy steel chain around his neck, a tall, wild-looking Indian, straining against his bonds, hatred flashing in his dark eyes, and fresh bruises on his near-naked body, was proudly presented to the gaping Colonel.

"Take a look, Colonel Buchannan!" said the beaming Cherokee Kid. "Can you believe it? An honest-to-God wild Injun! He's just what this old ailing show needs."

The Colonel stared at the creature, whose dark face was flushed, mouth skinned back over his teeth, eyes red with rage. When those anguished eyes met the Colonel's, the redman made some shapes with his lips, but no words came. Only animal sounds. And loud, rapid breaths that were drawn in rattling gasps.

"I've seen one of these creatures before," boasted the Cherokee Kid. "Spooky! His eyes were bloodred and he foamed at the mouth."

The Colonel made no reply. He continued to study the fierce, wild heathen struggling vainly against the imprisoning bonds. In the hot sunshine every muscle of his body strained and rippled beneath the filthy bronzed flesh. Inhuman sounds erupted from the chain-cinched throat. The big near-naked creature's appearance was that of a trapped animal. He radiated menace. He threw off a scent of danger. Threat shone from his wild dark eyes.

The Cherokee Kid continued hopefully, "Sure, we have Indians in the troupe—lots of 'em—but hell, they're all middle-aged or older and as fat and tame as old ladies. They couldn't scare a child. Look at this beast. He's totally wild. A throwback to the old days. A heathen that's still as untamed as his murdering, scalping ancestors." The Kid looked at the redskin and laughed. "Who knows? Maybe this one's the Stone Age creature the Pulitzer press has been warning the yahoos about! He'll scare the living hell out of them."

Colonel Buchannan continued to study the trussed Indian. He stepped up to the savage, looked him squarely in the eye, and said, "Savvy English?"

The Indian grunted, and again his lips made shapes, his eyes flashed, but no words came. Desperately he strained against his bonds. The chains around his throat clanked as he grunted and growled.

"The creature speaks no English," said the Kid. "I'm telling you, Colonel, he's an uncivilized savage and exactly what we need in the show."

The Colonel frowned, shook his white head, and rubbed his chin thoughtfully. He walked around and around the dirty, naked figure. Excitement caused the blood to rush quickly through his veins. Ever the showman, he could already envision huge crowds of curious spectators turning out to see the fragile, fair, refined Diane Buchannan and the fierce, frightening, untamed redskin.

The Beauty and the Beast!

No two ways about it, the savage would be a valuable drawing card. Already he could see the creature listed there on the program.

They would call him THE REDMAN OF THE ROCKIES!

Chapter 5

The news spread rapidly.

Within the hour everyone in the troupe, from the Colonel on down to the lowliest roustabout, was talking of nothing else. All were anxious to have a look at the Redman of the Rockies.

Including Diane Buchannan.

The mess tent was abuzz that noontime when she and Texas Kate passed through the long serving line. Tales abounded of how the Cherokee Kid, up in the mountains and temporarily cut off from his hunting party, was suddenly and brutally attacked by a wild, bloodthirsty savage. The Kid, caught totally off guard and unarmed, had been lucky to get away with his life!

Diane was as curious as the rest. She hurried through the meal, finished in minutes, and left Texas Kate lingering over her apple pie. Outside, Diane looked about, meaning to ask one of the performers where the Redman was being held. It wasn't necessary. All she had to do was follow the crowd.

She did just that.

Everyone was hurrying toward the livestock pens and animal cages located on the flats at the arena's far north side. Diane rushed to catch up and was just rounding the arena's large oval when she ran into her grandfather.

"Diane," he called, limped forward, and caught her by the arm. "Hold on a minute. Where you headed?"

"Where do you think?" she said breathlessly. "To see the creature."

The old showman shook his white head and gently drew her aside. "Child, you're to stay away from the Redman. He's a savage, totally uncivilized and highly dangerous. There's no telling what he might to do a pretty young woman like you."

"Isn't he restrained?" Diane was annoyed.

"Yes, chained hand and foot, but there's no assurance he won't break away. He's a powerful brute, and it's simply not safe to be anywhere close to him. You hear me? Don't let me catch you near him!"

"I won't."

Later that same afternoon Diane tiptoed forward.

Her moccasined feet made little or no sound on the dusty plain. Bottom lip caught between her teeth, breath held, Diane stole steadily closer to the unsuspecting Indian.

His back was to her. She knew he didn't see her, didn't hear her approaching. The relaxed attitude of his body indicated he had no idea she or anyone else was within a mile of him. His heavy, powerful arms were lifted. The fingers of both hands were curled around the slender bars directly before him. A long, shiny braid, its end bound with sleek otter skin, lay atop a massive shoulder. The other braid hung down his back.

Diane silently crept up on him. Her heart drummed in her chest. Her mouth was dry. She expected him to sense her presence at any second. She reached him, stood not a foot behind him. Slowly, cautiously she lifted her arms. Quickly she thrust her hands in front of his face and covered his eyes with her fingers, taking him totally by surprise.

For a split second the startled Indian did nothing. Didn't move a muscle. Didn't make a sound.

Then deep laughter rumbled from his massive chest and shook the old Indian's squat body. Diane laughed as well and withdrew her hands. He turned from the barred ticket cage to face her, his broad, wrinkled face alight with joy.

"Little Buck!" Ancient Eyes exclaimed happily as his gargantuan arms enclosed her in a bone-crushing embrace. "How you been, Little Buck?"

Laughing, Diane hugged the old Ute chieftain who never called her by any other name. To him she was not Diane; she was Little Buck. She had known Ancient Eyes all her life. Balanced on his knee, she had listened by the hour while he told fascinating stories of the old days he'd spent among his people. Happy days when he was young and strong and roamed the rugged Shining Mountains as proud and free as the soaring eagle. As wild as the winds that howled around the highest peaks.

Struggling to free herself from his steel grasp, Diane said, "I'm great, and you?"

Ancient Eyes released her. The broad smile remained on his wrinkled face; his black eyes glittered. "I old. How good can I be?" He shrugged dismissively.

"You'll never be old," said she. Then: "What are you doing out here at the ticket cage? Something going on inside?"

He grinned and confided, "Thought maybeso find tobacco or cigarette somebody leave. No luck. You have tobacco, Little Buck?"

Diane laughed. "No, but I'll help with the search. Come on." She took his arm and they strolled toward the newly constructed grandstands. On the way they bumped into one of the show's Rough Riders. Diane nudged Ancient Eyes, nodded toward a telltale yellow tobacco sack string dangling from the cowboy's breast pocket.

So Ancient Eyes was puffing contentedly on a hastily rolled cigarette when they left the obliging Rough Rider. On they strolled, reaching the grandstands. There in the hot afternoon sunshine they sat and visited, enjoying each other's company. They laughed and talked like a couple of kids.

Ancient Eyes was endlessly curious about Washington. Once, long ago, he had visited that distant place with Chief Ouray. There he had met the Great White Father, Andrew Johnson. He wanted to know about the new Great White Father, so Diane answered question after question.

Finally she asked one of her own.

"Tell me about the Redman." Diane was looking directly at Ancient Eyes' dark, lined face. She caught the strange expression that leaped into his obsidian eyes, saw the slight tightening of his mouth. "What is it? What's wrong?"

"Nothing. Nothing wrong," said Ancient Eyes.

But Diane was left with the uneasy feeling that something was bothering the old chief. Something he wouldn't talk about. Something to do with the Redman of the Rockies.

Sensitive to his feelings, Diane was sorry she had brought it up. Immediately she changed the subject. She asked how he'd like to watch her put her black show stallion, Champ, through his paces while she did some fancy trick riding on the horse's back.

"Break fool neck if not careful, Little Buck," Ancient Eyes warned.

"Have you forgotten who taught me?"

"Who?"

"You did!"

The old Indian grinned impishly. "I old man. Forget."

But Diane could tell by the look of pride shining from his black eyes that he hadn't forgotten at all.

The fierce August sun had finally began to slip below the Front Range of the Rocky Mountains on that same long summer's day. The dry, withering heat had lost its potent sting. The thin air was beginning to cool.

And Diane Buchannan, after having been thwarted more than once in her attempt to get a look at the Redman, was confident she'd now be successful. She had wisely planned this final excursion to coincide with the dinner hour.

Colonel Buck Buchannan's Wild West Show served three square meals a day prepared in specially equipped rail cars. The hours were set and strictly adhered to. The show people had to be at the mess tent during serving hours or miss the meal.

This was one meal Diane had decided to miss. While the others were congregated for supper she slipped from the rail car she shared with Texas Kate, moved quickly in the opposite direction of the mess tent, and was soon skirting the oval arena and on her way toward the animal holding pens.

The chatter of the diners faded and died away. The last of the day's light disappeared. Diane hurried into and down a dim narrow corridor between a maze of wooden corrals. The farther she went, the darker it became. Horses poked their heads over stalls and neighed and whinnied excitedly. She automatically put her forefinger perpendicular to her lips and whispered, "Shhhh!"

Ears laid back, eyes big, the high-strung show horses refused to quiet down. They put up such a racket Diane was afraid Shorty and his boys would hear them all the way over at the mess tent.

They didn't—but someone else did.

Diane finally saw the end of the narrow passageway directly ahead and was relieved. She walked faster. When she was no more than two or three feet away, a match flared. She stopped abruptly. Her eyes flew up to a man's face, partially illuminated by the orange glow. He was lounging against the last stall.

She took a step forward. He threw a long leg up across in front of her and hooked a bootheel over the third rung of the stall opposite, trapping her. He draped a forearm on his raised thigh and leaned slightly forward, revealing his face.

Smiling, he said, "Phil Lowery, Miss Buchannan. Billed and better known as the Cherokee Kid. Hope I didn't startle you."

Diane stood her ground. She looked directly at the smiling man and

said, "I don't startle that easily, Mr. Lowery. Now if you'll kindly let me
pass."

"Where you going? Maybe we could go there together."

"That isn't very likely, Mr. Lowery."

"Kid," he corrected, "call me Kid. Where *were* you going?"

"Surely it's of no interest to you." She glared down at his outstretched
leg, penning her like one of the animals.

The Cherokee Kid didn't lower it.

"You're wrong there." His gaze moved suggestively from her face
down over her slender body. "Dead wrong." His eyes slowly returned
to hers. "You're a very beautiful woman, Diane—may I call you Diane
. . . that is your name, isn't it?"

She sighed with annoyance. "I had no particular destination in mind,
Mr . . . Kid. I was simply taking a walk."

"I see." He nodded, puffed on his cigarette. "Well, your grandfather
would want me to caution you about roaming around down here
alone." Finally his long leg went back down to the ground. He took her
arm. "Know what's down here? Wild animals and wilder men."

"And I suppose you're one of those wilder men," she said contemptuously, making it clear he couldn't frighten her.

The Cherokee Kid smiled and ushered her out into the dusk. "I might
be," he said. "Care to find out?"

"Certainly not."

"No? I don't believe you. I think you're curious."

"You're dreaming," she replied bitingly.

He ignored the sarcasm. "I'll walk you back to your quarters." His
fingers continuing to encircle her upper arm, he said, "Maybe you'll
change your mind by the time we get there."

"Don't bank on it," she said, more irritated with him than he could
possibly have imagined. It seemed there was a conspiracy—and everyone in the troupe was in on it—to prevent her from seeing the Redman!

When the edge wore off her disappointment, Diane found the Cherokee Kid a pleasant enough companion. He was far more forthcoming
than Ancient Eyes when she questioned him about the Redman. He
freely admitted that the wild creature had scared the living daylights out
of him. Said he'd had to fight for his life in the unprovoked attack.

At her door she turned to face him, got a better look at him. From the
mellow light streaming out the open door of her quarters she saw that
the Kid was not only tall and very strong-looking but also quite handsome.

His hair was a thick dark blond; his eyes were a sparkling green. His
nose was straight, mouth appealingly full, chin heavily cut. He was

clean-shaven. His white shirt was freshly laundered; his beige trousers were meticulously pressed, his boots shined. He was obviously dressed for an evening out.

"Well, good night, Kid. I'm tired, think I'll go to bed." Teasingly she added, "What about you? You going right to bed too?"

"Yes." He was quick to answer. "As a matter of fact, that's exactly where I'm going."

It wasn't a lie.

A quarter of an hour after leaving Diane, the Kid walked through the front door of Jennie Rogers's House of Mirrors, an establishment its owner called the "plushest whorehouse from the Missouri River to the West Coast."

A bevy of beautiful, elegantly gowned young women sat about on sofas of lush gray velvet in a spacious second-floor parlor. While a smiling black man played "A Bird in a Gilded Cage" on a dark walnut grand piano, the Kid stood in the room's entrance and looked the women over.

He knew what he wanted. Quickly he chose a slender, youthful-looking woman whose raven black hair spilled around her bare shoulders and down her back to well below her waist.

"That one," he told the madam, and Jennie Rogers motioned to the exotic-looking Cheralynn.

"The queen's suite, Cheralynn," the madam instructed when the dark-haired woman reached them.

Nodding, Cheralynn swished her long, flowing hair back off her face, took the Kid's hand, and led him down a silent corridor to a birdcage elevator fashioned of gold bars. There was barely room for two people inside. It was impossible to keep their bodies from touching. The tiny elevator had been Jennie Rogers's idea. She wanted her customers to start getting in the mood before they got upstairs.

It worked on the Kid. Exiting after the brunette, he could hardly wait to get her in bed.

"Jesus Christ," he muttered when Cheralynn led him into a spacious room containing only one unorthodox piece of furniture.

A long, narrow carpet of plush red velvet led across a floor of gleaming white marble to a raised dais. Upon that dais sat a high-backed throne of shimmering gold gilt. From somewhere high above, white rays of light poured down in a bright circular pool enclosing the golden throne in hot, luminous brilliance.

The Kid was intrigued. "What's it for?"

"Fantasies," said Cheralynn. "If a customer chooses, he can pretend to be a commoner who is allowed—ordered—to make love to his queen."

The Kid grinned. "Let's give it a try."

Minutes later, wearing nothing but his beige trousers, he marched up the long red velvet carpet to the raised dais. Cheralynn sat upon the gold gilt throne. She was believable as a sovereign in a hastily donned long, flowing gown fashioned of gold braid intricately sewn together. The gown's sleeves were long and tight; the bodice was snugly fitted and high-throated. The skirts were very full, swirling about the arms of the gold throne and concealing her gold-slippered feet.

A long gold lamé cape lined with soft white ermine was hooked at her throat, then swept dramatically to one side to fall down over the throne's arm and lie prettily in a gold and white ermine pool on the polished white marble. On Cheralynn's dark head was a crown of gold decorated with semiprecious stones. In her right hand was a golden scepter.

She spoke, and her voice was low, firm. "Come forward, my obedient subject, and state your reason for seeking an audience with your queen."

The Kid moved directly to the dais. He bowed from the waist. "Your Royal Highness, it is my duty and my urgent desire to make love to you. Grant me this, I beseech you. Bestow upon this wretched commoner this one wish."

"Come closer," commanded the queen.

The commoner climbed the dais's steps, stood before her. The queen lifted her golden scepter, touched it gently to his swelling groin, and said, "If your peasant's body responds to my staff of sovereign authority and readies itself properly to enter the royal flesh, then you may have your wish."

He bowed. Then his hands clenched and unclenched at his sides while the naughty majesty slowly molded and shaped his responsive male flesh, wielding her golden scepter in a most provocative manner. The Kid found it incredibly exciting to stand there before Her Royal Highness as she guided the scepter slowly up and down and all around until he thought he would explode.

The queen, licking her wet red lips with the tip of her pink tongue, watched that physical evidence of his desire expand before her eyes until he was straining and surging against the tight, confining trousers. Finally she took pity on him.

Lifting the scepter to tickle his hair-covered chest, she said, "No nobleman has ever boasted a more impressive erection. Come forth and do your duty—claim this royal flesh."

In a flash the Kid had skinned out of his pants, grabbed her by the hand, jerked her up off the throne, and sat down on it, his long bare legs apart. He drew her close, shoved her long golden skirts up, and was delighted to discover she wore nothing underneath. The elegantly gowned queen climbed astride her pulsing naked subject.

While the hot white lights spilled down over them, the gowned, caped, crowned queen allowed her big naked servant obediently to make love to her while seated on the throne of gold. Her grateful subject clung to the throne's golden arms and thrust rhythmically, glorying in the wet heat of the female flesh he could feel enclosing him but could not see because of the swirling golden skirts.

The accommodating monarch clung to the naked peasant's strong neck and expertly ground her bare bottom down on him, glorying in the sensations caused by that rock-hard male flesh which she could feel so intensely up inside but couldn't see for the golden skirts covering them.

It was great fun right up to the royal release. The Kid enjoyed the princely game so much they changed positions and played it again. Only this time he wielded the scepter. Afterward Her Highness, sagging against his damp chest, nuzzled her nose in the thick chest hair, gave a flat brown nipple a playful lick, and said, "There's a nice soft bed in the next room. Shall we go there now?"

"By all means, Queenie," he said, grinning like an imperial imp. "I promised a new friend of mine I'd go straight to bed."

Diane waited only until the Kid was well out of sight. Then she slipped back outside and hurried through the deepening dusk toward the corrals. She raced right through them this time, ignoring the indignant whinnying and snorting of the horses.

She hurried on to outlying pens and cages. Her anxious search didn't take long. She found the Redman *where* she expected him to be. And *how* she expected to find him.

Caged like an animal.

An identical cage, housing a powerful mountain lion, sat squarely alongside the Redman's. Heart in her throat, Diane ventured near the cages. She stood there staring, shifting her attention back and forth between the man and the beast.

Both restlessly paced their cages.

Both growled threateningly, low in their throats, as they watched her watching them. Their eyes gleamed with fierce hatred. Powerful muscles bunched and pulled in their long, lean bodies.

Diane shivered.

Which was the more dangerous? Human or animal?

She edged up closer to the mountain lion's cage. His head lifted, revealing a distinctive diamond-shaped patch of raven fur beneath his tawny throat. He snarled and swiftly pounced, shooting a sharply clawed paw through the restraining bars. Diane gasped and jumped back in fear.

When her pulse had slowed, she moved toward the Redman's cage. He stopped his restless pacing, stood flat-footed, and stared unblinkingly down at her. His face was granite hard; the eyes, locked on her, were black and menacing. The cheekbones soared; the nose looked as if it had been broken. The mouth was full yet appeared alarmingly cruel. Coarse, tangled black hair reached almost to his bare bronzed shoulders and was streaked with silver around his mean-looking face.

A soft suede leather loincloth tied atop one bronzed hip and a wide beaded band encircling his throat were his only clothes. Long, leanly muscled arms hung at his sides. His bare bronzed feet were planted firmly apart in a proud, defiant stance. Those dark, hypnotic eyes dared her to step closer.

Boldly Diane threw back her shoulders and stepped closer to the near-naked savage. Then screamed and jumped back in panic when the Redman leaped like lightning, thrust a bare arm through the restraining bars, and reached for her.

Her heart pounding in her chest, she backed away, her frightened eyes riveted on those long, grasping fingers, that dark right wrist upon which a wide silver cuff bracelet flashed in the summer twilight.

Chapter 6

The big day had finally arrived.

➵➵➵➵ The afternoon's parade down Denver's wide Broadway Street had been a smashing success. People lining the sidewalks and leaning out the windows of tall buildings had no idea that a major disruption had occurred just prior to the parade's start.

It had been decided that the Redman of the Rockies would take part in the grand parade. Expensive color flyers had been hastily printed up, extolling the beauty of the refined trick rider Miss Diane Buchannan and the wildness of that totally uncivilized and highly dangerous brute, the Redman of the Rockies.

As it turned out, the Redman proved to be almost *too* dangerous. Shorty Jones had waited until everyone in the parade procession was lined up in place. Then the skinny little animal wrangler, cigarette dangling from his lips as usual, carried a rope, steel wrist irons, and a heavy chain to the Redman's cage.

The strategy was to cuff the creature's wrists together, loop the linked chain around his neck, mount him astride a big paint pony, and tie his bare feet underneath the horse. The Cherokee Kid, mounted on his big gray gelding, would then lead the paint pony and the nearly-naked savage right down Broadway, allowing every man, woman, and child a good, long look at this savage beast, the Redman of the Rockies.

Shorty stepped up to the creature's locked cage. The key to the cage had been taken from its secret hiding place in Ancient Eyes' quarters. Other than the old Ute chieftain, only Shorty knew where it was kept.

Key in hand, Shorty unlocked the barred door, opened it, and stepped up inside.

And grunted in shock and pain when the fierce Redman knocked him flat on his back. The cigarette flew from Shorty's mouth. The chains and steel cuffs fell from his hands. The Redman exploded from the unlocked cage and ran so swiftly he was a hundred yards from the exhibition grounds before anyone could react. Shouts and yells of warning went up from the troupe. Diane, astride her black stallion, turned in the saddle and stood in the stirrups. She drew in a quick breath when she saw the nearly naked Redman sprinting barefoot across the plain, a picture of graceful ferocity.

The Cherokee Kid and a half dozen mounted Rough Riders wheeled their horses and galloped after the fleeing savage. Despite their inequitable advantage, the Redman almost managed to elude them.

Running for his very life, the creature raced with lightning speed toward the foothills to the west, his silver-streaked raven hair streaming out around his noble head. His long bronzed legs were churning with swift, long-strided precision when all of a sudden a bare foot struck a sharp rock or he sprained an ankle. His powerful, fluid gait abruptly changed. Any hope he'd had of getting away disappeared with that one misstep.

The Cherokee Kid spurred his gelding forward and managed to catch up with his prey. Hugging the lunging mount with his knees, the Kid leaned down, snagged a handful of the Redman's flowing black hair. He yanked hard. The Redman's body was jerked backward. He stumbled, fell to his knees, struggled up again.

The Rough Riders encircled him. A well-thrown rope fell over the Redman's bare shoulders and tightened around his chest, trapping his arms at his sides. A couple of riders dismounted, wrestled the Redman to the ground, and tied his hands behind him. The Kid stayed in the saddle. Smiling, he led the recaptured Redman back to the fairgrounds. Applause rose from the troupe as the Kid cantered his mount, purposely making the Redman run and stumble on his injured foot to keep from falling.

The runaway redskin was promptly placed back in his cage and the door securely locked. He would still have a part in the parade—couldn't disappoint the public—but he'd remain behind bars, locked safely in his cage. The wheeled flatbed supporting his cage would be drawn down Broadway by a quartet of horses.

While the workmen made the necessary adjustments, the Colonel reined his mount over alongside the Kid.

The Kid looked up, shook his blond head, and said, "That was a close one, Colonel. I'm afraid that savage is nothing but trouble."

"On the contrary, Kid," the master showman calmly replied, "he's a godsend. We'll make his attempted escape a part of the show."

The Kid frowned. "You mean . . . no, I don't think—"

"This is not the East, Kid. The people in Colorado still remember the Meeker Massacre. We'll set the creature free in the arena. Let him attempt an escape." The Colonel smiled broadly, blue eyes twinkling, and added, "Then you'll ride in and recapture him to the sound of deafening applause."

Beginning to nod, the Kid said, "Imagine the screams and pandemonium when we turn him loose."

"I can, Kid! Why neither Pawnee Bill nor any other wild west show in the country has an act to compare."

After the parade, members of the troupe seized the opportunity to rest, to take a long breather before the evening's eight o'clock opening performance.

It was a very still, very hot August afternoon. The streets of Denver were now nearly deserted. Workers and shoppers and those who had viewed the parade had fled to the haven of their homes to relax, cool off, and have their evening meals before returning to town for the opening presentation of Colonel Buck Buchannan's traveling extravaganza.

Diane was not resting. She was restless. She strolled alone down the quiet city streets, stopping to look in store windows, lingering before a fancy restaurant to read the menu posted outside the door. She made a sour face. None of the offered fare sounded good. She wasn't hungry, though it was well into the supper hour. She blamed the dry Denver heat for her lack of appetite.

She wandered aimlessly on down the street to where the sidewalk ended. Across an empty city block stood the fairgrounds. Diane stopped and smiled guiltily, realizing she was very near the Redman's cage, realizing as well that she'd been heading there all along. She'd simply taken a detour, choosing the long way around so that no one in the troupe would see her.

Diane crossed the street and plunged determinedly through the empty, weed-choked lot, pushing dead sunflowers out of her path, yanking irritably when her lacy petticoat snagged on a thorny bush. She reached the far side of the block and was about to step down into the dusty street when she heard a whimper, some laughing and scuffling.

She paused, turned her head, listened, and heard it again. She went immediately to investigate, a frown of puzzlement on her face. She came upon a couple of young ruffians behind an old boarded-up warehouse. The large teenaged boys were crouched on the ground, tormenting a tiny, terrified white kitten.

Diane was horrified. She shouted at them to stop and raced to the kitten's rescue. Her eyes flashed purple fire and she angrily grabbed one of the boys by his shirt collar. She snatched him up with such force it startled him. He came stumbling to his feet, covering his face with his arms, cowering before her.

"Get out of here, both of you!" she snapped commandingly. "You ought to be ashamed of yourselves, abusing a poor dumb animal!"

She released the boy's collar with a forceful shove, and both bullies turned tail and ran as fast as their legs would carry them. Her jaw hard, chin squared, Diane shouted after them, "How would you like to be treated like you were treating this defenseless creature? You're a disgrace to mankind!"

Her eyes lowered and the severe expression on her face softened immediately. She went down on her knees, her long skirts swirling out around her. She very slowly, very gently picked up the trembling kitten and clutched it to her breast. She cradled the scared, meowing little creature close, stroked the soft white fur of its quivering back, and murmured soothingly, laying her cheek to its head.

When the kitten had calmed and quit shaking and mewling, Diane rose to her feet. Holding the tiny ball of white fur against the side of her bare throat, she went in search of its mother. She walked briskly about in back of the warehouse, calling loudly.

In seconds a relieved old mama cat came flying through the tall weeds of the vacant lot. Diane went back down on her knees and quickly gave the kitten over. Then stayed as she was for a long moment more, kneeling on the ground, watching the heartwarming, demonstrative reunion.

Someone else was also watching.

Someone had silently witnessed Diane Buchannan's sudden flash of anger toward the pair of heartless young bullies. Had mutely observed her surprisingly admirable display of bravery when she straightaway confronted the rough-looking pair with no thought to her own safety. Had been an entranced bystander when she comforted the frightened kitten with the inborn tenderness of a protective young mother toward her own precious offspring.

Someone had seen it all.

His dark, impassive face softening ever so slightly when the beautiful raven-haired woman hugged the furry white kitten to her breast, he watched unblinkingly from his barred cage across the dusty alley.

The fierce Redman of the Rockies.

Chapter 7

By sunset the fairgrounds' newly constructed grandstands were filled to overflowing. Extra folding bleachers had been hastily added to stretch the seating capacity. It was as if not only the city of Denver but the entire state of Colorado had turned out en masse for the nighttime premiere performance of *Colonel Buck Buchannan's Wild West Show*.

As the appointed hour approached, the heart of every performer beat a little faster. Opening-night jitters were nothing more than a building excitement, a tingling anticipation which caused the blood to surge swiftly through veins, pulses to quicken pleasantly. The troupe was experienced and totally confident. All the same the performers felt vitally alive and childishly eager to get out there before the huge, expectant crowd and do their stuff.

All was ready.

Run-throughs had gone smoothly. The lights had been tested and retested. The dusty arena watered down. Huge, colorfully painted backdrops stood just outside the show ring, arranged numerically, their numbers corresponding to the show segments in which they would be used.

So now, as the still summertime darkness settled over the Queen City of the Rockies, Colonel Buck Buchannan's Cowboy Band serenaded the last of the straggling spectators into their seats, a late change had been made on the show's agenda. One not listed on the printed programs.

The eager crowds filling the fairgrounds were in store for an even more exciting evening than promised.

SHOWTIME.

The oval arena was totally dark. The crowd in the packed grandstands sat in darkness. The brief flare of matches, the scattered glow of cigarettes sprinkled orange pinpoints of light throughout the bleachers. It appeared to be a giant gathering of luminous orange fireflies. The hum of a thousand separate conversations competed with the band's playing of martial and show tunes.

And then . . .

All at once the band went into a loud fanfare. At the same time bright calcium flares blazed to life, illuminating the empty arena as wild west banners slowly descended. All conversation stopped. Every head turned. Each pair of eyes focused on the lighted arena's south entrance gate.

Loud cheers and whistles greeted him as that grand old gentleman of the Plains, Colonel Buck Buchannan, galloped into the arena astride a glorious white stallion with wild, glowing eyes. Horse and rider, caught and framed in the blue mirrored spotlight, were a sight to behold.

The Colonel was dressed all in snowy white gabardine. His shirt and trousers were heavily fringed and decorated with gleaming silver embroidery. The trousers were stuffed into handmade leather boots; the boots' tops inlaid with silver. On his hands were fringed white gauntlets, and atop his white head a white Stetson was cocked at a jaunty angle.

His magnificent white steed, Captain, was equally well turned out with fancy trappings of white and silver. His long white mane and strips of wide silver ribbon had been meticulously plaited together into a dozen perfect, gleaming silver and white braids. Saddle and bridle were heavily embellished with silver.

The wide smile on Colonel Buck Buchannan's face was brighter by far than the calcium flares. The Colonel reared Captain up on his hind legs and lifted his white Stetson in a sweeping salute to the audience. A crescendo of applause erupted as the mighty stallion turned around and around on his two hind legs, the man on his back seated militarily straight.

Flowers were tossed at the Colonel and Captain as they began a tour of the ring. One hand loosely holding the reins, the other proudly waving his Stetson, the Colonel hailed his adoring gallery. The white stallion pranced, strutted, cantered, and danced to the music, leaping softly in the light.

So entranced was the crowd by the old master showman and his trained white stallion it took a minute for them to realize that other performers had followed the Colonel into the arena.

Colonel Buck Buchannan's Wild West Show was officially under way, the extravaganza opening with a colorful Grand Review. The fast-paced spectacle left the audience breathless. Featured performers galloped into the ring and pulled up sharply on their horses right in front of the packed stands. Some mounts reared as the Colonel's white stallion had done. Others bowed. Still others pranced back and forth.

The smiling, waving stars made a full circle around the arena and followed the Colonel out into the darkness as the rest of the cast entered. First came the big bell wagon, all bells clanging loudly, the heavy wagon being pulled by the renowned Belgian horses weighing a ton each. Next the old-time chuck wagon, making a perfect figure eight in the arena. Then the gilded lion cage, bars close together, tawny mountain lion snarling and pacing inside. Other cages decorated with mirrors and gold gilt and housing wild animals paraded into the ring.

Then in rode the Indians, led by Ancient Eyes in colorful war bonnet, his lance raised. Feathered and painted and shrieking war hoops, a contingent of Utes and Pawnees and Arapahos rode their bareback paint ponies into the light.

After the Indians, dozens of Mexican vaqueros in bright, colorful serapes and oversize sombreros. Next the Cossacks and Bengal Lancers, all in native costume. Then the Rough Riders and charros. And suddenly the big arena was filled with cowboys, on foot and on horseback, herding along steers, buffaloes, mules, and horses.

The shouts of the riders, the whips' lashes, the neighs, bellows, and snorts of the animals, the creak of saddle leather, the colorful costumes, the stirring music—sounds and sights of the magnificent spectacle. With remarkable precision and pace, hundreds of men and animals moved around the arena and back out into the dark recesses outside.

Right on their heels a special carriage rolled in, carrying the famed female sharpshooter, Texas Kate. She was smiling and waving, basking happily in the loud applause. Her graying brown hair was tightly curled around her broad, beaming face. She wore a fringed blouse and shirt, bolo tie, and boots. The front of her blouse was covered with marksmen's medals.

The carriage stopped in the arena's center. Texas Kate stepped down into the spotlight with pistol, rifle, and shotgun. She was always first on the program. Years ago the Colonel had designed the show to graduate in excitement. Aware that shooting and shouts might unnerve the women and children in the audience, he brought on Texas Kate very early in the performance.

Kate started very gently, shooting only with a pistol. It worked perfectly. The young children and the nervous women in the audience saw a smiling, harmless woman out there and soon relaxed. When Texas Kate had their total trust, she switched to the rifle and gradually increased until she was shooting with full charge. Skillfully she prepared the audiences for any frightening act that might come later.

For a good half hour the trigger-talented Texas Kate put on a shooting exhibition unlike anything the paying crowd had ever seen. Bullets cracked and objects exploded as the smiling sure-shot female marksman hit stationary targets, moving targets, flying targets. Texas Kate beat her own record when she hit a total of forty-nine out of fifty glass balls tossed into the air. At thirty paces she hit the narrow edges of playing cards. She perfectly plugged silver dimes tossed into the air.

The finishing segment of her routine was the crowd's favorite. Texas Kate's quiet assistant, the skinny little cowboy who had driven her carriage into the arena and tossed the glass balls, the cards, the dimes for her, now shyly moved into the spotlight, waving a package of cigarettes in his hand. Propmen, hidden in the darkness, rolled into place a protective brick barricade behind him.

Shorty Jones was not actually a performer, but he assisted Texas Kate in her act. For two reasons. First, nobody else in the troupe volunteered. Second, Shorty seized any opportunity to be around Texas Kate. Shorty Jones had been secretly, silently sweet on Kate for more than a decade. He'd never told her in so many words, but he suspected she knew. Trouble was, she didn't care. She was still waiting for another man. Shorty knew he could never hope to measure up to the missing Teddy Ray Worthington.

Shorty stepped back against the temporary barricade, shook a readymade cigarette from his pack, stuck it into his mouth, and lit up. Texas Kate picked up her pearl-handled pistols, held them high in the air, then paced off fifty feet. She turned and immediately fired ten shots in rapid succession, first with one hand, then the other, snipping an nth of a degree from Shorty's lighted cigarette with each shot.

She shot so fast and so accurately that her incredible performance was over too soon to suit the screaming crowd. People were still whistling and begging for more when Texas Kate, allowing Shorty to help her back up into the carriage, waved as she was driven out of the spotlight and into the darkness.

The applause finally died away.

Silence.

Then a shout from a man out in the audience. "Where's that Beauty? Bring on the Beauty!"

From another section of the grandstands. "Beauty! We want the Beauty! The Beauty and the Beast!"

"Beauty and the Beast!" Others took up the chant. "The Beauty and the Beast! Beauty and the Beast! The Beauty and the—"

Shouting, yipping scouts and vaqueros and bawling steers, untamed horses, and charging buffaloes filled the arena, drowning out the shouts, commanding the crowd's attention. Lassos whirled through the air, encircling hooves, necks, ears, and even tails of the thundering herds. Nimble vaqueros leaped from horse to horse, from horse to ground, from ground to horse.

And then the Rough Riders—the tough gristle and bone cowboys— led by the blond, handsome Cherokee Kid astride his snorting chestnut stallion. They were the real thing, these men, wild and rough, the last of a rugged breed being slowly pushed off the plains by progress and civilization. They galloped like the Wild Bunch into the arena, guns blazing, scaring spectators and scattering the troupe.

In a stirring finale the riders joined forces and staged an old-time roundup. They cut cattle from the herd, roped and branded them. Soon all disappeared in a cloud of dust.

When the dust settled and the applause subsided, a faint throb of drums filled the air. Into the ring marched the proud redskins as the drums grew louder, faster. Lances raised, feather bustles and head-dresses fluttering in the breeze, the old war chiefs and their braves went into their symbolic tribal dances to the riotous approval of the audience.

However, the crowd's captivation with the Indians' colorful cere-mony was short-lived. The Indian the people most wanted to see was not dancing to the drums. He was not in the arena. The Redman of the Rockies was nowhere in sight.

As quickly as they had come, the Indians danced their way out of the arena as the throb of the drums grew muffled and died away.

Again there was silence. And again darkness as the calcium flares were lowered and turned out. Seconds passed. A pinpoint of soft blue light suddenly appeared in the darkened arena's center. The light grew bigger. And bigger. The growing mirrored spotlight picked up a horse and rider. A slender black-haired woman and a sleek black-coated stal-lion. Neither horse nor rider moved. They might have been an incredi-bly lifelike statue, save for the slight breeze from out of the east lifting the ends of the woman's raven hair, the stallion's flowing black mane.

The temporarily dazed crowd came roaring to its feet as a dazzling smile began to spread over the pale, perfect face of the rider.

"Beauty!" they loudly hailed her. "Beauty! Beauty!" they shouted ex-citedly to the slender raven-haired woman astride the magnificent black stallion. Diane was nothing less than spectacular. Dressed in black satin shirt and tight-fitting black leather trousers, her tall, shapely body mounted up on the big black horse, she looked every inch the western queen, not to be crossed. She was the envy of every woman in the audience, the dream girl of every man. She went immediately into her routine.

The noise subsided when, with only a soft-spoken command to Champ, the big black wheeled about and went into a fast, dirt-flinging gallop. When the stallion reached top speed, Diane shot to her feet on his back.

For the next half hour Diane commanded the attention of the crowd with her daring riding and roping skills. She leaped to the ground while the black stallion sprinted across the arena. Then leaped back astride his back. She slid down underneath his neck, slipped down his long, flowing tail, rode the big creature in ways no one would have thought possible.

She got out her lariat and put on a roping exhibition that was every bit as thrilling as the fancy riding. She lassoed the black's neck, his belly, his ear, his tail. She roped one front hoof, then two. She spelled out her name with the rope, drawing oohs and aahs as, one letter at a time, she wrote out "Diane" with the spinning, perfectly tossed rope. The crowd stomped its feet and cheered when she tossed the lariat up into the grandstands. She climbed on Champ's back, wheeled him left, and went into her final act: the mounted somersault.

Loud applause, whistles, and shouts of "Bravo, Beauty! Bravo, Beauty, bravo!" escorted her out of the arena. Exhilarated, out of breath, Diane slid down off Champ's back just outside the entrance. She tossed the reins to one of the waiting wranglers and watched as the black was led away.

In the dim light she backed into something, turned, and saw that it was the Redman's cage. For a second her eyes met those of the creature. He gave her a wild-eyed look that made her shiver. He continued to look straight at her as his cage rolled away. Diane stood there for a moment, feeling faint and foolishly frightened.

The roar of the crowd drew her attention to the arena. They were screaming, "Redman! Beast! It's the Beast! The Redman of the Rockies!"

Diane drew a shallow breath, shook her head, and started to walk away. She changed her mind. Glancing quickly about, she climbed the arena's tall fence to watch and was appalled by what she saw.

The Redman's cage was being slowly wheeled around the inner perimeter of the ring by the burly Leatherwood brothers. Every few yards the Leatherwoods stopped and called for anyone in the audience who wanted to get up close to the fierce beast to come on down.

Diane was astounded to see the preponderance of women who scrambled down out of their seats to crowd around the Redman's barred cage. Through violet eyes narrowed in disgust she watched as women, young and old, pretty and plain, gathered around the Redman, twittering and gasping and laughing nervously. Clearly they were not totally repelled by the nearly-naked beast.

Diane felt a funny quiver race up her spine as she observed the women practically fighting one another to get closer to the Redman. Sex and mystery were bound together in the beautiful, wild creature. That's what drew all those foolish women to his cage. Diane was revolted.

But she didn't leave.

She continued to sit there atop that wooden fence while the Redman's cage moved slowly around the big arena. The excited females of Denver continued to swoop down to the cage, and Diane couldn't believe her eyes when she saw pretty girls who were obviously from fine families tossing ribbons from their hair into the creature's cage. Lacy handkerchiefs and fresh-cut flowers were pitched inside amid peals of high-pitched feminine laughter.

Diane gasped, then held her breath when a very foolish young blonde ripped a pearl button from the collar of her summer dress and held it out on her palm to the Redman, sticking her hand right through the restraining bars of his cage. Diane silently waited for the untamed savage to grab the girl and pull her roughly up against the bars, perhaps even hurt her badly.

The Redman never moved.

He didn't reach for the blond woman; he didn't take the offered pearl button. He stared at the silly woman with fierce hatred shining out of his dark eyes. His cage rolled away. The pouting blonde threw the button at him and flounced back to her seat.

Diane took a much-needed breath.

Finally the cage had made a complete circle. It was back at the arena's entrance. Diane, from her vantage point on the fence directly beside the arena gates, could see the Redman inside. He looked furious, as if he deeply resented being shown off like an animal.

Diane automatically lowered her eyes. She wished they would hurry and roll his cage outside the lighted ring. What were they waiting for? Why had they stopped there inside the arena?

She found out.

Davey Leatherwood unlocked the cage and released the Redman. To Davey Leatherwood's—and the audience's—shocked surprise, the enraged Redman attacked Leatherwood with his bare hands. Striking with the swiftness of a serpent, the slim Indian wrestled the big, powerful white man to the ground. He pounded Leatherwood's face with his fists; blood spurted.

Women screamed and men shouted.

Danny Leatherwood quickly dragged the Redman off his baby brother, turned, and smiled up at the crowd as if it were part of the act. But the smile left his face when the Redman, struggling free of his grasp, turned and threw a punch that caught Danny Leatherwood squarely on the chin, knocking him to his knees.

Before either Leatherwood could react, the Redman took off running. Screams of fear and excitement rose from the crowd as the nearly-naked savage raced across the dusty arena in an honest attempt to escape. He was almost to the north fence when the mounted Cherokee Kid and the armed Rough Riders thundered into the arena.

The Redman never stood a chance.

He was ridden down by the Rough Riders, but only after they had toyed with him, as a cat does with a mouse. The enraged Redman was run back and forth across the ring, almost getting away, not quite making it, while the riders laughed and yipped and played to the appreciative crowd.

At last the Redman was caught. Weak and out of breath, his long legs and bare chest glistening with sweat, he was roped by the smiling mounted Cherokee Kid. By then the angered Leatherwood brothers were bearing down on the trapped Redman.

"Try taking a swing at me now, you red bastard." Danny Leatherwood stepped up close, stuck out his chin, his taunt spoken too softly for the crowd to hear.

His arms pinned to his sides, the Redman struck with his teeth. A loud yelp of pain went up from Danny Leatherwood as he reached for his bitten, bloodied earlobe. The crowd gasped and murmured.

The Cherokee Kid swiftly dismounted. While the Leatherwoods held the savage, the Kid clamped heavy chains on the ferocious Redman's hands and feet and dragged him back to his cage.

Diane sat there unmoving atop the arena fence.

She felt almost sick.

The crowd loved it.

Chapter 8

❊❊❊❊ After the show the Colonel and Mrs. Buchannan hosted an opening-night party for the entire troupe. The celebration, held inside the fairgrounds arena, was as big a success as the show.

By the time the performers bathed, changed clothes, and wandered back down for the party, the troupe's talented propmen had miraculously transformed the dusty arena into a magical place which hardly resembled itself. A smooth wooden-floored dance pavilion bordered with baskets of fresh-cut flowers and hand-painted scenery set the mood. A raised dais was in place near the dance floor for the Cowboy Band. The calcium flares circling the arena burned low, casting only a soft, mellow light over everything. A long makeshift bar stood just inside the entrance gates. Behind that bar Shorty, with the habitual cigarette hanging from his thin lips, and Ancient Eyes, with a white dish towel tied around his wide middle, were pouring drinks.

Diane arrived just as the Cowboy Band went into a rousing rendition of "Oh, Dem Golden Slippers." Smiling, she hugged the Colonel, congratulated him on the show's success—the highest one-night gross in two years—then leaned down and kissed her grandmother's cheek. The frank and protective Ruth Buchannan patted Diane's slender back and whispered in her ear, "You look lovely, dear, but that dress is liable to get you in trouble around these wild Rough Riders."

"I can take care of myself, Granny," Diane whispered back, disengaged herself, and strolled toward the bar.

She knew what her grandmother meant. Her yellow dotted swiss dress was pretty and certainly stylish, but perhaps the low-cut neckline was a bit too daring for the frontier. Along Washington's sophisticated Embassy Row the dress wouldn't have drawn a second glance. Diane shrugged bare shoulders dismissively and stepped up to the long bar.

"Can't a lady get a drink around here!" she said, pounding a fist down atop the gleaming wood.

"Sure can. What'll it be, Miss Diane?" Shorty's eyes were narrowed against the cigarette smoking drifting up into them.

Before she could reply, Ancient Eyes said, "Soda pop for Little Buck!" He shoved an ice-cold root beer across the bar to her.

Diane shook her head, then reached out and took the offered glass bottle. "Isn't anybody in the troupe willing to treat me like a grown woman?"

"I am," came a low voice from behind her.

She quickly turned. And bumped squarely into the hard, ungiving chest of the Cherokee Kid. Her open bottle of root beer splashed onto his clean white shirtfront.

"Oh, my Lord . . . I'm sorry," Diane apologized as she reached into the low-cut bodice of her yellow dress, withdrew a lacy handkerchief, and began awkwardly blotting the staining soda from the Kid's shirtfront. "I *am* sorry."

The Kid smiled. "You won't have to be sorry if you'll do me one small favor."

Diane's violet eyes lifted to his. "Name it."

"Dance with me." He took the soda bottle and dampened handkerchief from her.

"I suppose it's the least I can do," she said.

"The very least."

He set the bottle aside, dabbed the last traces of root beer from his shirt, and guided her toward the dance pavilion. She stepped into his arms and was still there hours later when the band played the closing tune, "After the Ball."

The Kid hadn't allowed her out of his sight the entire evening. He politely but firmly turned down all the eager cowboys and vaqueros attempting to cut in for a dance. He totally monopolized her time. When the party ended, he didn't ask if he could walk her back to her quarters. He just did it.

At her door he said, "I want to see you again."

She turned to face him. "Considering the circumstances"—she cut her eyes around—"it would be hard *not* to see me again, don't you think?"

"You know what I mean." He stepped closer, so close she had to tip her head back to look up at him.

"Yes," she said, "I know."

She studied him thoughtfully. The moonlight shone on his dark blond hair. His green eyes burned with interest. His impressive shoulders strained the white fabric of his shirt and pulled tightly across his chest. He was a very attractive man, and it would be fun to have someone show her around the city.

Diane laid a flattened palm on his muscular chest. "I'm told the Brown Palace rents bicycles. We could go for a ride sometime."

The Kid's large, square hand closed firmly over hers. "I'll come for you in the morning at nine sharp." He leaned down, kissed her cheek, whispered good night, and left.

Diane stood in the moonlight watching him walk away. He seemed a perfect escort: handsome, likable, a polished dancer. Yet the minute he was out of sight, she forgot about him. She turned, started to go inside, changed her mind. It was very late, but she wasn't the least bit sleepy. If she went inside, she'd only disturb the slumbering Kate.

Diane sighed, sat down on the stoop, kicked off her black dancing slippers, and wrapped her arms around her knees. She reached up, slipped the restraining ribbon from her hair, and let the long tresses cascade down around her bare shoulders. She threw her head back and looked straight up at the heavens. She inhaled the sweet night air deeply and studied the pale silver moon and the brightly twinkling stars.

She felt suddenly the way she'd felt so many times when she was a child and lay out on the lawn of Granny and the Colonel's big northern Arizona ranch house, staring up at the night sky.

Dreamy. Restless. Yearning.

Diane sighed again and let her thoughts wander back over the evening. The laughter and music and dancing. The successful standing-room-only show with all its color and pageantry and excitement. And, she hoped, large profits. The exhilaration of performing before a large audience, the sweet satisfaction of hearing the applause. The thrill of watching the other top performers . . . the . . . other . . .

The Redman of the Rockies leaped into her mind, shoving aside everything else. Her brow knitted as she saw again the foolish ladies rushing down to the Redman's cage. She frowned and bit the inside of her bottom lip at the unwelcome recollection of seeing the poor creature race across the dusty arena in a hopeless attempt at escape.

Diane exhaled.

What, she wondered, had the Redman been doing while she and the others danced and enjoyed themselves at the cast party? Could he hear, from his cage down by the animal pens, the music and the laughter? Had all the merriment of which he was not a part kept him awake?

What was he doing now? Was he still restlessly pacing in his cage? Or was he sound asleep? Was he dreaming of another life? A life far better suited to his wild ways?

Diane rose to her feet.

Warily she looked up, then down the long row of rail cars lined up on the spur. All were dark. Everyone was sleeping. That one chance in a million gave her this opportunity.

She looked down at her shoes and promptly decided she could move faster and quieter barefoot. So she peeled her silk stockings down her long, slender legs, took them off, and stuffed them into the toes of her slippers.

She stepped off the stoop. Again she looked around, took a deep breath, lifted the skirts of her yellow dotted swiss dress, and ran as fast as she could toward the darkened arena. When she reached the arena's high enclosing fence, she followed its curve northward and all the way around to the far side.

She wisely chose not to go through the horse stables this time. It took five minutes longer, but she skirted the many stalls housing the show ponies and managed to reach the rest of the animal holding pens without causing a disturbance. At last she spotted the distinctive twin cages fifty yards ahead, their steel bars glittering in the moonlight.

With her goal now in sight Diane hesitated.

What was she doing down here? It was the middle of the night. She should be safely in her bed, not wandering around down among the animal holding pens. What if someone should see her?

Holding her skirts up around her knees, Diane stood there feeling foolish and nervous, debating with herself whether or not she should proceed or turn and hurry home before she was caught.

The pull of the Redman was too strong. She was helplessly drawn to his cage. She felt as if she simply had to use this chance to study him closely when no one else was around.

Heart beginning to thud against her ribs, Diane ventured forward, tiptoeing on bare, dusty feet. In seconds she stood directly before the twin cages and was incredibly relieved to find both man and mountain lion sleeping peacefully. Here was her opportunity to examine them at her leisure.

First she stepped up to the big cat's cage and immediately smiled. The ferocious mountain lion appeared totally harmless as he lay there on his back, paws in the air, golden eyes tightly shut. She had the foolish urge to reach inside the cage and gently stroke the exposed white-furred tummy rising and falling so rapidly with his deep, quick breaths. She knew better than to try it. Although in slumber he seemed as tame as a tabby, the big beautiful cat was highly dangerous.

"Never wake a sleeping tiger." The familiar phrase ran through Diane's mind.

She moved away. Silently she stepped up to the Redman's cage. For a long moment she simply took satisfaction in the pleasing picture of the fierce Redman sprawled out before her in deep slumber. Soon an embarrassed smile spread over her face. It was indeed a guilty pleasure to look upon such a beautiful creature of another race.

He, like the cat, lay upon his back. His silver-winged raven hair flowed at the sides and fell over his high forehead. His sharp-boned, fierce-eyed face looked almost boyish in repose. That full mouth was relaxed just enough to lose some of its natural cruelty.

Diane's intense gaze moved down over his face, past the wide beaded neckband encircling his throat, to his naked torso and long, leanly muscled arms. His shoulders were wide and sculpted. His chest was smooth and bronzed and fell away beneath his ribs, tapering to a flat, almost concave belly.

Diane swallowed hard.

The brief loincloth the creature wore rode low around his prominent hipbones. Fully visible was his navel, below which a thick line of raven hair curled down inside the covering breechcloth. Casting only a momentary glance at the groin straining against the supple leather, Diane's eyes traced the lines of his bare, perfectly shaped legs. One knee was bent, the sole of a bare foot resting on the hay-strewn floor. The other leg was stretched out full length.

Her gaze moved slowly down the hard thigh, past the knee, over the calf, and to the bare bronzed foot. Then very slowly it came all the way back up, noting with unconcealed interest the fact that even well above the point where his rock-hard thigh met his hip joint, his smooth skin was all of one color: a beautiful dark golden bronze.

Diane was positive that if she reached out, tugged on the narrow leather thong riding the small indentation below his hipbone, and carefully peeled back the covering loincloth, the part of his body which was never exposed to the sun would be the same pleasing hue.

Suddenly the wispy hair at the nape of her neck lifted, as if someone had walked over her grave. She was overcome with an eerie feeling that the creature was watching her. Her face immediately reddened. Shame burned her cheeks. Her head snapped up, and she looked quickly at his face.

And froze.

His eyes were open, shining in the dark. He hadn't moved a muscle in his long, lean body, but those dark eyes were wide open and staring straight at her. Fear and guilt warred within her.

How long had he been awake? Had he seen her make that fully unguarded and shamefully intimate inspection of his body? Diane tried to speak, couldn't. She began to tremble, raised her arms, and hugged herself, unwittingly causing the neckline of her gown to slip lower between the swell of her breasts.

The Redman's eyes, black, clear, and incredibly calm, continued to regard her with icy hatred. His teeth gleamed in the darkness and Diane felt a chill up her spine. The moment he awakened he radiated an anger that seemed volatile and dangerous. And something else as well.

A sense of dark, almost mystic sexuality.

Suddenly overcome with terror of the caged beast, Diane whirled and ran away, vowing as she ran that she would *never* come near the creature again.

Never!

Chapter 9

Diane and the Cherokee Kid rode their rented bicycles out to the point where the Platte River converged with Cherry Creek. The initial part of the ride was relaxed, leisurely, and enjoyable. Then the Kid made the mistake of challenging Diane to a race. A fiercely competitive young woman, she wasted no time in taking him up on his dare.

Pedaling as if the devil were after her, she tore down the dusty street, dark hair flying around her face, teeth gritted in determination. She managed to beat the Kid to a shade-covered, grassy spot beside the narrow, swiftly flowing Cherry Creek. Exhausted but delighted to have won, she hopped off the bicycle and dropped it down on the grass. Out of breath, sides aching, she sank to the ground herself and fell immediately over onto her back.

She laughed triumphantly, flung her arms up over her head, and breathed deeply. She sighed, enjoying the outing, the warm, beautiful morning, and the awesome scenery surrounding her. She went into new peals of laughter as she lifted her head and watched the Kid come puffing up, his bike wobbling, his broad chest heaving from exertion.

He stopped a few yards away, threw a long leg over, and let his bicycle fall where it was. Forehead and throat beaded with perspiration, he came to where Diane lay flat on her back. He looked down at her, blotted his brow on a muscular forearm, and fell to his knees beside her.

"I won," she said, smiling up at him. "I won."

"No," he corrected, struggling for breath, "no, you didn't." He stretched out on his stomach beside her. "I won."

"You! How do you figure?"

Heart still pumping rapidly, he said, "You wanted to beat me so badly you half killed yourself to do it."

"So? And you didn't?"

He shook his head and grinned. He lifted a hand and touched his forefinger to her bottom lip. "Now you're so exhausted I've got you where I want you. Lying here too weak to fight me off."

"Don't count on it," she warned, continuing to smile easily.

"I mean to kiss you, Diane Buchannan," he cautioned, smiling just as easily.

"I know," she replied, looking straight up into his green eyes, arms staying as they were, flung up above her head.

The Kid moved his hand to her narrow rib cage. His fingers gently curved around her waist. He leaned down and kissed her, his mouth warm and eager on hers. Diane's arms didn't come down to twine around his neck. But she did kiss him back, turning her head a little, molding her lips to the gentle pressure of his.

As soon as the Kid lifted his blond head, she pushed on his broad chest, sat up, and said, "I'm starved. Let's ride over to Pell's Fish House for lunch."

She shot to her feet while the Kid sat there on the ground, stunned by her abrupt manner, disappointed that his kiss hadn't had a more lasting effect. He was accustomed to having women sigh and swoon when he caressed them. His green eyes narrowed as he watched Diane dash merrily over and jerk up her bicycle. He had the uneasy feeling that this overly independent raven-haired beauty meant to lead him a merry chase.

That unpleasant prospect annoyed him. He felt his temper rising, was struck with the strong desire to grab her right off that damned bicycle, fling her back down on the summer grass, and kiss her until she knocked off all this haughty foolishness and sighed his name in rapture.

He exhaled heavily. He couldn't do it. He had to swallow his pride and take the time and patience to woo this one properly. She wasn't just another woman with whom he wanted to go to bed. She was Diane Buchannan, the Colonel's only granddaughter. It appeared the heartless little bitch enjoyed playing games. Well, he would let her play.

Smiling again, the Kid rose to his feet, brushed the grass blades from his trousers, hurried to climb on his bicycle and overtake the beautiful, maddening woman. For once in his life he intended to play his hand right. The Colonel was quite fond of him; he was sure of it. In the two years he had been with the troupe, Colonel Buchannan had been right there to bail him out of a couple of scrapes. And instead of preaching to him, the old showman had laughed, clapped him on the back, and said, "Kid, you remind me of myself when I was a young man. Why, back before I married my sweet wife, Ruthie, I was quite the hell raiser."

Pedaling up the street, the Kid was silently making plans. Plans that involved the laughing young woman racing breezily ahead of him. Almost from the minute he had joined the troupe he'd begun looking forward to the day when the Colonel and Mrs. Buchannan were too old to travel.

Soon after meeting the lovely Diane, the aging couple's granddaughter and only heir, he'd been stuck by the idea that if he and Diane were to marry, the old man might step aside sooner. Being married to the granddaughter wouldn't be all that bad. She *was* very beautiful, and he had no doubt he could take her down to size, train her to be the kind of wife every man wanted. Sweet. Passionate. Loyal. Patient. Obedient. Willing to accept his occasional indiscretions without complaint.

Marrying Diane Buchannan was definitely the answer. Then the show, and the girl, would be his.

The Kid pulled up alongside Diane. When she glanced over at him, he turned his most winning smile on her and said, "Diane, I didn't—I didn't mean to frighten you back there."

Her dark, perfectly arched eyebrows shot up and her violet eyes flashed with derisive laughter. "Kid, you couldn't frighten me if you tried!"

Stung by her unexpected retort, he wisely kept his bruised ego to himself. Docilely he rode back into town with her, making small talk, doing his best to charm her. They shared a hearty meal at Pell's Fish House, and afterward he again followed her lead as she climbed back on her rented bicycle and rode off down toward the fairgrounds.

Diane didn't consciously head straight for the Redman's cage. At least she told herself she didn't. But minutes after reaching the fairgrounds, she was rolling to a stop directly before the barred cage, her anxious eyes searching for the creature.

She got off the bicycle, moved up closer to the cage's steel bars, and peered in at the reclining Redman.

"Isn't he something?" The Kid's voice came from just behind. He discarded his bicycle and came to stand at Diane's elbow. "A real throwback. A dirty, ignorant Stone Age Neanderthal."

The Redman, lying down in the shade at the back of his cage, turned a bored, scornful gaze on the gawking pair, then yawned and stretched his legs apart and clasped his hands behind his head. His mouth fixed in a hard, thin line, he flexed the muscles of his upper body, causing his taut stomach to cave in under his ribs, the flat belly to fall away from the covering loincloth.

"Diane, stay away from down here unless I'm with you," the Kid warned. "If he should get loose . . ."

"Yes, I will," Diane murmured, unable to take her eyes off the relaxed Redman. The creature showed no emotion. None at all. Did he feel anything? Was there anything they could say or do that would capture his attention?

Diane realized she was being thoughtless and maybe even unkind, but she caught herself longing to get a rise out of the Redman of the Rockies. To evoke some kind of emotion. Looking straight at the Redman, Diane moved a step closer to the Kid, slid her hand up around his big arm, and, pressing the hard biceps with restless fingers, murmured, "I sure enjoyed our morning together, didn't you, Kid? It was lovely being off alone, far away from the others. Just the two of us." Her voice was low and coated with honey.

Pleased but baffled, the Kid said, "It sure was. Only thing is, it didn't last long enough."

Diane smiled knowingly and pressed her dark head to his shoulder. She gaily flirted with the Kid, flirted as she'd not done all morning. She laughed softly and squeezed his big arm, pressed herself close. She looked into the Kid's eyes and leaned up on tiptoe to whisper in his ear so the creature couldn't quite hear. Actually what she whispered was nothing more than teasing nonsense, but the big blond man smiled and nodded and looked immensely pleased.

While the pair laughed and whispered and flirted, Diane stole quick, curious glances at the caged creature, lying in his shaded cage not ten feet from her. When she saw that his dark eyes were closed and his bare chest was rising and falling rhythmically, she felt let down.

The savage was sound asleep!

Unreasonably disappointed, she promptly pulled away from the Kid and said, "It's getting late. I must go to my quarters at once."

Puzzled by her mercurial mood changes, the Kid said, "Well . . . wait, I—I'll go with you."

"No." She stopped him. "You have to return the bicycles to the Brown Palace. Don't you?" She turned and walked away.

Frowning, he scratched his head and called after her, "Have a late supper with me tonight after the show?" No response. "Please, Diane. Have dinner with me."

"All right," she called over her shoulder, not bothering even to glance back at him.

* * *

The Cherokee Kid tried hard to impress the beautiful Diane Buchannan. He spent his free time in an all-out attempt to fascinate, excite, and overwhelm her with his masculine charm. He took her on a carriage ride through the city park one afternoon. The next day he took her up into the foothills, where they picnicked in a lush green valley a thousand feet above the city.

He escorted her on window-shopping forays past the May Company, the Denver Dry, the big Daniels and Fisher store, and Buerger Brothers. She was unlike the other show girls he'd known. She didn't drag him inside the fine stores, hoping he'd spend money on her. She was more than content with window-shopping. He found that very refreshing.

He squired her to Denver's fanciest restaurants, including the elegant Tortini with its private, intimate dining salons, the Brown Palace's dark and cozy Ship's Tavern, and the Hotel Windsor's opulent dining room with its diamond dust mirrors, marble floors, Brussels carpet, and hand-carved furniture.

Together they toured the Tabor Grand Opera House, that gaudy self-monument erected by the late, flamboyant silver king. They wandered through the sprawling Richthofen Castle, ambitious folly of the Prussian nobleman Baron Walton von Richthofen. They toured the huge Tivoli Union Brewing Company, graciously sampling the foamy brew. They sipped nose-tickling phosphates at McMahan's drugstore, caught a Sunday matinee melodrama at the ornate Broadway Theater, and ventured into the posh Inter-Ocean Club for a round of roulette one midnight after the show.

The bold and well-informed Diane tried to persuade the Kid to take her down to Denver's red-light district. He refused. She was disappointed. She'd heard of Mattie Silks and Jennie Rogers and was dying for at least a look at the outside of the gaudy Market Street houses.

"Have you seen their places?" she asked the Kid.

"Certainly not," was his quick reply, and he hoped his face wasn't red as he grinned, fondly recalling the fun and frolic on the golden throne at Jennie Rogers's.

The Cherokee Kid showered Diane with sentimental gifts, compliments, and more attention than he'd ever afforded any one woman in his life. But it was not easy to impress Diane Buchannan. She was not one of the sweet, simple farm girls who showed up at the fairgrounds with stars in their eyes and dreams of romance and adventure in their hearts.

Diane Buchannan had been "raised on the road." As a child she'd had private tutors from the age of five. She had traveled the world over, met influential people from every walk of life. She had sat on the knee of Queen Victoria—when the troupe appeared in Europe, had been received at the White House by three different administrations.

As a grown woman Diane had had dozens of rich, handsome young men vie for her affections.

She wasn't falling right into his arms the way the Kid had hoped.

He had no intention of giving up. The stakes were too high.

Colonel Buchannan was firmly in the Kid's corner. The Kid had managed, very skillfully, to pull the wool over the old man's eyes. Almost everything he had told the Colonel regarding his past had been fabricated. Lying came easily to the Kid. He had been doing it with great success all his life. So the Colonel didn't see Philip Lowery—the Cherokee Kid—for the kind of man he really was. The Kid was ambitious and selfish and had little respect for his fellow troupers. He possessed, indeed, all the essential qualities of success.

The old showman had noticed that the young couple had become almost inseparable. He was pleased. The prospect of having his overly adventurous, headstrong granddaughter safely married was more than appealing. His blue eyes twinkling, he offered the anxious Kid a slice of sound advice regarding the wooing and winning of his beautiful granddaughter.

"It'll take a man of iron will, strong heart, and sensitive manner to tame Diane Buchannan."

Chapter 10

Diane just couldn't get the Redman of the Rockies off her
➤➤➤ mind.

She seized every opportunity to pass the cage of the hard-featured
savage. Untamed and dangerous he might well be, but physically he
was a superb specimen and Diane found herself alarmingly intrigued by
him.

She told herself it was a harmless fascination, no different from that
which she felt toward the tawny mountain lion caged beside him. She
relished watching both, especially when they were unaware of her
presence, and reasoned that the fierce savage was as different a species
from her as the big male cat. Therein lay her captivation. It was perfectly normal. It was not the least bit unhealthy to be dazzled and
drawn by the beautiful pair.

Diane secretly acknowledged that the creature had a disarming way
of looking sideways at her whenever she passed his cage. What did it
mean? What was going on in his head?

On occasions, when she was feeling unusually curious and coura-
geous, she'd stop, step up close to the barred cage, and study him
thoughtfully; it seemed by turns to amuse, then enrage him. She could
have sworn that a time or two she caught a teasing light shining out of
the dark eyes, a minute lifting of his cruel lips into something resem-
bling a smile. By the same token there was no doubt in her mind that
on a couple of occasions her very presence had filled him with unrea-
sonable fury.

* * *

Monday morning.

Diane awakened very early. The first thought that popped into her mind was the Redman of the Rockies. She hastily dressed and wandered down to the holding pens shortly after sunup.

The Redman's cage was being hosed down. The roustabout wielding the high-pressure hose carelessly pummeled the Indian with the full force and blast of the water.

Stopping a few yards away, Diane watched in stunned horror as the great power of the water gushing forth from the big fire hose pinned the Redman at the center of his cage. He stood with his feet apart, fists clenched at his sides while the driving force plastered his shoulder-length black hair to his head, caused his eyes to close, turned his bronzed face to the side, and beat on his bare chest and belly with a thrust that would have brought a lesser man to his knees.

Not this beautiful beast. The defiant creature was so tightly coiled he seemed to be straining against his own flesh, as though he were wearing invisible chains. But he didn't knuckle under. He didn't make a sound, didn't try to escape the brutal assault of the water.

Diane's heart raced in her chest as she watched the proud savage stand there silently enduring this cruel, unnecessary punishment.

She shouted a warning. The roustabout shut off the hose. The savage's wet-lashed eyes opened.

"Drop that hose and get out of here!" she snapped at the thoughtless workman. The man shrugged, laid the hose down, turned and walked away, shaking his head.

Diane moved up to the cage. To her surprise and puzzlement, the silent savage who had suffered so impassively—who had not so much as raised a hand to shield himself against the stinging water—became abruptly, inexplicably enraged.

And his fury was directed right at her.

Astonished by his reaction to her intervention on his behalf, Diane stared in mute terror as the Redman grunted like an animal and clawed at the wide beaded band encircling his throat. His eyes were fierce and mean beneath the water-matted dark lashes. His teeth were bared like a wolf's, feral and frightening.

He advanced and retreated toward the cage bars. He gripped the cold steel cylinders and tore at them with superhuman strength, his bronzed biceps bulging, a vein throbbing on his forehead, his dark face scarlet with fury.

His barbarous behavior affected the mighty mountain lion caged beside him. The great cat went into a frenzy. He snarled and pounced and thrust furry, lethally clawed paws out through the bars. He raced wildly about the cage, throwing himself up against the walls, keening and hissing as if he wanted to tear Diane to pieces.

Diane couldn't move.

She stood there rooted to the spot, entranced. She was seeing the pair completely unveiled. Raging out of control. Totally wild and unthinking. She looked again at the Redman's sharp, predatory eyes. Those dark animal eyes flashed with menace, and she was positive it was her presence that had set him off.

Even as she studied him, the Redman's raging ceased. He withdrew to the far side of his cage. There he slowly lowered himself to the floor. He sat with his knees bent, his back against the wall. Rivulets of water and sweat trickled down his dark face, his sleek body. Beads of water clung to his long eyelashes, the tip of his once-broken nose, an earlobe.

The silver bracelet flashed on his right wrist as he lifted his hands and swept the thick, wet hair back from his face. He moved no more. There he remained. Sullen, silent, impenetrable.

The mountain lion gave one last teeth-baring growl, turned majestically, and leisurely pranced away. He lay down at the back of his cage, paws out before him, head held high, diamond patch of dark fur under his throat exposed. His golden eyes were fixed on the silent man in the next cage. He purred plaintively, low, and very softly in the back of his throat, as if he were offering solace to the brooding, silent savage.

Diane backed away, shaken.

She turned and hurried off. She walked fast. She headed straight for the custom-built rail car her grandparents shared. Her mind was made up. She would tell the Colonel to release the Redman of the Rockies. It wasn't right to hold him.

Diane now saw it all clearly, how much the show had fallen. It was bogus, stale, warmed over. A self-parody. The bizarre chase of the Redman had been concocted and staged out of desperation, not choice. Too pathetic to be worthy of the show's honored past. She'd tell the Colonel as much. Tell him this very morning.

She knocked loudly at her grandparents' quarters. The door opened, and her grandmother stood before her.

"Good morning, Granny." Diane smiled at the tiny white-haired woman. "I know it's early, but I must talk to the Colonel!"

From inside boomed the voice of the Colonel. "It's Diane? Good, good. Come on in here, Diane! I want to show you something."

Diane stepped inside, saw the Colonel seated at the table, poring over a stack of account books spread out before him.

"Honey," he said, lifting blue, sparkling eyes to her, "I've got wonderful news! *Colonel Buck Buchannan's Wild West Show* has drawn larger crowds here in Denver than we've pulled in years! Three matinees and four nights in a row playing to standing-room-only crowds!" He laughed and clapped his hands like an excited little boy. "And it's all because of you and the Redman of the Rockies. The Beauty and the Beast. It's you and that savage the folks turn out to see." Chuckling happily, he looked closely at Diane, saw that she wasn't laughing with him. "What is it, child? What is it you came to ask me? What do you want? Tell the old Colonel and he'll get it for you."

Diane smiled weakly at her dear grandfather. And she said, "Nothing, really. I just wondered if it might be a good idea to add a horse race to the show's program. Cowboy McCall against Iron Shirt and Mexican Bob and—"

"Yes! I like it! We'll throw in a Cossack and an Arab for good measure! Ruthie, did you hear that? Our little grandbaby is a chip off the old block or my name's not Colonel Buck Buchannan!" Gleefully he added, "At this rate Pawnee Bill will never get his hands on my show!"

The Denver engagement was rapidly drawing to a close. Crowds continued to jam the fairgrounds. Members of the troupe were thrilled; they were actually being paid again. A holiday mood prevailed, and cast members congratulated one another and laughed more than usual.

Even Shorty joked good-naturedly, "The Colonel don't pay me much." He drug his bootheel back and forth through the dust. "Twenty dollars a week and all the manure I can take home."

Diane laughed and thought it a shame that Shorty was unable to show more of his humorous, fun-loving side to Texas Kate. If only he could unwind a little around the constantly joking, wisecracking Kate, he might get somewhere with her.

Diane was still smiling as she and the Kid left Shorty and wandered on aimlessly through the grounds. Accompanying them were a couple of the Rough Riders and their most recent sweethearts. One of the women casually suggested they visit the Redman's cage.

Immediately annoyed, Diane glanced sharply at the redheaded show girl. She said nothing, however, and went along with the group. As they approached the cage, Diane's violet eyes narrowed as she searched anxiously for the Redman.

His wild black shoulder-length hair billowed while he roamed his cage like a wounded animal. He sensed their presence, stopped his pacing, and stared coldly at them.

The redhead moved up close to the bars. "My goodness. His face would scare little children, but that body . . ." She laughed nervously, then added, "His thighs must be made of bronzed steel."

"Never you mind his thighs," warned her Rough Rider escort.

The Redman's cold black eyes were riveted on the fawning redhead. But not for long. Diane deliberately—perversely—danced by the Redman's cage. The leaded hem of her skirt flew above her knees as she swayed her hips seductively. Without looking at him, Diane knew those black eyes now rested entirely on her.

The Kid clapped his hands as she strutted about, and the others joined in the fun. Soon the entire group was mocking and making fun of the caged Redman, Diane as guilty as the rest. She childishly teased and taunted him, just as she did the ferocious mountain lion caged beside him.

But even as she goaded and teased the tall Indian behind bars, she felt shame and remorse. Guilt over her mean and unforgivable behavior grew after they'd left him. She was conscience-stricken and miserable. She kept seeing his eyes. Couldn't get them out of her mind.

There was a brain behind those dark, wild eyes!

Diane's misery increased with that night's sold-out performance. She couldn't keep from watching what she knew would make her feel worse than she already felt.

She sat on the arena fence and watched the Redman's crowd-pleasing portion of the show. Pity and a deep sense of guilt mingled in her breast. Disgustedly she watched as the cage was wheeled around the arena and laughing women came down to stare and poke at the Redman. Then sadly she watched as the cage was thrown open, and the magnificent savage—prodded and baited—again tried a futile escape.

Her eyes closed in agony when the Cherokee Kid and his Rough Riders thundered into the arena to ride the Redman down.

She couldn't watch anymore.

She turned, dropped to the ground outside the arena, and walked away. She felt mentally exhausted and wished she had no after-show engagement with the Kid. With feet of lead, she trudged toward her quarters while screams and loud applause from behind signaled the recapture of the Redman.

It was then, hearing those deafening shouts of approval, that Diane made her decision.

She would release the Redman of the Rockies.

Chapter 11

ᗢᗢᗢ Diane reluctantly joined the Kid for a late supper after the show. But she cut the evening short, pleading a headache.

Actually it was more like a heartache.

She was troubled. She'd made up her mind to release the Redman, and with the decision came an unsettling mixture of serenity and distress. She was sure it was the right thing to do, so she felt good about it. It would be a terrible setback for the Colonel and his troubled troupe, so she felt bad about it.

She'd come out from the District of Columbia for the sole purpose of helping her aging grandfather save his beloved show. When she threw open the Redman's cage, she would be slamming the door on the Colonel's dreams.

Diane lay awake in her narrow berth, restlessly tossing and turning. It was very late; she'd left the Kid hours ago. It had to be nearing three or four in the morning. In the bunk across the room Texas Kate, lying flat on her back, snored softly, making strange little whistling sounds through her nose. They were getting on Diane's already frayed nerves.

Sighing, she sat up, looked over at Kate, and ground her teeth. She threw back the bedcovers, rose, and lifted the silk robe from the foot of her bed. In the darkness she tiptoed to the small sitting room, pulling the compartment door closed behind her.

Diane drew on the blue silk robe, lifted her long, tousled hair free, and moved toward the front door. She opened it, poked her head out, and looked around.

It was so late the moon had gone down and the stars were rapidly fading. It was very dark. Every rail car in the long show train was dark as well.

The entire troupe was sleeping.

Tying the robe's silk sash loosely at her waist, Diane stepped outside. The August night was surprisingly cold, and Diane wore almost nothing. Her pale blue gown and robe were of the softest silk and lace. A strong breeze from out of the east knifed right through the flimsy fabric. She pulled the robe's lace-trimmed lapels tightly together and shivered.

Diane knew she should turn around, go back inside, and get into bed, where she belonged.

She stepped down off the stoop and sprinted on bare feet toward the northern end of the big arena looming before her in the darkness. She never once looked back, completely comfortable that everyone else was sound asleep.

Almost everyone was.

But in a darkened rail car near the very end of the train Ancient Eyes was wide-awake. In his favorite chair before an open window the old Ute chieftain sat in the chill morning darkness, staring out at the past. His broad, ugly face was expressionless.

Suddenly his glazed black eyes widened, then focused when a slender dark-haired woman dashed across his line of vision. He gripped the worn arms of his easy chair, leaned forward, and squinted.

Then murmured soundlessly, "Little Buck!" He swallowed hard, watched in disbelief as she made her sure, swift way around the circumference of the big arena and disappeared into the thick darkness. Again he whispered, "Little Buck!" and argued with himself about going after her.

He rose from his chair, pulled the colorful blanket more closely about his naked shoulders. But he sat back down. Little Buck was fiercely independent and possessed a volcanic temper. She would be furious if he followed her. She was no longer a child. She was a grown woman. A grown woman who was going somewhere in the middle of the night wearing only her nightclothes.

Ancient Eyes' barrel chest tightened. He'd seen what was going on. Little Buck was constantly in the company of the Cherokee Kid. Likely she was going to him now. The old Ute shook his head sadly. It was painful to stand quietly by while the girl he loved as if she were his own flesh threw her life away on a man like Philip Lowery. Lowery wasn't worthy of Little Buck.

Ancient Eyes sighed wearily. He'd told the Colonel—right from the beginning when Philip Lowery had first joined the troupe—that he thought Lowery was ambitious and unprincipled, would cause only trouble. But the Colonel liked Lowery, had refused to listen. Now the Colonel seemed fully approving of the growing relationship between Little Buck and the Kid.

So it was up to him.

The troubled Ute threw off his covering blanket, rose, and hurriedly dressed. He silently stole from his quarters and out into the enveloping darkness.

Diane was cold and out of breath when she reached the Redman. At the adjacent holding pen a lantern hung from a pole. The lantern cast a wide circle of mellow light which softly illuminated only one end of the creature's cage, the end where its bars met those of the lion's. That portion of the lion's cage was lighted as well.

Diane stopped and stared.

All that was visible of the Redman were a pair of long, leanly muscled bronze legs stretched out full length. The pool of light stopped just short of where his brief loincloth began. A bare bronzed foot rested against the bars separating him from the lion.

And as unbelievable as it seemed, a soft, furry paw was pressed flat against the sole of the Redman's bare foot. Diane's fascinated gaze followed the cat's paw up to where the lantern's light ended at a powerful tawny shoulder. She couldn't keep from smiling.

For a long moment Diane stood quietly between the lantern and the cages, unmoving, not making a sound.

The Redman sensed her presence there in the darkness even before he smelled her perfume. Silently he turned his head. And he watched her watching him.

Her hair, the color of midnight, shimmered with blue under the flickering light of the lantern. Flailing in the wind, that coal black hair whipped around her pale, perfect face and slender shoulders.

The Redman's dark eyes moved down over her slender ivory throat. The lacy lapels of her blue silk robe had partially parted. Visible to his searching gaze was the swell of her full breasts, a fleeting glimpse of pale, rounded flesh.

The muscles in his naked belly tightened. His hands, lying at his sides, flattened against the rough planks of the cell floor.

At that instant a strong gust of night wind hit her full in the face. Her eyes automatically closed against its force, and she struggled to stay upright. The loosely tied sash of her pale blue robe came undone. The robe immediately caught the wind and billowed out behind her, the sashes whipping uselessly, the lacy hem of her nightgown swirling up around her bare knees. She reached for the pole supporting the swaying lantern.

As she stood there in the wind against the lantern's light, her slender body clearly outlined through the soft blue silk, the Redman could see the chill-hardened nipples of her beautiful breasts piercing the gown's filmy bodice. The soft, shiny silk hugged her small waist, clung seductively to the flare of her hips, and pressed enticingly against the soft feminine V between her pale thighs.

Holding the pole with one hand, attempting to get a grain of sand from her watering eye with the other, Diane remained totally unaware that the Redman was awake, that his burning black gaze was riveted to her.

The wind died slightly. She released the pole, managed to rid her tearing eye of the stinging sand, then pulled her robe securely around her body and tied it tightly. She lifted her head, looked again at the Redman's cage.

And stood there frozen.

Her hand clutched her throat and her eyes stared fearfully. The Redman was sitting up, his bare shoulders and dark head dominating the pool of light. He was looking straight at her. His dark face was set; his cruel lips were a thin, tight line. He appeared sinister, like a raven on a tombstone.

Diane was suddenly overcome with fear. She retreated from the creature, stumbling blindly backward among the painted flats and show props. Out of the light she stopped, watched him warily. He rose to his full, impressive height, staring still, searching for her in the shadow.

Even with him chained or behind bars and standing totally still, there was something violent and unpredictable about the creature. Diane sucked in her breath at the sight of him. She felt terribly cold, at the same time uncomfortably hot. She was unreasonably frightened. She felt faint, almost dizzy.

Her face flushed with heat.

There was, about the mysterious Redman, a constant palpable threat of sex—intermingled with sudden violence. The savage exuded an erotic menace. And Diane, though terribly afraid of the fierce, untamed brute, was helplessly drawn by that sexual threat.

She trembled violently. She stood there concealed in shadow, watching him, wondering if it was safe to move closer. Wondering if she should turn away. Leave this very minute. Abandon her foolish plan to release him.

No.

No, keeping him caged was inhumane. He was a wild and beautiful creature who should be free to roam his beloved mountains. Just like the great male cat caged beside him. Both should be free. Both *would* be free. And soon.

Diane stood there in the chill night wind and stared at the harshly handsome Redman gripping the steel restraining bars. The powerful muscles were straining against his smooth bronzed flesh as if his entire being were silently screaming for release. It was appealing. It was heartbreaking.

It was a wrong that had to be righted.

She was going to do it.

She still wasn't sure just how or when, but she *was* going to set them both free.

The Redman sank slowly back down to the floor. He wrapped long arms around his bent knees and bowed his head. His loose, long hair swung forward, spilling over his bare, upraised arms. In that position he seemed far less menacing. Almost vulnerable.

Cautiously Diane approached. His head immediately snapped up. He sniffed the air as an animal does. He had caught the scent of her body. She forced herself to remain calm, to continue moving closer. Bravely she stepped up very close to his cage, expecting him to leap up any second and frighten her half to death.

To her relief the beast remained seated. He lowered his long legs, crossed them, and then crossed his arms over his chest. She advanced even nearer. He stared straight at her. She was snared, perversely enthralled by him. Their gazes locked.

After a long tension-charged moment of silence, Diane softly asked, "If I set you free, you wouldn't hurt me, would you?"

The Redman gave no reply. His arms came uncrossed. He reached up and with long, tanned fingers touched the wide beaded band encircling his throat. His dark eyes flashed. He made strange desperate, groaning sounds but didn't speak a word.

Diane shook her head. He didn't understand. Or did he? She had to be sure. She tried another tack. She goaded him, baited him, tried to make him angry.

No response.

She grew bolder. In mock seduction she flirted with him. She wet her lips with the tip of her tongue, puckered, and made little kissing sounds in the air not a foot from his hard-featured face. She drew in her breath, put her hands on her hips, and bent one knee forward in a provocative pose.

Nothing.

She smiled and whipped her head around, sending her long, tumbled hair down over her right shoulder. She drew a section of that shiny black hair up in her hand and presented it to the staring creature for his closer inspection. Boldly she reached right through the bars that separated them while her heart pounded with fear.

Still no response.

Only those strangely beautiful eyes staring at her. Dark, flashing eyes which she had never been this close to before. Cold, measuring eyes that held her in thrall. Deep, fathomless eyes which at odd moments appeared to be a deep navy blue instead of black.

Chapter 12

→→→ Texas Kate yanked a wire curler from her hair with a balled fist, dropped it on the vanity, and stared at herself in the oval mirror, one stringy curl dangling down on her forehead.

"Lord, it must be nice to be so young and pretty you don't have to do anything but wash your hair." She glanced in the mirror at Diane, dressing hurriedly behind her.

No sooner had she spoken than another close clap of thunder rattled the rail car windows, drowning out Diane's reply. Kate flinched, then shook her curlered head. The morning had been bright and clear. Now, shortly after lunch, dark, ominous clouds had boiled up over the mountains and were moving steadily eastward. The sun had completely disappeared.

It was Wednesday, the twenty-eighth of August. The final performance of *Colonel Buck Buchannan's Wild West Show* was scheduled for this very afternoon, not an hour away. The Denver engagement would then be completed. Unless the threatening afternoon thunderstorm postponed the show until evening.

"That lightning's movin' this way and—hey, you're getting decked out a little early, aren't you?" Kate wrinkled her brow. "Lord, child, it's still an hour till show time, and it looks like it might come a downpour any minute."

Stepping into her black leather trousers, Diane said, "I have an errand to run."

"Errand? Why, honey, if you want something done, get one of the boys to do it. Need something from town? Send Shorty; he'll be glad to help out. He's always obliging me that way."

Diane sucked in her breath, buttoned the last button of her tight black leather pants. She stepped up behind Kate, laid her hands atop the older woman's stout shoulders, smiled at Kate in the mirror, and said, "Now I wonder why?"

Kate's eyes met Diane's in the mirror. "Why, you know Shorty. That skinny lil ol' animal wrangler is as good as they make 'em, that's why."

"Yes, he is," Diane agreed. "But don't you think it's a bit more than that?" A perfectly arched dark eyebrow lifted.

"Oh, get on out of here! You know I'm a respectable married woman and my Teddy Ray's a jealous man." Kate chuckled heartily, her springy gray-brown curls jiggling with her laughter. "You young folks . . . all the time thinking about love and romance."

Romance was the last thing on Diane's mind that hot, cloudy August afternoon, but she grinned and nodded as she presented her left wrist to Kate. Kate quickly fastened the cuff of Diane's black satin blouse, then picked up a hairbrush and pulled it through the tight curls framing her face. As a final touch, Texas Kate took a rabbit's foot dipped in rouge and dabbed it generously on both fleshy cheeks.

Diane shoved her long dark hair atop her head, secured it with a silver clasp, and said, "I have to run. See you after the show."

"That storm breaks, there won't be a show."

Diane didn't answer. She rushed out, turning worried eyes up to the darkened sky. Jagged streaks of lightning pierced the thick blackness in the west, crashing down atop the jutting mountain peaks, the echoing thunder jangling Diane's taut nerves. The scent of rain was heavy on the still air as she hurried down the lengthy line of parked rail cars until she reached the one near the end. Ancient Eyes' quarters.

Diane knocked loudly on the door, praying he wouldn't answer. Praying the rain wouldn't postpone the afternoon show. Praying her secret plan would go off without a hitch.

She waited, nervously tapping her moccasined toe on the wooden stoop. She knocked again, pounding with her fist. She called his name several times.

Then exhaled with relief. She'd known he wouldn't be in his coach at this hour. In his old age Ancient Eyes had turned into a creature of habit. One of his habits was to dress early in his Indian show finery and wander down to the exhibition grounds to hang around the wranglers while they readied the stock for the show. He liked to trade tall tales and smoke their ready-made cigarettes and hand out unwanted advice.

This was her chance. Feeling only slightly guilty, she slipped inside

Ancient Eyes' private domain. Blinking in the shadowy dimness, she silently cursed the approaching storm. The leaden sky had cast the entire compartment into murky darkness, and she didn't dare risk lighting a lamp. Clasping her bottom lip between her teeth, Diane went in search of the key.

The key to the Redman's cage.

She spent several minutes looking in chest drawers, atop the eating table, in bookshelves. She thumbed through a thick, yellowing scrapbook, smiling fondly at the old Indian's touching sentimentality. She hurried into the sleeping compartment, lifted a pillow from his tidy bunk, and tossed it down again.

Then jumped, startled, when a gruff, raspy voice from out of the shadows said, "This what you're looking for, Little Buck?"

She whirled about to see Ancient Eyes, his long eagle feather headdress streaming down his broad back, filling the dim doorway. In his hand was a silver key, gleaming in the half-light. His broad, ugly face broke into a wide smile. He winked at Diane.

She smiled. "I could never fool you."

"No," he said. "I know you come, Little Buck."

She followed him back into the sitting room and watched as he deliberately placed the silver key inside a carved wooden box that sat in plain sight atop the chest she had searched. He looked at her. She nodded knowingly.

Diane anxiously sat down while Ancient Eyes took off his feathered war bonnet, placed it across the table, and then slowly lowered his girth down into his favorite worn easy chair.

"Tell me about the Redman," Diane bluntly commanded. "Tell me everything."

Ancient Eyes' broad smile faded and the light in his dark eyes dimmed. He looked grim. With no further coaxing from Diane he told of the deed that had been weighing heavily on his heart. As she looked intently into his flat black eyes, he spoke of that day he would never forget.

"It was on the Monday afternoon when troupe train steam into Denver . . ." As he began to speak, the first drops of summer rain started falling.

The old Ute chieftain told how the hunting party—he, Shorty, the Cherokee Kid, and the Leatherwood brothers—had left the troupe's train just prior to its arrival in Denver. The five of them had ridden their horses down the ramp and headed immediately toward the foothills. The plan had been for the Kid and the Leatherwoods to trap a mountain lion for the show.

He and Shorty had tagged along to enjoy some trout fishing in the high country's clear snow-fed streams. Once in the mountains they didn't see much of the younger men. That first afternoon and most of the next day the boys were busy setting up trap cages to catch a big cat.

Before dawn on Wednesday morning he and Shorty rose and left camp while the others slept. They trekked in a zigzag path up the timbered slopes in search of a better fishing hole. A mile from camp, high up beside a rocky stream bed by a gentle waterfall, they found the ideal spot and settled in for a pleasant morning.

Around nine o'clock they heard a loud commotion coming from below: the crashing of underbrush, the snarling and whimpering of an animal. He and Shorty exchanged looks. He laid aside his fishing pole and took up his field glasses. Squinting, he swept the powerful glasses in a wide searching arc over the pine- and juniper-dotted terrain below until he reached a grassy clearing where a big mountain lion had been lured into one of the trap cages and was frantically trying to free itself.

The lion was halfway out of the trap when the Cherokee Kid and the Leatherwoods came rushing into the clearing. They tossed a wire mesh net over the big male cat, and then the Kid started beating the trapped, frightened animal with an ax handle, bringing it down again and again across the lion's head and back.

All at once a lean Indian from some distant tribe leaped from out of nowhere onto the Kid's broad back and pulled him off the wounded, panicked cat. The Kid bellowed like a bull and shouted for the Leatherwoods. Danny Leatherwood grabbed at the Redman while Davey shoved the lion into the cage, then turned and tossed the steel mesh net over the Indian's head.

The brothers pulled the Indian away from the Kid and tightened the net around him. The Kid immediately whirled about and turned the ax handle on the restrained Redman. With the full force of his big, powerful body behind it, the Kid swung the ax like a baseball bat, bringing it down across the Redman's chest. The Kid delivered blow after punishing blow to the Indian's chest and belly and thighs. Finally, brutally, to his throat.

Ancient Eyes told how he shouted loudly and Shorty blew shrill warnings on his silver whistle as the two of them went plunging down the mountain in an attempt to stop the madness. But it was too late. When they reached the clearing, the injured Indian and the wounded cat were caged.

Concluding, Ancient Eyes said sadly, "I as bad as the Cherokee Kid. Not tell the Colonel." He shook his white head regretfully. "I see how happy the Colonel is when Kid show him Redman and I keep quiet. I shame myself. I shame the Colonel."

Diane was outwardly calm when she gently patted the broad, stooped shoulder of the old Ute and murmured softly, "Don't feel bad, Ancient Eyes. Now we'll fix it, you and I."

The threatening afternoon thunderstorm turned out to be nothing more than a brief, cooling summer shower. At show time the sun was shining brightly from a cloudless Colorado sky. The troupe performed its last rip-roaring show before an enormous crowd, and the successful Denver engagement of *Colonel Buck Buchannan's Wild West Show* became history.

From the minute the final performance ended, it took only three hours to strike the grandstands and sets and load the train. Diane observed the well-coordinated operation with keen interest. She watched closely as the caged Redman and caged mountain lion were loaded into an animal car directly ahead of the train's caboose. The car was left unguarded.

With the rest of the troupe Diane boarded the train for departure to Salt Lake City, Sacramento, and then on to their San Francisco winter quarters. Wearing a smile and a cool summer frock of pale purple, she stepped up into a comfortable day coach near the front of the train. It was just past sundown when the locomotive steamed out of Denver. Leaning out the window, Diane waved and blew kisses to the crowds lining the tracks.

When finally she turned away from the window, she was annoyed to find the Kid lounging in the seat beside her. The sight of him now sickened her. She could picture him viciously wielding an ax handle against the defenseless creatures. She gritted her teeth with disgust.

Ignorant of her contempt, the Kid turned his most disarming smile on her, draped an arm along the back of her seat, and said, "Better sit back and relax, it's a long ride to Salt Lake." He gave her shoulder a squeeze.

"I'm exhausted," she said, quickly rising. "I'm going to retire to my sleeping compartment."

"Tired already? Why, we haven't even left the lights of Denver behind. Are you feeling all right?"

"I'm fine, thank you." She brushed past his knees with a curt good night and waved away his suggestion that he walk her back to her quarters.

Diane left him quizzically gaping after her. Never looking back, she hurried through the long train, car by car, slipped into Ancient Eyes' empty compartment and took the silver key from the carved wooden box. Then she moved quickly on down the line until she stood just outside the final rail car door separating her from the caged Indian and the big cat.

Diane took a deep breath of the cool, clean air, opened the door, and slipped inside, her heart hammering.

In the darkened car two sets of gleaming eyes locked on her as she made her way to the center loading doors. She slid back the heavy doors and again stood for a moment in the wind, wondering if she was doing the right thing.

In her mind's eye she could see the wild, beautiful pair—man and beast—turn grateful gazes on her as she unlocked the doors of their cages and set them free. She imagined herself watching happily as they leaped to the ground and sprinted gracefully toward the foothills, the night winds blowing the silver-streaked raven hair of the Redman and the black diamond-decorated tawny fur of the cat.

Smiling, Diane went first to the big male cat's cage. She unlocked it and heard her heart beat in her ears as she threw the cage open and stood aside. Just as she had envisioned, the sleek, beautiful mountain lion bounded out of the opened cage, took two long strides, leaped from the train, and disappeared into the night.

Diane sighed with relief and closed the empty cage.

She moved to the Redman's barred cage, carefully avoiding those dark, penetrating eyes. Her heart was really pounding now. She was so nervous she had difficulty fitting the key into the lock. After several stiff-fingered attempts, she slid the silver key into place, heard the click, quickly turned it, and unlocked the door.

She hesitated for a final second, then jerked the cage door open wide and shouted, "Go!"

In the blinking of an eye the Redman was out of the cage and towering over her, his bare chest glistening with sweat, his harshly handsome face set in hard lines.

Instinctively Diane cringed and took a step backward. But his right arm shot out like a striking serpent, the silver bracelet flashing in the shadowy light. Firm bronzed fingers tightly encircled her fragile wrist and he pulled her to him.

Their eyes met for a fleeting second, and in that second Diane thought she read a flicker of hesitation in the fathomless black depths.

Then it was gone.

The Redman of the Rockies swept her up into his arms, tossed her over his left shoulder, and leaped down from the train.

Chapter 13

Diane screamed her outrage.

➳➳➳➳ But there was no one to hear her except the Redman.

With Diane tossed over his shoulder, the Indian hit the ground running and within seconds was fifty yards away from the railroad tracks.

After the initial shock Diane's keen brain began to function with the usual clear, unemotional reasoning. She fully realized she was being captured by a wild, primitive creature and she *had* to be rescued immediately.

So she screamed to the top of her lungs, braced her hands on the Redman's bare back, and levered herself up so that she could lift her head. She shot an arm up in the air and waved madly, praying she would be seen from the train. Surely there'd be at least one member of the troupe who would look out the window, spot her waving, and know immediately that the Redman had snatched her.

It didn't happen.

The troupe's train continued to roll on down the tracks, picking up speed, growing smaller and smaller before her horrified eyes. The locomotive snaked steadily off into the distance and any hope of being quickly rescued vanished along with the fading caboose.

Diane continued to scream, but it was no longer in an attempt to attract attention. She screamed with rising fear and frustration. The Redman abruptly shifted Diane, sliding her down into his arms, placing a hand beneath her knees, the other at her waist. He slammed her up against his hard chest so forcefully Diane's head rocked on her shoulders and she almost lost her breath. Her flushed face was inches from the Redman's. Her eyes automatically went to his.

The Indian was not looking at her. He stared straight ahead, his dark, unblinking eyes fixed on the western horizon. He sprinted across the valley in long, fluid strides, uncaring that she was screaming and sick with terror. His stony coldness added fury to Diane's rising fear. She hated him for what he was doing and she wanted to hurt him. She doubled up her fists and beat on his bare chest and smooth shoulders, hitting him as hard as she could.

But her glancing blows to rock-hard muscle and bone hurt her hands so badly she was forced to stop. Still, the need to inflict pain was so great she wildly clawed at him, digging her fingers into his smooth bronzed chest, deriving a small measure of satisfaction from the feel of his flesh giving way under her sharp, raking nails. She drew blood and felt almost light-headed at the sight of it.

But not for long.

The Redman's total lack of reaction to her vicious attack further frustrated Diane. She squirmed and struggled, hoping to break his stride. Furiously she kicked her sharp heels back against his knees and thighs, attempting to throw him off-balance. She wasn't successful. The savage sprinted swiftly on, his fluid stride never broken, his graceful gait unchanged.

Diane continued to scream and kick and plead. And knew in her heart that all the screaming and kicking and pleading in the world wouldn't save her. Her captor wasn't a man, but an animal. A wild, uncivilized beast without reason or logic. A cruel, merciless savage with no heart and no conscience.

Diane finally went limp against him. She looked again at that dark, saturnine face and wondered what it would take to get through to him.

"This is a big mistake," she loudly informed him. "*I'm* the one who let you go! *I* unlocked your cage. *I* released you!" Her voice rose to a shrill shout. "*I* saved you, damn it! Can't you understand that? Can't you understand anything?"

No response from the stone-faced Redman. He showed no emotion at all. A chilling thought ran through Diane's mind. He would show no more emotion when he brutally murdered her. A shudder ran up her spine. She wedged her right arm between their bodies, pressed her sharp elbow in his abdomen, and braced herself so that she could lean as far away from him as his firmly gripping hands allowed. She whipped her head around as well, determined not to look at him again.

Diane studied the horizon, dark, jagged mountain peaks against a purpling sky, and cold fear gripped her wildly beating heart. The savage was taking her up into the Rocky Mountains. If he managed to get her to his wilderness stronghold, her fate would be forever sealed. She would never come back down!

Merciful God, she silently prayed, *help me, please help me!*

Despair swept over her in a drowning wave and Diane began to cry. Her eyes filled with tears, which quickly overflowed and splashed down her hot cheeks. Her slender body soon shuddered with her racking sobs.

And still the heartless Redman ran.

Through her blinding tears Diane caught sight of an animal's light-reflecting eyes flashing from out of a distant squawbush. Blinking to clear her tear-blurred vision, she watched a limber-spined cougar leap from out of the underbrush and upon a high rise of rock. She recognized the diamond-throated mountain lion—the one she had released.

The cat stood poised now, unmoving, atop that high rock spire. Diane frantically wondered if the Redman saw the dangerous cougar looming there against the darkening sky. She quickly glanced around. The Indian's dark, chiseled face and cold, merciless black eyes gave nothing away. But he didn't alter his course. He ran straight toward the tall rock obelisk.

Filled with a new kind of terror, Diane slid her arm from between their bodies, wrapped it around the Indian's back, and instinctively nestled closer to his solid chest. Burying her head on his shoulder, she closed her eyes tightly as they neared the waiting mountain lion. Her jaw clenched in dread, Diane was certain that any second she would feel the sharp, slashing teeth and deadly, tearing claws sink into her flesh as the big cat leaped from his perch and killed them both.

She heard a low, vibrating growl and couldn't keep from opening her eyes. She looked up. They were directly below the rock rise, the big cat now just above their heads, his golden eyes flashing in the last of the twilight.

And then they had passed by him.

Safely.

Diane peered cautiously over the Indian's shoulder. She watched as the beautiful beast leaped down from the spire, raced after them, passing them closely with long, ground-eating strides, and disappeared into the thick chaparral.

Mentally and physically exhausted, Diane sagged against her captor, too tired to cry or kick or shout any longer. Despair and helplessness had drained her of the needed energy. She realized she was beaten. There was to be no immediate escape. There was nothing she could currently do but preserve what little strength she had left and keep her wits about her.

She was tired to the bone, but obviously the Indian was not. He continued to run at that same, long-legged pace, and he looked as if he could run forever. They were leaving the flatlands behind now, ascending into the rugged foothills west of Denver, quickly gaining elevation. With animal grace, the loinclothed, moccasined Redman picked his sure way over huge, tumbled boulders, leaped across deep ravines, expertly ducked low limbs of scrubby junipers and scattered piñon pines.

Up the timbered slopes he carried her until they were totally swallowed up in a dense forest of towering ponderosa pines and silvery Douglas firs. Diane tensed anew as the thick darkness enveloped them. But the impenetrable savage continued running through the trees as if he could see in the dark, the way an animal does.

Her eyes closed; her head drooped onto the Redman's shoulder. She felt the tickle of beads from the wide neckband encircling his throat and moved her head slightly. With her face buried in the curve of his neck and shoulder, Diane caught the savage's scent: a unique, masculine, surprisingly clean scent that was far from unpleasing. With her sight temporarily missing, her other senses were heightened. She hadn't noticed, until now, that the Redman's breath was loud yet even and slow despite his exertion. Or that his raven hair, brushing against her cheek, was as soft and silky as her own. Or that the long bronzed back she clung to was smooth and deeply clefted in perfect symmetry.

Diane blinked when abruptly they emerged from the pine forest, bursting out into a high, wide mountain valley. Hope sprang into her breast when she saw a narrow dirt road which cut through the rolling meadow, leading upward. The road had to lead somewhere! Perhaps to a small mountain community. Or to a remote cabin.

Her heart leaped with joy when the Redman reached the narrow lane, turned, and started up it. That's when it dawned on Diane. The Redman meant to ransom her. He aimed to trade her for money. Why hadn't she thought of that before? That was it! It had to be. What other use could he possibly have for her?

Excitement and hope causing the blood to rush through her veins, Diane quickly dabbed at her eyes with the back of her hand. Since the Redman neither spoke nor understood English, it would be up to her to handle the necessary transactions. She rehearsed exactly what she would say to the people with whom he intended to bargain. She would assure them that if they paid for her release and let the savage go, she would see to it they were generously rewarded.

They topped a rise, and sure enough, fifty yards ahead on a gentle incline sat a big, roomy ranch house with all its lights ablaze. Diane felt almost giddy with relief. There was no doubt in her mind that within those walls resided a big, strong rancher, his wife of many years, and a houseful of children, some of whom were half grown.

Diane was staring so intently at the warm, inviting-looking home, she didn't notice when the Redman left the dusty lane to circle widely around the perimeter of the yard. As soon as she realized that his intent was *not* to go up the house, she knew she had made the wrong assumption. So she immediately opened her mouth to cry out.

And found it covered with a firm hand as the Indian lowered her to the ground and followed her down. Unable to make a sound with his long fingers clamped tightly over her lips, Diane rolled her eyes questioningly, clawed at the covering hand, and kicked her feet.

A bare, hard-muscled thigh came over her knees, pinning her legs to the ground. Not bothering to look down at her, the Redman drew Diane's left hand around his back, trapping it between him and the ground. He forced her other hand down to her side and slid his knee up higher to cover and capture the hand.

For what seemed an eternity to Diane, she was forced to lie silently on the ground beside him. An early moon climbed above the tall pines and a rising night breeze carried with it the first chill of approaching autumn. It was agony knowing that while she lay there, unable to scream, salvation was less than a hundred yards away, inside that big ranch house.

There was no way she could signal to them. The Indian's long fingers stayed over her mouth; his lean, powerful body continued to press so close to hers she could feel the fierce heat emanating from him. She lay flat on her back; the Redman was stretched out on his side, his full weight supported on one elbow, knee and thigh draped over her.

It struck her that he couldn't possibly lie in that position for long. It was bound to be uncomfortable. He would have to shift sooner or later, and when he did, maybe she'd get the chance to scramble away from him.

The Redman never moved.

While Diane squirmed and fidgeted and tossed her head in agony, the Indian lay perfectly still, in the same position, not moving a muscle. He displayed no discernible distress of any kind. Didn't appear to be uncomfortable.

Long minutes passed.

An hour.

Miserable, Diane twisted her head about. She found she couldn't see the ranch house from the low swale where they lay, but she spotted the gleaming golden eyes of the mountain lion in the distance. Those awe-some eyes, shining out of the thick blackness of the bordering forest, were not stationary. They moved continuously as the big male cat paced back and forth. Diane watched uneasily, knowing the lion was watching them, wondering when he would race across the meadow and attack. Her head turned to the side, gaze riveted to those constantly roving golden eyes, Diane considered alerting the Redman of the lion's presence. But how? She couldn't make a sound.

She sighed, turned her attention away from the lurking cougar back to the savage.

Incredulous, she looked up at him. The attitude of his dark head had not changed an nth of a degree. Disbelieving, she stared at his dark, chiseled face, at the sharp, predatory profile, silvered by the moonlight.

His obsidian gaze was riveted to the lighted ranch house. He didn't look down at her although she was sure he could feel her eyes on him. His long dark eyelashes never lifted or lowered restlessly. He rarely blinked. The cruel, sculpted lips never twitched or parted. Not once did she see him swallow.

And yet, even though he was as still as a statue, there was an animal alertness about him. She had no doubt he would be able to sense any attempted escape well before she tried it. She had to remember—at all times—that she was not dealing with a rational, logical-thinking man. This creature who could lie in one uncomfortable position for hours was a primitive, murderous savage who could scalp and kill her without batting an eyelash.

Inwardly trembling, Diane lowered her gaze from the moon-silvered features to the bronzed naked torso. She blinked at the sight of the damage her clawing nails had done to his smooth chest. Several long slashes reached all the way down to his hard, flat abdomen. Clotted, drying blood was clearly visible in the shallow furrows. She wondered if she had hurt him. She wondered if anything *could* hurt him.

While she was staring at his nail-scratched chest, she noticed the slight, almost imperceptible pull of biceps in his long left arm. The next thing Diane knew she was on her feet, with the Redman holding her close against him, hand still over her mouth.

Her eyes anxiously went to the big ranch house, and her heart sank. The lights no longer burned inside.

Chapter 14

✦✦✦✦ With one strong arm clamped firmly around her waist, the Redman half carried, half dragged Diane toward the whitewashed barns and outbuildings located far back behind the darkened ranch house. Just outside the sprawl of sheds and stables he abruptly stopped, turned his head, and sniffed the air like an animal.

Then he urged Diane forward to a slant-roofed stable. In the open doorway the Indian again stopped and drew Diane around in front of him. His fingers still firmly covering her mouth, he pressed her back against his tall, lean body.

His free hand went to her waist. Diane felt those long dark fingers tugging determinedly at her narrow purple sash belt and stiffened in alarm. The sash slid away and was his. At once his hand came atop her right shoulder, and a fierce shudder surged through Diane's tensed slender frame. She screamed—only a faint whimper got past the covering bronze fingers—when he yanked on the short, puffy sleeve. The fragile fabric easily gave way.

The heartless beast meant to rape her! To tear the clothes from her protesting body, then forcefully take her here in the moonlight where they stood. Dear God, what kind of animal was he? Why here? Why now?

She squirmed furiously, her eyes wild with horror. Her dainty purple cotton sleeve, torn completely loose from the dress, whispered down her bare arm and off. Trembling violently, she quickly crossed her arms over her breasts, terrified his next move would be to rip the dress's low-cut bodice down to her waist.

She sputtered and choked when the cool, calm Redman parted the fingers covering her lips, stuffed the torn dress sleeve into her mouth, then secured it by tying the purple sash behind her head. He waited a heartbeat, and she realized he was making sure she was properly gagged. Diane struggled and strangled and again attempted to scream. The only sound that got through the smothering fabric was a faint moaning whine.

Satisfied, the Redman was again in motion. He moved out of the bright moonlight and into the darkened barn, taking her with him, propelling her with one strong hand clutching both wrists, pinning her arms behind her. Inside he paused and Diane presumed he was as blinded as she. She could see nothing. But there was the strong, definite scent of horseflesh filling the close darkness.

She surmised that the foolish savage meant to steal one of the rancher's mounts. She wanted to laugh at his stupidity. She knew the second the stabled ponies caught the scent of humans, they'd put up such a racket the big rancher would come running, she hoped with a loaded shotgun in hand.

She began to count in her head, sure she wouldn't make it past five before the horses smelled danger. When she reached ten and all remained quiet save for the very soft blowing of an unseen animal, Diane was dismayed and baffled. She was further dismayed when the Indian, taking her with him, stole through the thick darkness as if he could see clearly.

Diane knew all there was to know about horses, so she had no idea how he was able to locate and quickly gentle a high-strung stallion. But that was exactly what happened. Enfolding Diane in a long, bare arm, he drew her up against his hard length in a close, revoltingly intimate embrace and stood there patiently, soundlessly stroking and soothing a horse that she couldn't even see in the thick darkness.

Within a few short minutes the Indian had managed to find everything he needed. With a long, soft leather strip he bound Diane's wrists together in front of her. He took a bridle down from its peg, a saddle from off a sawhorse, and got both on the stallion with no apparent trouble. He picked up a couple of extra horse blankets and strapped them behind the cantle. He found a large sheathed hunting knife and stuffed it down into his breechcloth. He tossed some soft batwing chaps over his arm, snagged a pair of silver-embellished spurs with his index finger, jerked a battered Stetson and a canteen down from an old hat-rack beside the barn door.

Throughout, he drew Diane along with him by the leather bands securing her wrists. She knew he was ready to depart when she felt his strong hands come around her waist. He lifted her up across the saddle and immediately swung up behind her. She felt those steel arms enclose her. Seated across the saddle as she was, her hands bound so that she couldn't easily hold on to anything, Diane had little choice but to lean back against the Indian's solid chest. She did so, fully expecting the inconsiderate brute to send the stallion galloping from the barn at top speed.

At an unseen, unspoken command the powerful steed went into motion. But the big mount didn't gallop or lope or even canter out of the barn. The stallion walked slowly, prancing a little proudly, moving unhurriedly out into the bright moonlight. There the Redman gently neck reined the responsive beast in a wide, gentle half circle, turning him away from the ranch, pointing him up toward the mountains.

Steeling herself for the sudden burst of speed which would surely come now, Diane turned more fully to the Indian, pressed her head against his shoulder, focused her eyes on the wide beaded band encircling his throat, and waited. And soon grew exasperated.

The mute savage *never* did what she expected him to do. Now well out of sight of the ranch house, he continued to walk the stallion in a slow, leisurely gait, as if he were taking his favorite sweetheart out on his favorite pony for a romantic ride in the moonlight!

Diane's burning hatred of the Redman grew as the stallion pranced happily across the grassy, gently undulating meadow, skirting the rugged base of the mountains. She'd always prided herself on possessing the uncanny ability to know pretty much what was going through a male's mind. Few times had she been surprised. Most men, she had learned early in life, were overgrown boys and far from complex. She had yet to meet the man who wasn't easy to read. Until now.

But, then, she was forgetting; her captor was not actually a man. He was a big, dangerous brute whose preferred primitive existence was but an example of his Neanderthal instincts. She couldn't be expected to understand the mind of an animal.

Wondering if the ignorant aborigine ever intended to take the gag from her mouth, Diane was astonished when, abruptly, as though *he* had read *her* mind, he lifted his right hand. The wide silver bracelet on his wrist flashing in the moonlight, he tugged the knot loose from the purple sash and let it fall around her shoulders. When she felt his fingers inside her mouth, Diane was highly incensed. But she was grateful when he pulled the damp, choking fabric out.

She coughed and swallowed repeatedly and drew several long, deep breaths while her captor sat behind her, observing her closely from beneath hooded lids. She felt his intense gaze and raised her bound wrists up before him, nodding and motioning for him to untie her hands.

The savage didn't obey. Nor did he shake his head or nod or in any way indicate that he had understood what she asked. Foolishly, futilely, as people are wont to do when attempting to communicate with a deaf person, Diane shouted loudly, "My hands!" She lifted them higher, directly up before his face. "Untie my hands. Please!"

The Redman curled a finger around the leather strap holding her wrists together and forced them back down to her lap.

"No, no!" she yelled. "Untie them! I want you to untie my hands!" Again she lifted her hands in front of his face. Again he lowered them, his moonlit face impassive, dark, hooded eyes unreadable.

"You untie my hands this minute, do you hear me?" she screamed at him. "The leather is rubbing my wrists raw and it's your fault! So you untie them right now before—before—" She sighed, beaten, and her head sagged forward on her chest. She muttered contemptuously, "Oh, God, don't you understand anything? Is there no way I can get through to you?"

The creature rounded his shoulders and squinted furiously, but Diane never saw it. Her hair had come unbound hours ago and it swung forward now, curtaining the side of her delicate-boned face. She jumped when she felt the Indian's hand on her hair. He gently swept it back off her face, carefully tucked it behind her ear. Her head quickly snapped around; her narrowed gaze shot up to his face.

His dark eyes peered straight ahead into the impenetrable distances. Mystery hovered in the shadows beneath the high bones of his cheeks. Menace threatened in the lines of his sculpted mouth. Diane shivered and lowered her eyes, struck anew by the potent danger this strange savage embodied.

Contrite, she vowed she'd not shout at him again or make faces or scratch and kick. How was she to know what might set him off? She'd be more careful. The last thing she wanted to do was enrage him. She'd felt the strength in those lean bronzed hands enough to know he could choke the life out of her without even breaking into a sweat.

Diane trembled. She was deathly afraid of this tall, slim Indian with the fine, sinewy face and glittering dark eyes. She felt, at the same instant, strangely drawn to this man who seemed not really a man at all but a big, beautiful beast.

Not wanting to touch or be touched by him again, Diane hooked her bound wrists around the saddle horn, stiffened her spine, and leaned up and away from her captor. She would ride like that from then on, no matter how long or how far they were to travel.

Purposely pitching her voice to a low, pleasant register so that he couldn't dare guess what she was saying, Diane told the Redman, "I'm doing this—leaning up this way—because I can't stand to have you touch me."

The Indian's impassive gaze flicked to her face. She smiled at him and, speaking in deliberately sweet tones, murmured, "You filthy animal. You loathsome beast, you make me sick. You bring out the very worst in me and I hate you for it."

The Redman's unwavering black gaze was fastened on her face. Diane looked directly into those black eyes and could tell that he understood nothing. His expression never changed.

So she continued to bare her soul. Very softly she said, "You see, right from the beginning, when I first saw you in that cage, you frightened me, yet you fascinated me. I wanted to free you, and, I'm afraid, it was as much for my sake as for yours." Diane paused, shaken by her spoken confession as she faced the unpleasant truth about her motives for freeing the Redman.

More afraid than ever, she quickly warned, "I'll get away from you! I'm smarter than you; I'll find a way. Yes, I will, Beast, I will." She paused, then quickly added, "You don't mind if I call you Beast, do you?"

His black, passionless eyes dismissed her, lifted to the trail ahead. Diane drew a ragged breath, looked nervously about at their surroundings, and wondered why he didn't turn the stallion directly up into the mountains. He continued to guide the mount more north than west. In time they rounded a timbered hillock and Diane spotted a wide scattering of lights situated directly beneath the ascending ridges of the towering Front Range. She concentrated, attempting to get her bearings.

The town spread out before them. Was it Central City? Blackhawk? No, that couldn't be. They were too far north.

As the Redman reined the stallion toward the winking lights, the city's name dawned on her. Boulder! The pristine mountain hamlet of Boulder lay straight ahead. Again Diane was filled with hope. Even if the Redman didn't take her into town, he surely meant to camp close by. Then, if she could only manage to escape during the night, she'd have no trouble reaching Boulder.

Hope grew as the lights of Boulder grew brighter, nearer. Hope faded as the savage purposely avoided the town, keeping the stallion on the outskirts, continuing on a northwestern route. When Diane realized he had no intention of riding into town, she screamed loudly, knowing it was a waste of breath. He let her scream, made no attempt to stop her. And when, screaming and pleading, she looked at him, his face still wore the same hard and inscrutable expression.

As the last lights of Boulder died away behind them, Diane's futile screams died away as well. When she realized she'd succeeded only in making her throat raw and sore, her shoulders slumped with defeat. On they rode in silence, climbing steadily, finally angling more westward. They moved up through a wide, high valley bordered on both sides by timbered cliffs rising hundreds of feet into the air.

The moonlight disappeared as they rode deeper into a wide canyon between the towering peaks of Colorado's Front Range. The chill of the high country night settled in with the darkness, and Diane was suddenly cold. And she was tired. Her back felt as if it would break from the uncomfortable position. Sitting up and away from the Redman had taken its toll, and she couldn't help speculating on how it would feel to lean back against the warmth of that solid bronzed chest.

She would die before she'd do it. She gritted her teeth to keep them from chattering and straightened her sagging shoulders. If she was cold, well, he was surely colder since he was the same as naked. And if she was tired, so was he. And she could damned sure ride as long as any man.

Or beast.

After a couple of cold, tiring hours of riding in darkness, they climbed up out of the canyon and into the silvery moonlight. But Diane never knew it. By then she was sound asleep.

She was blissfully unaware that somewhere back inside the cold canyon, she had dozed off. The Indian had sensed it the moment she fell asleep. Never altering the long, reaching strides of the big stallion, he reached up, unhooked her bound hands from the saddle horn, untied her wrists, and gently, carefully laid her back in the crook of his strong right arm, pressing her dark head to his shoulder.

He rode on.

Erect but easy in the saddle, Diane unconsciously snuggled closer to his warmth. Her soft lips fell open against his bare flesh as she sighed softly in her sleep.

A faint smile briefly twisted the Redman's set mouth and momentarily warmed his too-old dark eyes.

Chapter 15

High above the village of Boulder, the Indian guided the sure-footed stallion across the steeply dipping sandstone conglomerates making up the Fountain formation of the Flatirons. Then on along the three-thousand-foot Royal Arch of the Rockies' Front Range and into the Flatiron wilderness.

The moon had paled and was going down when the Redman finally pulled up on the lathered stallion. The stars were fading from view as morning approached. Carefully the Redman chose a lush but narrow valley where the alpine grass was already beginning to change color with the promise of an early autumn.

There, in the looming shadow of the jagged-topped Indian Peaks, a tributary of South St. Vrain Creek flowed slowly through the small, twisting meadow, its surface as smooth as glass.

For a long moment the Indian remained mounted. The winded stallion stomped and blew while the Redman's narrowed eyes slowly scanned the darkened valley. In seconds he had chosen the spot where they would sleep. The low lip of a canyon wall would shelter them from the winds and shade them from the rising sun.

Early-morning dew was falling and the air had grown cold with the nearing dawn. The Indian looked down at the woman sleeping in his arms and an expression which was almost paternal came into his dark eyes. It vanished quickly, but he took care not to waken her. He tossed the stallion's reins to the ground and the big mount immediately lowered his head and began cropping the rich grass.

The Indian reached one long arm behind him and unstrapped the extra horse blankets from behind the cantle. Then he dismounted with such agile grace the woman in his arms made only one soft little gasping sound, inhaled deeply, and snuggled closer.

And slept on.

When he reached the lip of the canyon, the Indian knelt on one knee to spread a blanket. The woman slumbered on as he gently laid her across it. Again he looked at her, his dark eyes narrowed.

She was sound asleep, her silky black hair fanned out over the blanket, her right arm bent at the elbow, the open palm facing upward. That slender arm was bare up to her shoulder where he had torn the sleeve away. The low bodice of her pale purple dress revealed the alluring swell of her ivory breasts, rising and falling rhythmically with her slow, even breaths. The purple skirts, wrinkled and twisted about her slender body, lay swirled up around her knees. Knees that were pale and shapely and covered with nothing but the sheerest of silk stockings. On her feet were sharp-heeled slippers fashioned of soft white kid.

Stone-faced, the Redman removed her slippers, set them nearby, and noticed the curious wiggling of her toes. At the same time she sighed luxuriously in her sleep. A hint of a smile touched his hard lips. He drew the spare blanket up over her and carefully tucked it in around her shoulders.

He stayed on his knees a moment more, his dark, scrutinizing gaze slowly traveling back up to the pale, fragile face. Thick, dusky lashes were closed over those remarkable eyes. Eyes unlike any he'd ever seen before. Large, luminous eyes of an incredibly beautiful violet hue. Expressive violet eyes that darkened appealingly to purple when she was angry or frightened.

Her small, perfect nose had a haughty, aristocratic tilt even in slumber. But a pair of soft, full lips, slightly parted now, suggested the promise of fiery sexuality.

The Redman's mouth tightened, and a muscle spasmed in his firm jaw. He shot to his feet, turned, and ducked out from under the rock overhang. He unsaddled the stallion. He removed the bridle and hobbled the big beast with the long leather reins. He slapped his spread hand lightly against the horse's gleaming withers, and the stallion responded just as he wanted. The animal stepped forward a couple of paces; the reins pulled, the bit clanked. The Redman was satisfied.

The stallion went back to grazing, and the Indian walked the few steps down to South St. Vrain Creek. On the grassy banks he crouched on his moccasined heels and filled the empty canteen with cold, clear water. He turned the canteen up and drank thirstily, then refilled it and laid it aside.

He took the hunting knife from his breechcloth, unsheathing the wide-bladed weapon from its protective leather. He drew a calloused thumb along the blade's edge. Razor-sharp. Pleased, he raised it to his neck. Placing the blade's pointed tip between his throat and the scarlet beaded neckband, he sliced away the unwanted adornment with one swift outward thrust. The captive neckband fell away. He caught it, laid it beside the filled canteen, and again rose to his feet.

Knife in hand, he tugged loose the narrow leather string tied atop his right hip. His loincloth fell away, and he stood there naked in the cold gray dawn. He absently rubbed his blood-streaked chest, drew a long, deep breath, and stepped into the creek's clear, shallow water. He waded quickly out until the water reached to his waist.

He placed the sharp-edged hunting knife between his strong white teeth, pushed away from the stream's rocky bottom with his feet, and swam with long, graceful strokes across the creek. The creek's far boundary was a high wall of ragged rock. He placed the knife up on a shelf of rock and tested the water's depth. It just topped his wide shoulders.

The perfect depth for a brisk morning bath.

The Indian rolled over backward in the icy water, allowing his silver-streaked black hair to fan out and become fully saturated. He floated for a few peaceful minutes, feeling his tired, bunched muscles unwind and jerk.

He turned over onto his stomach, lowered his head, and plunged beneath, fully submerging himself. He swam underwater for as long as he could hold his breath. Then he broke the calm surface and gulped air down into his aching lungs.

He went to work.

With deft hands he massaged his itching scalp and drew his fingers through the wet thick hair. Over and over again. He shoved the hair off his face and concentrated on washing the dried, clotted blood from the long claw marks going down his chest. He winced and gritted his teeth, silently cursing the pale beauty responsible. The deepest scratches bled anew as he carefully cleaned them. He allowed the ice-cold water to close the opened wounds.

He thoroughly washed the dust and dirt from his long, lean frame, and when he was clean, he leaped up onto the rocks. Water sluicing off his naked body, he shivered from the cold, pushed his sopping blue-black hair back off his dark face, and patiently waited for the rising of the sun.

He sprawled naked on the rocks, his eyes closed. He sensed a presence. His eyes swiftly opened. His narrowed gaze shot across the creek to zero in on the woman. She was just as he'd left her, sleeping peacefully, her face turned in his direction.

He reached out, picked up the sharp knife, turned his dark head, and looked up. A hundred feet above, lolling lazily on a flat shelf of sandstone, was the diamond-throated big cat. Resting on his belly, paws out before him, the huge mountain lion yawned broadly, throwing back his great head, golden eyes closing, sharp teeth bared.

The Indian laid the knife down and relaxed.

It was summer, so daybreak came early. In half an hour the sky had turned from gunmetal gray to scarlet red and then to white gold with the rising sun. The naked Indian sat there, luxuriating in the changing degrees of light and warmth. Under the rapidly heating sun, beads of water evaporated from his lean bronzed body. The scratches down his chest became a rosy pink. His wet long hair began to lose much of its moisture.

Leaning lazily back against his rock bench, the Redman again looked across the creek. From his perch up on the rock wall, he could clearly see the dark-haired woman sleeping on in the peaceful silence. His eyes remained fixed on her until the sun finally rose high enough to cast reflections on the placid creek.

The Indian turned his attention away from the sleeping woman. He gripped his bare, spread knees, leaned over, and looked straight down into the water. And saw his face as clearly as if he were staring into a mirror. Bracing his bare heels against the rocks, he leaned lower, reached down, and scooped up a double handful of water. He splashed his face with the water, then splashed it yet again. He took up the sharp knife, leaned out and shaved meticulously, using the creek's clear surface for a mirror. Black whiskers disappeared under the gliding pull of the razor-sharp blade. When no stubble of beard remained on cheeks, chin, or throat, the Indian again washed his smooth bronzed face.

With knife in hand, he rose, stretched up on his bare toes, stood poised there for a moment, and came back down. Then he picked his way around and across the narrow creek on dry, scattered boulders just upstream.

He re-dressed in his breechcloth and moccasins and joined the sleeping woman under the lip of the granite wall.

Diane lay on her side, now facing away from the creek. The blanket had slipped from her shoulders, was down around her waist.

Cautiously the Indian lay down beside her so that her back was to him. He stretched tiredly out on his back, folded his arms beneath his dark head, and quietly yawned. He could feel the glorious relaxing of muscles throughout his long body, the slow, creeping release of consciousness.

He was about to drift off completely when Diane stirred restlessly, turned over onto her back, and tossed her head, flinging a lock of tousled raven hair across his cheek and a bare slender arm over his naked chest.

He immediately froze.

He held his breath, sure she would wake up.

He slowly turned his head, looked at her, and saw the slight quivering of her soft bottom lip. Then felt the minute shivering of her slender frame against his length.

His heart stopped beating when she rolled over to face him, snuggled right up against his side, her chilled, slim body seeking warmth. Her face was an inch from his upstretched underarm. He could feel her warm, moist breath on his tingling skin. She squirmed still closer. The tickle of her long dark eyelashes against his flesh sent an involuntary shudder through him.

The Indian never for a second considered turning and enfolding her in his arms. He stayed just as he was, flat on his back, while she unconsciously cuddled closer, a soft pale hand pressing against his flat belly, a dimpled knee sliding up his long, bare leg.

Deprivation had long been part of his training to become a man. A lifetime of closely guarding and governing his emotions and desires made it possible for him to lie beside the pale, beautiful woman without touching her. This remarkable control had made him a sought-after lover among beautiful, insatiable women. He was capable of making love on demand, no matter the time, the place, or the circumstances.

That rigid control worked just as effectively the opposite way. His mind had conquered his body more than once, and when necessary, he could prevent annoying, unwanted physical arousal. He exercised that power now.

He ground his teeth as Diane's soft breast pressed against his ribs. Perspiration dotted his damp hairline when her wiggling toes dug into his bare calf. The muscles of his flat belly tightened when her sliding knee unwittingly nudged the soft leather of his loincloth up and away from his groin. The slight pressure exerted by her moving knee pulled loose the leather knot tied atop his right hip, the knot holding his breechcloth in place.

The Indian swallowed hard but did not move. He called on all the powers he possessed. He commanded his mind to control his body. He closed his tired eyes and exhaled deeply, slowly.

And fell asleep.

Chapter 16

Diane began to stir.

Her eyes fluttered halfway open, then slipped closed. Then opened again. Yawning, she lazily squinted, struggling to see in the deep shadows enveloping her. She was on her back. An unusually low ceiling looked totally foreign. It appeared to be fashioned of rock.

In the foggy consciousness that followed awakening, Diane tried to understand what she was seeing, where she was, what was happening. She lay totally still, listening. She heard low, slow breathing that didn't sound like the snorting, whistling sounds made by Texas Kate.

Slowly Diane turned her head, and her sleepy eyes widened with fear and disbelief.

The Redman of the Rockies was asleep beside her!

It all came back in a rush of remembering. Paralyzed with terror, Diane couldn't budge, couldn't scream. Only her widened eyes moved as she lay there silently staring at the sleeping savage.

He lay stretched out flat on his back, his long arms raised and folded beneath his dark head. Diane's frightened eyes slid slowly, warily up to his chiseled face. Sooty, long lashes were closed over those menacing dark eyes. High, prominent cheekbones cast shadows on his smooth bronzed cheeks. The nose, which had apparently been broken, added an almost humanizing touch to his harsh, chiseled features. The cruel, hard mouth, slackened a little in sleep, appeared fuller, softer.

But still dangerous.

Diane's eyes cautiously moved down from his face to his throat. The beaded neckband was missing. Purple and yellow bruises were clearly visible on his bare throat. Diane experienced a brief flash of empathy. Frowning, her gaze moved on. His smooth bronzed chest was marred with long, mean-looking pink streaks. Diane bit her trembling bottom lip. She was the one responsible for those deep scratches. She could still feel his flesh giving beneath her sharp, raking nails.

Her gaze dropped lower and she softly winced.

The knotted thong that held the savage's skimpy loincloth in place had come untied. The tiny leather apron had slipped down his flat brown belly and rode dangerously low on his pelvis. Only his groin was covered. Everything else was bare. That splendid masculine body was fully exposed to her nervous, guilty scrutiny.

Tense but curious, Diane silently stared at the interesting juncture where his hard-muscled thigh joined his slim hip. She studied the prominent hipbones. The drum-tight belly. The indentation of his navel. The thick black line of curling hair leading down from his navel. The shadowy hint of raven curls peeking from beneath the low, loose loincloth.

Diane closed her eyes.

She tried to think, tried to get hold of herself. Quickly she reviewed exactly what she had seen and heard upon awakening. She'd seen a shadowy rock cave, the Indian sleeping beside her, and the cave's sunny opening on the far side of him. She'd heard the savage's deep, even breathing and the clanking of a metal bit outside.

She put it all together in an attempt to determine what her chances were of getting away. The sleeping Indian was between her and the cave's opening. The stolen stallion was likely hobbled a few yards away. If she could manage to get past the savage without waking him, she'd be able to catch the horse and ride to freedom. She might not have such an opportunity again.

Diane cautiously opened her eyes. Her nervous gaze climbed slowly, steadily back up to the Redman's face. And she froze. His dark head had turned. His merciless black eyes were wide open and fixed on her. For what seemed an eternity to Diane, they both lay perfectly still, staring at each other.

It was she who broke the strange spell.

Diane quickly lurched up into a kneeling position. She threw a bare foot across the Redman's body, meaning to lunge quickly over him, shoot to her feet, and run for her life.

But he was far too swift for her.

He caught her with one foot on either side of him. Diane screamed when he gripped the skirt of her purple dress and yanked her down hard atop him. His hands immediately encircled her waist. He anchored her astride his hips and defensively turned his head to the side when she struck out at him.

Frightened and furious, Diane began to cry as she wildly pummeled his dark face and naked torso with her fists. Irrational, self-destructive, she sobbed and shouted, "Let me go, or I'll kill you! I will, I'll kill you! You dirty, stupid savage, I hate you!"

While she slapped and hit him, her fear and temper worsened. Her sobs grew louder, her threats wilder.

"You disgusting animal! You heartless beast," she wailed shrilly, "I'll cut your heart out with that damned stolen knife! I will, I mean it. Do you hear me? I mean it, I do, I do!"

Her face grew flushed and hot; her tangled hair whipped around her head and tumbled into her eyes. She was blinded by tears, and her heart pounded so furiously she thought it would explode. Desperate, she used every ounce of her strength fighting him, too irrational to consider the futility of the assault.

Her arms finally grew weak and heavy from hitting her impervious captor. The Indian endured the raining blows without retaliation. He calmly held her waist with both hands, riding out the storm, waiting patiently for her to calm down or tire out.

Diane was nowhere near calming down.

She could feel herself slipping over the edge. Knew she was losing all rationality but couldn't stop herself. She screamed and sobbed and beat wildly, frantically on the supine savage. She could hear her piercing screams filling the small chamber, the screams of a madwoman. She tried to stop and could not. She was out of control, growing wilder with each passing second.

Screaming loudly. Sobbing uncontrollably. Bucking violently against the hard, unresponsive body beneath her.

The Indian realized that the frightened, angered woman riding him so recklessly had become totally hysterical. So he did what he had to do. He raised a hand and slapped her hard with his open palm.

And felt the pain of the blow shoot right through his drumming heart. He gritted his teeth so hard his jaws hurt.

Diane gasped in stunned surprise, and a loud sob died on her lips. Her tear-filled eyes widened with shock. She stared down at him as her slender body continued to jerk reflexively, and she sniffed and fought for breath.

But she stopped crying.

For an instant she stayed poised just as she was, kneeling astride him. A hand lifted in the air, her knees viciously grasping his trim waist, her heart racing so fast her breasts rose and fell rapidly, straining against the low purple bodice.

Then every bone in her body seemed to go limp. She sat wearily back down on him, her bottom settling on his groin and hips. Her knees lost their tenacious grip, fell slack against his ribs. Her spine became limber; she drooped helplessly forward. And put up no struggle when the Indian gently drew her down to him. Her elbows touched the blanket beneath him; her hands came to rest on his biceps. Her fingers curled naturally around the hard, solid muscle.

His hand cupped the back of her head. He gently pressed her face down on his left shoulder and swept the dark, tangled hair from her red-rimmed eyes and back off her face, the wide silver bracelet flashing on his wrist. Diane sighed heavily and allowed herself to sag fully down on him. Her slender body still jerked slightly with involuntary tremors, so she didn't object when she felt his strong but gentle hands skimming soothingly down her bare upper arms and over her back. His firm fingertips tenderly stroked her back, curiously comforting.

Totally wrung out, Diane felt any traces of lingering tenseness being expertly rubbed away by his gentle, unhurried hands. Her temple touching his smooth tanned jaw, Diane closed her stinging eyes and willingly gave herself up to a few needed moments of total relaxation.

She inhaled deeply and was struck again by the clean masculine scent of the savage. He smelled as if he'd just stepped from his bath, all scrubbed and fresh and sun-warmed. Diane sighed softly when she felt the Redman's fingers cautiously sweep aside her long, tangled hair and go to work on the knotted muscles in her neck.

She moaned softly as he dexterously took away the kinks and knots. His fingers, which had been so temperate on her back, were now strong, determined to expel all traces of tenseness. It seemed to Diane that she had never been quite so relaxed in her life. She didn't know how that could possibly be, but it was a fact. So she let herself appreciate the tranquillity of the moment, a precious interlude without thought or fear.

The savage seemed as content as she to lie there beneath her, unmoving, posing no immediate threat. Perhaps in every ongoing life-or-death struggle a truce is called from time to time so that both sides can recoup. She'd gladly recoup while she could. She'd lie here and rest up for the fierce skirmishes ahead.

The pair continued to lie quietly in the deep shadows under the cliff. The Indian stretched out on his back, the woman draped astride him, her knees hugging his sides, hands slipping down to clutch his ribs.

It wasn't long before what had started out to be a restful, relaxing respite became something else altogether.

At first Diane was only vaguely aware of her compromising position. Soon she became vitally aware. Her head rested on the savage's bare shoulder; her lips were a scant inch from his bruised throat. Her breasts, spilling from the low bodice of her dress, were flattened against the solid wall of his naked chest. She was astride his body, one knee on each side of him. Somewhere in their struggles her skirt had come up, and one of her knees and part of her thigh were totally bare.

Flesh touched flesh.

Worse—far worse—her buttocks and open thighs were pressing intimately against his pelvis and groin.

The sight of his slipping loincloth flashed through her mind, and Diane didn't have to wonder if the tiny piece of leather had come entirely off. She knew. Nothing was between them except the slithery satin of her underpants.

Horrified, Diane could feel the fierce heat of him rising against her, pressing the slick satin against that most sensitive of spots. And she could feel that awakened feminine flesh swelling, throbbing for him.

She lay completely still, hardly daring to breathe. Ashamed and frightened by what was happening to her, she felt her nipples tighten and press insistently against the Indian's hot, smooth chest. She suddenly became aware of his hands. The last time she recalled feeling them, they were compassionately massaging her shoulders. They no longer were. They were clasping her rib cage tightly, and the bronzed thumbs were urgently pressing the sides of her breasts.

From beneath veiled lashes, Diane watched the Redman slowly swallow, saw the muscles of his throat slide beneath the bruised skin. She heard his ragged intake of air, felt his rapid, heavy heartbeat against her breasts.

All at once the Indian, with amazing speed and agility, rolled Diane over onto her back and was lying atop her. His harshly handsome face loomed just above. Hot pinpoints of light glittered from the dark, scary eyes boring down on her. His cruel lips, hardened with passion or hatred or both, hovered inches from her own.

Diane fully expected to feel that brutal mouth cover hers in a kiss of fierce savagery. Torn between wanting it and fearing it, she turned her face away and felt the tickle of his silver-streaked hair brush her cheek. His hands quickly clasped her head on either side, and he forced her to look directly at him.

Terrified of the animal possession she knew was coming, Diane lay helpless beneath the naked savage, her frightened gaze riveted to his face. In agony she looked into those hot black eyes, unable to turn away because his hands held her in a tight, viselike grip.

She could feel the sexual power radiating from him, sensed the dangerous, aggressive passion consuming him. His breath was ragged and warm against her face. His body was so fiery it burned right through her clothes.

Yet he hesitated.

Diane stared into those burning black eyes and wondered if this was part of her torture. Did he want her to lie here helpless while he gave her time to dread his brutal violation of her body? Was this his way of prolonging the torment? Was he so canny and sadistic that he wanted to draw out the violent, degrading rape for as long as possible?

While Diane stared fearfully up at the dark mask of his face, his eyes suddenly blinked as though he were coming out of some kind of deep trance, and his face became human again. Still, she tensed with dread when his hands released their tight grip on her head.

Her breath came out in a strangled rush when his hand moved down between their bodies. She waited to hear the tear of fabric as he ripped her dress away.

It was she who blinked when he rose to his knees astride her. The dark hand that had so worried her was modestly holding the loose loincloth in place over his groin.

He rose to his feet, stood there astride her, and casually tied the leather string atop his right hip. Then without so much as a parting glance, he stepped over her and ducked out into the bright sunlight.

Diane sat up, terribly shaken and tremendously relieved.

And totally baffled.

"Signal Boz to stop the train! Get me my guns! Wire the governor!" A distraught Colonel Buck Buchannan shouted the orders as soon as Texas Kate told him the news.

Texas Kate had awakened that morning to find Diane missing from their compartment. Sensing trouble, she hurriedly dressed and made her way to the Colonel's coach, asking everyone she met if anyone had seen Diane. Nobody had.

As she approached the open door of the Colonel's quarters, Texas Kate heard loud, excited voices. She paused, listened, and learned that the Redman of the Rockies had escaped during the night.

Texas Kate felt her heart hammer against her ribs. She knew at once that the savage had taken Diane from the train.

Kate rushed into the crowded coach, and all conversation stopped as she shouted that Diane was missing!

* * *

". . . and after the governor's been wired," the Colonel now bellowed, "have someone contact the authorities and—"

"Wait," said the Cherokee Kid, interrupting, "if we bring in the governor and the law, adverse publicity will cripple advance ticket sales and enable Pawnee Bill to cash in on our troubles."

"Damnation, Kid, that savage has my only granddaughter! Do you expect me to—"

"Colonel, I'll go after her. I'll take the Leatherwood brothers. We'll leave right now while the trail's still hot."

"I'll go with you," said the Colonel, shaking his white head decisively.

"Buck, you can't," his worried wife, standing at his elbow, quickly cautioned. "You can't ride far with that lame leg. You'd only hold the boys up, and every minute counts."

"Mrs. Buchannan's right," said the Kid. "We'll have to ride hard to make up for their head start. I'll get her back for you, Colonel. I swear it." He paused then, appeared suddenly self-conscious, and added softly, "I won't let that savage harm her. Sir, I'm in love with Diane." He lowered his head, looked as if he were on the brink of tears.

Touched, the Colonel gripped his shoulder. "Go get her, son!"

Chapter 17

The Indian struggled to awaken. He thrashed restlessly about, fighting to emerge from a nightmare's numbing horror. His head tossed from side to side and he muttered unintelligible words. His bronzed face and bare chest were covered with a sheen of perspiration. His eyes rolled rapidly beneath the closed lids.

After several agonizing minutes of flailing about, at last he broke the bonds of sleep, bolting upright in his bed, his black eyes open wide with panic. His breath came in painful, labored gasps. His heart thundered in his naked chest. He looked anxiously around and took a small measure of reassurance from the familiar surroundings.

But a sense of deep foreboding lingered.

Ancient Eyes swung his feet to the floor. He sat on his bunk, both hands clutching the narrow mattress, commanding his racing heart to slow its beat. Telling himself he'd had a terrible nightmare, a bad dream. It meant nothing, nothing at all. A dream already growing fuzzy, half forgotten.

Even as the old chieftain reasoned with himself, his mood didn't lighten. Something was wrong. He could feel it. The disturbing nightmare was a harbinger of real peril. And now, wide-awake, he could hear the Spirits of the Afterworld whispering of some catastrophe.

Ancient Eyes turned, leaned across his bunk, and jerked up the window shade. He looked out, then shook his head worriedly, his white hair swinging forward into his dark, wrinkled face. Always he awakened before dawn lit the eastern skies. Had for years. Not this morning. The new day was already bathed in bright white light.

The Ute labored up from his bunk. Disregarding a nagging pain in his chest, he poured water into a basin and hurriedly washed up. Quickly he dressed. By the time he had donned a blue chambray shirt and denim trousers, he was again covered with perspiration.

His dark forebodings grew stronger.

Ancient Eyes didn't proceed directly to the dining car as was his custom. He wanted no breakfast this morning. He was mildly nauseated, probably a case of indigestion.

Besides, there was someplace he *had* to go, something he had to do. He had to see for himself.

The key to the cage was missing from its carved box. Had Little Buck been successful in her daring act?

Ancient Eyes started through the cars, heading toward the train's rear. As he made his way steadily but slowly back, the gloom that hung over him deepened. He glanced out at the countryside rolling past the windows and frowned as the sun abruptly went behind a cloud. Suddenly it was dark, and in that darkness all his fears were magnified.

It was an omen.

An evil omen.

The sun itself was frightened. It was hiding behind the clouds, afraid to come out.

Ancient Eyes was frightened, too. And curiously tired. He had just gotten out of bed and had slept hours longer than usual, yet he couldn't recall being quite so tired ever before. His legs were so weak and heavy he could barely lift them. The annoying nausea was growing worse, and he was perspiring profusely. At the same time he felt as though he were chilled to the bone.

A young Mexican charro brushed past the old Indian. Ancient Eyes caught his sleeve, pulled him back. "Tell me, Arto," he said, "what is it? Something has happened?"

The slim Mexican hunched his shoulders, rolled his brown eyes, and said, *"Dios,* Ancient Eyes, have you not heard? The Redman of the Rockies get loose! He kidnap the Colonel's granddaughter!"

The charro hurried on his way. The old chief sagged against a compartment door. His broad hand went up to clutch at his aching chest. The pain was now almost unbearable. He felt as if he might black out. But Ancient Eyes laboriously steadied himself, turned, and anxiously started making his way toward the front of the train.

All his fault. It was his fault. He alone was responsible. He would go at once to the Colonel and admit it. Tell him everything. Start at the beginning with the day they found the Redman and how the Kid and the Leatherwoods had beaten the defenseless Indian. Tell how he himself had foolishly showed the kindhearted Little Buck where he kept the key to the Redman's cage.

Ancient Eyes manfully ignored his worsening pain, his growing weakness. He knew now that he was seriously sick, but that made no difference. If this was to be the day of his death, he *had* to clear his guilty conscience. He had proved unworthy of the trust placed in him. He had to confess his unforgivable failings to his old white brother before he passed on to the Great Mystery.

Ancient Eyes inched his slow way through the cars, sweat pouring down his broad, ugly face, his vision becoming blurred. On he struggled, propelled by a strong sense of duty, ignoring the concern of worried troupe members calling to him, asking if he was ill.

Determined to make it to the Colonel's coach under his own power, he shrugged off all attempts of aid. Blindly stumbling on, the heartsick Indian finally sagged to his knees, choking and clutching his chest. A fellow show Indian swiftly leaped out of his seat and caught the aged Ute before he fully fell.

The concerned Arapaho, cradling the old war chief in his arms, shouted, "Get the troupe doctor! Looks like Ancient Eyes is having a heart attack!"

"No . . . no . . ." choked Ancient Eyes, "take . . . take me . . . must see Colonel."

"You're not seeing anybody but the doctor," cautioned the Arapaho. "Now stay quiet, old one. Be still."

Ancient Eyes felt consciousness slipping away. Frantic to stay awake, he grabbed the Arapaho's shirtfront. "There's something . . . must . . . tell . . ."

"He's passed out," said the Arapaho to those nervously gathering around. "Quick, help me carry him to the hospital car!"

Diane waited a few minutes, then rose, folded the blanket, and ducked out of the rocky cave into the bright morning sunlight. The Indian, leisurely gathering kindling, never looked up. He didn't acknowledge her presence.

Frowning, she warily watched him go about his tasks. He took his time; none of his moves was hurried. He did everything with an exquisite grace. Staring at the sharp-featured, loose-limbed creature, Diane was struck by the quiet, easy, reckless air that seemed to be a part of him.

She shivered.

She was deathly afraid of him. More afraid of him than she'd ever been of anything or anyone in her life. Strangely she would have been far less frightened if he behaved in a manner that might be expected of an untamed beast. He didn't. But he exuded a quiet, understated menace, and she knew he was capable of sudden bursts of violence.

When he'd lain atop her inside the rocky cave, he had come close to taking her forcefully. There had been an animal ferocity about him, his desire an almost palpable thing. The tendons had stood out in bold relief on his bruised neck, and a vein had pulsed on his high forehead. Every sinew and muscle of his long, lean body had been rock-hard, tensed, poised. For attack? Brutality? Rape?

Diane shuddered. To think that she had been scared, but attracted, halfway aroused by the dangerous desire he had exuded. Shame made her face flush hot as she reviewed those anxious moments inside the shadowy cave.

The hot-eyed savage had come uncomfortably close to tearing her clothes off, and she had come shamefully close to allowing it. As appalled by her own bizarre stirrings of passion as she was by his, Diane was once again frantic to escape. Right this minute. It wouldn't be easy to slip away from the mute but ever alert Indian.

Even now, when those penetrating eyes were not on her, she had the feeling that he somehow knew exactly what she was thinking. Diane mentally shook herself. That was totally absurd! How could this uncivilized savage—a human being, yes, but no different from, no more intelligent than, an animal—possibly know what was going through her mind?

He couldn't.

Heartened, Diane casually glanced around. She'd been asleep when they'd ridden into the narrow meadow. She remembered nothing, was not totally certain which direction led back down to Boulder. She looked up at the sun in an attempt to get her bearings. Then lowered her eyes to the carpet of grass covering the narrow meadow. Clearly she saw the hoofprints leading up into the canyon.

Diane cautiously glanced again at the Redman. He had a fire started. He was now engaged in stripping the leaves from a long serviceberry branch, apparently making a fishing pole. Without giving it any further consideration, Diane dropped the blanket and took off running.

She'd covered less than forty yards when he caught up with her. A long arm came around her waist, stopped her in mid-stride, and reeled her back against his chest. Diane immediately squirmed about to face him, shouting angrily as she turned.

But she fell silent when he wrapped a hand around the front of her throat. He pressed her head back into the crook of his supporting arm, forcing her to look up at his sharp, angular face and into his dark, piercing eyes.

Those eyes were narrowed, snapping at her. With his hand wrapped around her throat, he applied gentle pressure with thumb and finger-tips, allowing her to feel the leashed strength in his powerful hand. A chill uneasiness swept over her as the strong sunlight glinted on the wide silver bracelet encircling his wrist. His message couldn't have been more clear had be been able to enunciate it carefully.

If he chose to do so, he could choke the very life out of her while they stood staring at each other. That was what he was telling her. What he wanted her to understand and to remember. That she had no chance against him. He could kill her with just one hand.

Swallowing with great difficulty, Diane nodded furiously and said, "I understand, Beast."

The words had no sooner passed her lips than his fingers loosened on her throat. Afraid to move until he completely released her, Diane stayed as she was, body braced against his, head resting in the crook of his raised arm.

The Indian's hand didn't *lift* from her throat. It slid down her throat, spread on her collarbones, moved unhurriedly to the bare swell of her breasts just above her low-cut bodice. Nervously Diane narrowed her eyes and ordered him to stop. The order was ignored.

His eyes became bold and dark and very intense. His hand moved with maddening slowness over the curve of her left breast, to her slim midriff, finally to her waist.

And fell away.

The tall Indian released her so swiftly Diane nearly lost her balance. She stared after him as he negligently turned his back on her and walked away. For a minute more she stood there, shaken by his easy dominance, angered by his arrogance. She had a good mind to take off running again!

Diane followed him back to camp.

She dropped down beside the fire, hugged her knees, and wished for something to eat, something to drink. As if he could read her mind, the Redman picked up the canteen, circled the fire, and crouched down on his heels beside her. He offered her the canteen.

Diane refused to take it. He shrugged, turned it up to his lips, and drank thirstily. As she watched the cold, clear water pour from the canteen into his open mouth, her hatred for him grew. He was a mon-ster, an insolent bastard!

Teeth grinding, she shot to her feet, walked the few steps to the creek, and knelt down beside the cold, clear stream. She tried, unsuccessfully, to scoop up handfuls of water and bring them to her lips. Each time she lost all but a drop or two of the precious water before she could get it to her mouth.

She jumped when the Indian tapped her on the shoulder. He knelt beside her, leaned down, scooped up a double handful of water, and offered it to her. Violently she shook her head, hoping he was able to comprehend that she wouldn't drink from his filthy hands if she'd been out on the hot Sahara desert for a week!

The Indian tossed the water back into the creek. Her snapping violet eyes on him, Diane watched as he stretched out on his stomach beside her. His hands on the grassy bank, his elbows supporting his body, he thrust his face far out over the creek. A lock of his silver-streaked black hair fell into the water, but he seemed not to notice. He lowered his dark face and drank like a cat, barely touching the water's smooth surface with his lips.

He lifted his head, levered himself back up into a kneeling position beside her. Looking straight at her, he wiped his wet lips on a forearm and pointed to the water. He was challenging her to give it a try, probably hoping she'd fall in, face first.

Diane gave him a wilting look, haughtily shoved her hair behind her ears, and confidently stretched out on her stomach. Recalling exactly the way he had done it, Diane positioned her hands evenly on either side, balanced her weight on her elbows, and leaned far out over the water.

She groaned with frustration when a large section of her long, flowing hair began sliding around the side of her left shoulder. The Indian's quick fingers reached out and gently plucked it up before it touched the water. Diane carefully lowered her face. She took small, refreshing drinks, lapping at the cold water, sucking it up with puckered lips, while her captor held her long raven hair up in one bronzed hand.

When her thirst was quenched, Diane lifted her head, levered herself up just as he had done, and sat back on her heels. Giving him a smug, triumphant look, she snatched her hair from his hand and tossed it back over her shoulder.

Then cringed when his hand lifted to her face. She leaned as far away as she could in her present position, but his hand followed. His middle finger touched her small, aristocratic nose and flicked away a diamond drop of water clinging to its tip.

"Thanks, Beast," Diane said grudgingly. Nodding, he watched as she bent her head and blotted her wet face on the skirts of her wrinkled purple dress.

The expression in his black eyes softened appealingly. A faint hint of a smile touched the cruel, sensual lips of the savage.

Chapter 18

But Diane never knew.

By the time she raised her head, not a trace of tenderness lingered in her captor's dark eyes. His lips were set in a stern line. His hard-featured face was again an unreadable mask.

He pointed to the creek, he pointed to her, and then he pantomimed washing by rubbing his palms over his long arms and bare chest. The message was clear enough. She was to take a bath in the creek.

Diane favored him with a false smile. Then, speaking in the softest, kindest of tones, she said, "Beast, I wouldn't take a bath with you if it had been a year since I'd last seen a tub." Continuing to smile, she rose to her feet, looked down at him, and added, "Believe me, the day will *never* come when I take my clothes off with you lurking around."

She turned and walked back to the campfire, hoping he *would* take a morning bath. If he did, she'd snatch up what few clothes he had, hop on the horse, and ride away, leaving him naked and afoot!

Nothing of the kind happened, and Diane was not surprised. She had never actually supposed that the wild, uncivilized creature would be interested in keeping his body clean.

The Redman caught a trout for their breakfast, cooked it in the open flame of the campfire, and shrugged indifferently when Diane refused even to taste it. Seated cross-legged beside her, he ate with relish, biting eagerly into the fish with sharp white teeth and then licking his lips until she wanted to smack him a good one.

When finally he had devoured the entire trout, he absently rubbed his bare belly, sighed, and stretched contentedly. Diane remained composed, purposely making her face as expressionless as his usually was.

However, her interest was slightly piqued when the savage reached for the beaded headband he'd removed earlier. He took the sharp hunting knife from its scabbard and meticulously cut the headband into small square pieces.

Forehead puckered, Diane watched, wondering what bit of madness he was up to now. When he finished his chore, he gathered up all the square pieces—except one—and placed them atop the sleeve he'd torn from her dress. He tied those beaded squares up in the purple fabric, shoved the small, tidy bundle down into his low-riding breechcloth, and resheathed the knife.

He rose to his feet, leaving one colorful beaded square of the butchered neckband lying on the grass. Supposing he had overlooked it, Diane automatically reached for it, meaning to hand it to him. The instant her fingers touched the beaded leather square, his moccasined foot came down gently but squarely atop her hand. Diane's head snapped up.

The Indian stood there towering over her, tall and dangerous-looking. His dark, menacing eyes were riveted on her and Diane felt a surge of uneasiness rush through her slender body. She had no idea why she'd displeased him, but obviously she had. He slowly shook his head from side to side, then lifted his foot from her hand.

Diane's first impulse was to snatch up the beaded square and sail it out into the middle of the creek. But she wisely checked herself. For some unknown reason, that worthless piece of leather and beads obviously meant something to the savage. So much so that he refused to move away until she completely released it. He continued to stand there just above; so close his bare, hard thigh was scant inches from her face.

Diane slowly moved her hand, wanting no extra trouble. She could only surmise that the strange exercise of his carefully cutting up the neckband, tying up the pieces, and placing one on the ground was some sort of foolish, primitive ritual. She shrugged, folded her arms over her chest, and gazed out over the creek.

"Whatever makes you happy."

The Indian immediately stepped away, and Diane felt her breath escape in a rush. Pretending total disinterest, she stole glances at him as he went about preparing for their departure. He had the stallion bridled and saddled within minutes, the blankets strapped behind the cantle, the filled canteen hooked over the saddle horn.

Diane's violet eyes darkened with unintentional curiosity when he shook out the pair of stolen leather chaps, then whirled them around his tall body, buckling them behind his trim waist. Deftly he smoothed the worn leather around his long right leg, buckled it beneath his firm buttock and behind his knee, then did the same with the left leg.

Diane, watching him from beneath dark, veiling lashes, found his newly donned getup offensive. True, at least the fronts of his bare legs were now covered, but the cut of the chaps accentuated that distinctly male part of his anatomy that needed no emphasis. The apron of the skimpy loincloth which was designed to hang loose was now pulled tight over his groin.

He looked like a blatantly sexual bronzed god standing there vainly in the sun, torso naked, leather snugly encasing his flat belly and lean flanks and long legs. And ample groin. Diane was disturbed by his raw masculinity. She thought him base and crude, and the sight of him was unsettling, yet she couldn't take her eyes off him. He looked downright indecent when abruptly he crouched down on his heels, legs spread apart, and buckled the silver-trimmed spurs to his moccasins.

Diane felt her face flush with heat. She swiftly averted her gaze until he turned and walked away. Then her eyes lifted and followed him. Finally she was tempted to laugh. From the rear it looked as if the savage were attired in some silly peekaboo costume fashioned for bawdy frolic and play in a whorehouse!

Diane's face turned scarlet when her traitorous thoughts turned embarrassingly naughty, and she envisioned the harshly handsome savage wearing the leather chaps just as he was now—but *without* the breechcloth underneath.

Before she could completely collect herself, the Indian returned, leading the saddled stallion and wearing the stolen Stetson on his head. He stepped up close. While the stallion nudged at his bare bronzed shoulder, he held out his hand to Diane.

Ignoring it and his piercing eyes, she sprang to her feet. He stuffed the reins down into the low-riding chaps and put his hands to her waist. Diane anxiously pushed them away. Brushing past him, she stepped up to the stallion, grabbed the horn, and put her foot in the stirrup.

"Beast," she said over her shoulder, "I have no intention of riding draped across the saddle so that I have to look at you all day." She effortlessly pulled herself up, swung a long, slender leg over, and settled herself astride, modestly pulling her full purple skirts down over her knees and tucking them around her legs. "You disgust me," she said, pushing her hair back behind her ears, "you foolishly suppose that I'll forget you're an animal, but that will not happen. Flaunt your disgusting masculinity all you want; to me you'll never be anything but a beast." She paused, looked down at him, and smiled. "Ready, Beast?"

The granite-faced Redman looped the long reins over the stallion's neck and swung up behind Diane. He took off the Stetson, set it atop her head, and waited. She knew he expected her to object, to snatch off the hat and throw it on the ground or shove it back at him. So she didn't do it. She pulled the brim low on her forehead, secretly grateful that she wouldn't have to endure the alpine sun's harsh glare all day.

A pair of long bronzed arms swiftly enclosed her. The Indian gently touched the stolen spurs to the stallion's belly, and they were off. To where Diane did not know.

As they rode out of camp, Diane tipped her head back and looked up. On the rim of a rocky crag above the narrow creek, a pair of golden eyes gleamed in a sleek, regal head and a huge tawny body crouched as if ready to leap. Diane stared up at mountain lion, and the lion stared down at her.

Calmly lowering her eyes, Diane thought that the magnificent beast on the rocks above posed far less of a threat than the magnificent beast riding behind her.

Hours passed as the mounted pair rode higher into the wild, rugged Front Range of the Rockies. Across broad and beautiful meadows they traveled. Past fast-flowing crystalline streams. Through dense dark forests of lodgepole pines and Douglas firs. Up steep, jagged rocky summits. Down gentle, sparsely timbered slopes. Over narrow, treacherous precipices. Under gigantic, balanced boulders.

As long as they were atop the moving stallion, Diane knew she was in no immediate danger, so she was partially able to relax. But the long, tiring ride gave her plenty of time to think about the gravity of her dilemma. She could only imagine what lay in store for her, and the possibilities were limited. Her captor aimed to make her his squaw, or give her as a present to another savage, or barter her for goods.

Or kill her.

Diane's narrowed violet eyes lowered to the dark, powerful arms enclosing her, to the lean hand loosely holding the reins, and the wide silver bracelet on his wrist. His hand moved, and she studied his fingers. They were long and slender, and his nails were clean, smooth, and tapered.

The wispy hair lifted on the nape of her neck. Vividly she recalled having that hand wrapped around her throat. There was so much leashed strength in those long fingers the savage could have snapped her neck as if it were a brittle twig.

Diane experienced a shuddering ripple through her entire body.

She forced herself not to dwell on the chilling prospect of her fate. She would think of something else. Someone else. Her thoughts turned to those she most loved. The Colonel and Granny Buchannan were surely worried sick about her. And Texas Kate. And Shorty. And poor Ancient Eyes. The Ute chieftain must be right now blaming himself for what had happened when the fault was really hers. Bless his old heart.

The Cherokee Kid didn't warrant much of her concern. If there was blame to be shared, he deserved a healthy portion. He should never have beaten the Beast or brought him down out of the mountains. On the other hand, she could count on the Kid to lead the search, and with a little luck, maybe he'd find her in time to save her from the savage.

Diane's slender shoulders slumped. She'd left her position in Washington, D.C., for the sole purpose of helping out her grandparents. Instead she'd managed to add to their problems. Besides their worry for her safety, there was the show to think about. Gossip had a way of spreading quickly. Her capture at the hands of the Colonel's own chosen star attraction would bring damaging scandal to the already troubled troupe.

Pawnee Bill was probably already circling like a shark tasting blood.

More immediate worries again took precedence as the long day ended and they stopped for the night. Beneath the northeast face of the soaring fourteen-thousand-foot Longs Peak, they pitched camp just below the Roaring Fork waterfall on the banks of Lake Chasm. The water cascading over the rocks caused a loud, constant roar.

Supper was more fire-blackened trout caught in the lake, and Diane was so hungry it tasted good. When bedtime came, she tensed. Would this be the hour of her violation and death? Forced to sleep wrapped in the Indian's powerful bronzed arms, she lay in wakeful agony for what seemed forever until she could no longer hold her eyes open.

More than once throughout the chill mountain night, she awakened from her fitful slumber to find those dark, penetrating eyes calmly watching her. Each time her breath caught in her throat and her heart stopped beating. A frightening electricity filled the air between them, and she was rigid with fear.

And yet the expression in his intelligent eyes was baffling. What was he waiting for? Why not rape, scalp, and kill her and be mercifully done with it?

Morning came at last, and Diane was grateful to be alive to face the new day. They set out early and as they rode away, Diane noticed that the Indian left behind another cut square from the red beaded headband.

Soon the sun was high and hot, and the atmosphere was so thin the harsh rays poured down in unfiltered heat. Diane pulled her Stetson low. She grew faint and tired and found it difficult to breathe.

The altitude didn't bother the Redman. He guided the stallion higher and higher into the mountains and never showed any signs of discomfort. It appeared he knew exactly where he was going, though he seemed in no particular hurry to get there.

Under different circumstances, the awesome scenery would have been greatly appreciated by Diane. Summer mists and fog veiled the splashing Columbine Falls on the Roaring Fork. The fierce September sun flushed the peaks along the Continental Divide above Sprague Lake. In the deep shadow of Indian Peaks a fringe of lacy autumn ice decorated the edges of Red Rock Lake.

She caught the flash of big-horned sheep and white-tailed deer crossing a meadow of wild flowers. Saw bluebells and pink moss campion and indian paintbrush carpeting the high country glade. Heard the autumn-quiet murmur of crystal-clear water flowing down Hidden Valley Creek. And finally admired the quaking aspens in September's waning light, the fragile leaves still sprinkled with raindrops from an afternoon shower.

The savage selected the mouth of majestic Granite Gorge for their night's lodging. When they dismounted, the last vestiges of light reflected on the surface of Glacier Creek as it cascaded over the edge of Ribbon Falls. All too soon darkness fell.

With the evening meal behind them, Diane sat across the dying campfire from the Indian. She kept hoping he would grow sleepy and lie down without her. She herself was so weary she could hardly sit up, but she was determined to wait him out.

So the two of them sat there silently in the night while the moon climbed toward its zenith in the black, cloudy sky. A cool wind blew up, causing the orange flames of the fire to dance.

Finally Diane felt as if she could no longer stand to have his eyes calmly observing her, the firelight reflected in their dark depths.

She rose and wandered down the sloping bank of Glacier Creek. She stood there in the moonlight, knowing those dark, fathomless eyes were still on her. She could feel them. There was no escaping those eyes. There was no escaping him. Diane shook her head dejectedly.

Since the Redman had captured her, she had pleaded, cursed, cried, punched, prayed, bullied, and quaked in fear.

Nothing had worked.

Diane sank down to the grass, wrapped her arms around her knees, and sighed wearily. The wind rose and blew the clouds away.

And there she sat under a starry sky so bright she could make out the contours of the land on either side of Glacier Creek. She looked up at that starry sky, and in final frustration, like a child, she wistfully murmured aloud, "Star bright, star light, first star I see tonight, I wish I may—"

"I wish I might"—a deep voice, barely above a whisper, interrupted in perfect, accentless English—"have this wish I wish tonight."

Part Two

Part Two

Chapter 19

➤➤➤➤ "Do you see the necklace of stars almost directly above you?"
That low, masculine voice softly continued. "That's called Co-
rona. And there, just off to your left is Polaris. There's the Great Bear
. . . Io and her son. . . ."

Diane's lips fell open in shocked disbelief. Were her ears playing
tricks on her? She slowly lifted her head. A tall, ghostly apparition, now
more chillingly frightening than ever, her captor stood between her and
the moon. The dark, mysterious figure with the jet black hair, penetrating eyes, and gleaming white teeth could speak!

The sound of his deep, strangely monotonic voice turned the blood
in her veins to ice water as he calmly proceeded to educate her on the
stars and constellations.

". . . and off to the west, that's Orion. And there, just behind your
left shoulder, Pleiades rises." A long, bare arm lifted, and he pointed.
"Cassiopeia up in the northern sky, Draco directly overhead. Behind
them Boötes, like a great kite with the brilliant Arcturus glittering in his
tail."

His arm returned to his side. He fell silent and Diane knew by the
attitude of his head that he was looking directly at her. She could feel
those aloof, chilling black eyes fixed on her. For a long tension-filled
moment she sat there unable to react, displaying no emotion. Too astounded to move, too shocked to speak.

The Indian remained very still, very silent, waiting for some kind of response. Then, he quietly turned and walked away. When he did, Diane came out of her stupor.

She shot to her feet, hands balling into fists at her sides, her eyes flashing violet fire. All fear was momentarily gone, pushed aside by exploding anger. Screaming like a banshee, Diane flew at the taciturn Redman as he leisurely strolled back to the campfire. Propelled by blinding rage, she slammed into his back, threw her arms around his middle, and attempted to squeeze the life out of him. Straining with every fiber of her being, she applied all the pressure within her power. She gripped him with bone-crushing firmness, eagerly anticipating his strangled gasps and groans of pain.

She didn't get so much as a peep out of him. Frustrated, Diane angrily sank her teeth into the smooth flesh of his shoulder, viciously biting him. That did it. He flinched, and a soft moan escaped his lips.

Diane was elated.

But then the Indian easily unclasped her hands from around his body and, holding them both in one of his, turned to face her.

"Never," he coolly warned, "bite me again, Beauty."

"I'll bite you any time I get the chance, you bastard!" Diane snarled, struggling to free her hands from his firm grip. "You lied to me, you big beast! Deceived us all. Purposely tricked me!"

"No," he said evenly, "I did not."

"Liar! Impostor! Acting like you couldn't talk when all along—"

"I couldn't."

"Let me go, damn you," she snarled, frantic to free herself. "You *could,* too, talk! You just didn't want me to know it! Let me run my mouth when all along you understood every word I said. Damn you! I hate you, you—you—"

"Beast? That the word you're searching for, Beauty?"

"Yes! Beast! A fraudulent beast! You speak perfect English, and all this time you hid it from me! I could kill you for that! I demand that you let me go at once! Oh, God, you understood everything, were perfectly capable of talking! Were just pretending you couldn't!"

Abruptly the Indian released her. Diane staggered, almost losing her balance. His hands swiftly gripped her shoulders and steadied her.

Unruffled, he said, "Look closely at my throat, Beauty." Diane's eyes dropped to his throat. Even in the moonlight the nasty bruises were visible. "I couldn't speak until now, thanks to your manly lover."

"If you're referring to the Cherokee Kid," hissed Diane, "let me warn you that he's armed and on his way after me this very minute!"

"Beauty," said the Redman, "I'm counting on that."

His hands dropped from her shoulders and he slowly backed away.

She anxiously followed. "You—you were really hurt and couldn't speak?" He nodded affirmatively and took another backward step. Again she advanced on him, her anger still white hot. "Well, maybe you couldn't talk, but that's no excuse for acting like a wild man! You son of a bitch, you'd better let me go, you hear me. Let me go or I'll kill you, so help me God!"

He gave no reply.

He turned his back on her and walked away. Unhurriedly he headed toward the dying campfire.

His insolence burned Diane up. So he wasn't the least bit afraid of her? Well, fine! Good! All it showed was that he was too thickheaded to realize she meant every word she said!

Her violet eyes narrowed, Diane was tempted to fly at him again but thought better of it. That would do no good. He could easily subdue her, and she would have gained nothing. No, the thing to do was to be just as cool as he. To wait for the right opportunity. To bide her time until he least expected an attack.

Diane took a deep breath.

She would allow the savage to believe she had calmed down. She would pretend that her anger had cooled and that she wanted no further trouble. She would even go so far as to charm him subtly into letting his defenses down. Then . . . zap! She'd grab the knife, shove it into his bare belly, and flee.

Diane's slender shoulders lifted, then lowered. She pushed her hair back from her face, smoothed the skirts of her wrinkled, soiled purple dress, and went to join her captor. She sat down near but not too close to him, wrapped her arms around her knees, and said, "I apologize for my outburst."

He was looking into the fire, one long, bare leg stretched out before him, the other raised, a forearm draped atop it. His dark head didn't turn. He continued to stare into the dancing orange flames.

"No apology necessary," he said, his voice beginning to sound hoarse.

Diane gave a little nervous laugh and said, "You know my name. Won't you tell me yours?"

"Call me Starkeeper."

"Starkeeper," she repeated. "I like that. And it fits, doesn't it? You know so much about the stars. I suppose that's why they gave you the name?" He said nothing. She hurried on. "I find astronomy absolutely fascinating." She waited for a response, wishing he would turn his head to look at her. "Will you tell me more? I'm ever so ignorant on the subject and I—"

"Not now," he said, and rolled to his feet in one easy, fluid motion. He towered over her, the firelight playing over his tall, lean frame. "It's late. Time we get some sleep."

Diane smiled up at him, expecting him to offer her his hand. This time she would take it.

He didn't offer it.

Feeling her temper flare again, Diane carefully hid it. She rose unaided and said, "Yes, I'm quite tired; you must be, too." She yawned dramatically behind her hand, then said, "My goodness, are you as sleepy as I am? I can hardly hold my eyes open."

Wordlessly he took her arm and guided her to where they would sleep. There was no sheltering cave here, so he had spread the blanket on the soft grass directly below the towering west wall of Granite Gorge. The soaring cliffs effectively shadowed the spot from the distracting moonlight.

Diane commented on what a suitable place he had found, said she was certain she'd sleep like a baby here. Yawning again, she lay down on the blanket and steeled herself not to shudder when he stretched out beside her, so close his body almost touched hers. Deftly he swirled the spare blanket over them both, then lay down fully and folded an arm beneath his head.

Longing to move away from him, not daring to do it, Diane glanced up at his face. His eyes were wide open.

She said, "This place is simply beautiful, isn't it?"

Silence.

"The roar of the falls serenading us and the clear creek cascading over the rocks. It's so peaceful and—and—you know, I'm absolutely terrible with directions and geography. Where exactly are we right now?"

"Sleep, Beauty," he said in that same calm, impersonal tone, stretched, and closed his eyes.

Diane's gaze remained on his face. She smiled to herself. He was about to go to sleep. In only a matter of minutes he would drop off.

The Redman *did* fall asleep quickly. Unfortunately so did Diane. Which wasn't at all the way she had planned it. She struggled valiantly to hold her eyes open, but it was impossible. Minutes after lying down, both had fallen asleep. The exhausted pair slept through the chill night, Diane again unconsciously snuggling close to the warmth of the Redman's body.

But she did awaken first.

Diane began to rouse just as the first gray of dawn lightened the sky far above their heads. The deep rock gorge was still cloaked in nighttime darkness; it would be another hour before the sun's warming rays reached down inside the steep-sided granite canyon.

Slowly, cautiously Diane tilted her face. The Indian was still on his back, his eyes closed in slumber, one long arm wrapped around her. Her body was turned in toward his, pressed against his warm, solid length. Her face reddening, Diane could feel his hair-dusted thigh pressing boldly against the bareness of her own. She fought the impulse to shove down the wrinkled skirt that had ridden up during the night.

For a moment she stayed just as she was, watching him closely, making sure he was truly sleeping soundly. Satisfied he was, she warily began inching away from him, wiggling patiently, slowly out of his embrace.

When she was totally free—when no part of her body was touching his—she lay still for a while, again checking to be certain her movements hadn't disturbed him. He slept peacefully on, his breathing deep and even, the dark, chiseled face serene.

Diane could hardly suppress her excitement.

Her eyes remaining riveted to his face, she slid thumb and forefinger over the top border of the horse blanket, then slowly, steadily peeled it away from both their bodies. It took only a minute; it seemed like an hour. At last the blanket was completely pulled free. She laid it aside and once again waited, fearing the chill morning air hitting his near-naked body would awaken him.

He squirmed a little, twisting his bare shoulders and lean flanks as if attempting to nestle down deeper into the bed. Then nothing more. He slept on.

Diane agilely rolled into a sitting position. Turning, she reached across him, her eyes finally leaving his face. Her full attention rested on the sheathed hunting knife on his hip. Before her fingers ever touched the knife's hilt, she could almost feel its smooth solidness fitted firmly in her grasp.

Starting to come out of his deep slumber, the Indian became aware that someone was standing over him. He opened his eyes to slits, concealing their shine with thick lashes, to see the gleam of the knife blade plunging toward him.

Instinctively Starkeeper rolled to his side. He heard the dull thud of the knife stabbing the blanket and grass beneath. As he started to leap to his feet, he reached out, caught the ankle of his attacker, and with a quick turn, flipped her off-balance.

Starkeeper jumped to his feet and was about to leap on his foolish assailant but stopped the assault at the last instant when Diane's legs bunched against his chest, anticipating him. Realizing with surprise that the fiery Diane was almost as swift as he, he waited for her to spring to her feet.

She did so in a split second. Diane came at him with the knife, sharp blade held low, lunging furiously forward. Starkeeper pretended to step into the path of the knife, and she could taste sweet victory. Instead he reached out to grasp the wrist of her hand that held the knife. Using the momentum of Diane's thrust, he put out his near foot and jerked her past him, tripping her. She fell to her face on the ground, the knife still gripped firmly in her outstretched hand.

Starkeeper immediately fell atop her and straddled her but not before Diane managed to swiftly flip over onto her back to face him. Before he could lean down to pin her arms, she got the knife between them, ready to plunge it into his stomach. Astride her waist he was spread out over her, his hands on the ground on either side of her head. The tip of the knife was against his bare belly.

The moment of truth.

Their eyes were locked. Their breaths were coming in loud, short rasps. Both were furious. Both were frightened. It was the ultimate war of wills with the loser facing death.

Diane gritted her teeth and squeezed the knife's handle tightly, telling herself she could do it, she *had* to. It would take only a second. All she had to do was swiftly thrust the razor-sharp blade deep into his belly, and it would be over. She could do it, she knew she could. If only she could make herself quit looking up into his dark, compelling eyes.

Starkeeper stared straight down at her, willing her to look directly into his eyes. She couldn't do it; she couldn't stab him; he knew she couldn't. Not as long as he made her meet his gaze. She was fiery and forceful, but she was no killer. She didn't have the stomach for it.

Diane could feel her fingers trembling on the knife handle, could hear her heartbeat in her ears. She was weakening, and she knew it. She *had* to look away from him immediately. With great effort Diane began to turn her head.

"Look at me," he commanded in a deep monotone. "Look at me, Beauty." She obeyed, hating herself for it, unable to do otherwise.

Hating him when he smugly sat back on his heels astride her, rubbed his bare belly where the knife had pricked him, and said, "Beauty, if you're not going to kill me, I have things to do."

Diane sighed, and her raised arm fell away. Her fingers loosened on the knife; it dropped harmlessly to the ground beside them. Her violet eyes still on the man straddling her, she said tiredly, "Who are you?"

"I will show you who I am, Beauty."

"No! You tell me! Tell me who you are. Tell me right now!"

In the blinking of an eye he bent to her, his bare, broad chest crushing her breasts, his hands clasping her head. His mouth captured hers in a brutal, savage kiss, his tongue swiftly parting her lips and plunging inside. Caught completely off guard, Diane resisted, struggling against him, wishing she had killed him when she'd had the chance.

The long, devouring kiss continued, his mouth hot and demanding on hers, taking her breath away, scaring her, thrilling her. The invasive caress grew hotter, stronger the longer she fought against it. And Diane fought against it for as long as she possibly could. But the sexual fire he so effortlessly exuded was now blazing. His burning lips were reckless and ruthless; she'd never been kissed with quite so much passion in her life.

Her senses melting away in the blaze, Diane stopped struggling and eagerly responded to his fierce, frightening kiss.

At once his hard lips softened, his kiss became gentle, almost sweet in its tenderness. He lifted his head and looked down at the woman whose violet eyes had changed to a deep, appealing shade of purple.

Starkeeper lowered his voice to a whisper. "First, Beauty, I'll tell you a little about myself." He smiled at her as a sardonic light flashed in his black eyes. "And later I'll tell you a lot about yourself."

Chapter 20

"Yes . . . yes, that's better."

"Like this, darling?"

"Mmm . . . now a little lower . . . a little lower . . ."

"Here?"

"God, yes, yes."

Groaning softly, the naked man rolled up onto his elbows, his eyes humid and half closed. He smiled dreamily with building pleasure.

The beautiful young woman's long, silky hair fanned out on his belly was a pleasing sight. More pleasing still was her pale, bare bottom pointed skyward as she bent to him, her full, red lips and talented tongue toying with his blossoming erection.

"Oh, God," he groaned, lay back down, and reached for generous handfuls of her gleaming tresses. He took the blunt-cut ends of her shimmering hair, tickled his distended brown nipples, and sighed with bliss. With her hair deliciously tormenting him and her beautiful mouth licking and loving on him, he became so aroused his heart pounded in his naked chest and his bare toes curled.

When the beauty had brought him to the height of ecstasy, she lifted her head, tossed her hair back from her eyes, and smiled at him with wide, glistening lips.

"Baby, you're the best," he murmured, his big, prone body still tingling with tiny aftershocks. "God, I'd like to take you with me."

Her smile brightened. "You would?"

"Mmm, sure would."

She was stretched out beside him in an instant, her wet red lips pressing kisses to his tanned face, her hand stroking his broad chest.

"I'd like that very much," she cooed. "I want to go with you. Will you take me, really?"

"Tell you what," he said, a hand gliding down her slender back. "I'll make you a deal. Get me hot again in the next ten minutes, and I'll take you with me."

Her head shot up. "Oh, darling, I can. I will."

She did.

Using methods even he was not familiar with, the beautiful woman had him hard and throbbing within minutes, so excited he anxiously flipped her onto her back, spread her pale legs wide, and anxiously moved between. With his weight supported on stiffened arms, he drove into her with fierce, deep thrusts.

As nimble as an acrobat, she tilted her pelvis up to meet his driving force and at the same time leaned up to kiss and bite his chest until he quickly exploded within her.

Sagging down atop her, his body still joined with hers, he felt her fingernails scraping possessively over his firm buttocks, heard her say softly, "Lover, what's your name?"

"Phil Lowery," he replied, short of breath, heart racing, "known professionally as the Kid. The Cherokee Kid." He levered himself off her, fell heavily over onto his back.

"Kid," she repeated, "I like it. Kid. My name's Mary Louise Douglas, but I'm called Honey." She giggled and added, "I just thought of something funny. Isn't it true that all kids love honey?" She rose up on an elbow and tossed her long platinum white hair back over her shoulder.

He chuckled. "Sure, all kids love honey. This Kid sure loves his Honey."

"Oh, Kid," she said, and laughing happily, pressed her head to his shoulder and hugged him tightly, "when do we leave?"

"We?"

Her blond head shot up. "You promised if I could make you—"

"Now, Honey, I was teasin' you. You know that." He gently pushed her away, sat up, and swung his legs to the plush scarlet carpet of the garish gold and red bedroom. "I'd love to take you along, but I can't."

The platinum-haired Honey quickly scooted off the bed and fell to her knees between the Kid's legs. Her hands gripping his muscular thighs, she said, "Why not? I wouldn't be any trouble, Kid. I can cook and play the piano and—"

He leaned down and kissed her to shut her up. Then he playfully ruffled her white hair and said, "Honey, there's no kitchens or pianos where I'm going. I'm heading up into the high country to search for a missing woman. I should be on the trail right now. But this big old Kid loves his Honey so much it's hard to break away." He gave her his most winning smile, then added, "I really have to go, darlin'. My two compadres are waiting downstairs."

"Who is this woman?" Honey asked petulantly.

"The lady I'm going to marry," said the Kid matter-of-factly, "and if she knew I had been here in the Boulderado Bordello, tasting my sweet, gooey Honey"—he bent to her, kissed her pouting mouth— "she'd be plenty jealous."

"I hope so," said Honey. "What happened to this woman? How do you know you'll find her?"

"I'll find her," said the Kid, rising and reaching for his pants. "You remember I told you I own a famous wild west show?" Honey sat back on her heels and nodded. "Well, to get even with me, one of my Indian performers kidnapped my raven-haired fiancée." He pulled on his trousers.

Honey rose to face him. "What did you do to him that made him want to—"

Ignoring her question, he interrupted. "We have some good leads. A rancher four miles south of Boulder says they came by his place, stole a stallion from his remuda. I'll track 'em down."

"Well, Kid," said Honey, twisting a long platinum curl around her finger, "you had sure better hurry."

The Kid grinned. "Don't tell me my sweet Honey is suddenly anxious to get rid of me."

Honey grinned back at him. "No, I was thinking of your missing sweetheart."

He said, "This wasn't her fault, so no matter what happens, I'll still want her."

"Well, Kid, that's not exactly what I meant." Her emerald eyes twinkled, and she added naughtily, "After that Indian has made savage love to her, will she still want you?"

The Kid's grin instantly vanished. His suntanned face flushed with fury. He reached out and grabbed the smiling woman by her hair. Honey winced with shock and pain when the Kid hauled her up to him, viciously twisting her long white hair around his hand.

"You—you're hurting me," she complained, tears rushing to her eyes.

"Am I?" snarled the Kid. He slammed her naked body hard against his solid length, forcefully yanked her head back, and looked into her frightened eyes. "Am I really hurtin' you?"

"Yes! Yes, you are," she said, struggling, her hands impotently pushing him.

"Good," he said. "I'm glad. I came here for pleasure, not to hear your stupid observations about Indian lovers."

"I was teasing," she said, "I didn't mean—"

"The redskin hasn't been born that can take a woman away from me," he said. "You hear me? Hear me, bitch?"

"Yes . . . yes, I hear you," she sobbed. "Please . . ."

"Passion and punishment. That's what women need. All women. Keeps 'em in line."

Honey screamed as the Kid spun her around by her hair and abruptly released her. She crashed into the heavy carved footboard of the bed, then crumpled to the floor. She lay there sobbing in pain while the Kid coolly finished dressing.

When he was ready to leave, he came to her, nudged her ribs with the toe of his boot.

"Get up," he commanded. Honey cautiously raised her head, pushed her hair back, and looked up at him. Tears streamed down her red cheeks. She was paralyzed with fear. "I said get up!"

The Kid pulled the sobbing woman to her feet. She shuddered when he drew her close, unsure what he intended.

He kissed her. It was a long, slow, openmouthed kiss. When the kiss finally ended, Honey was no longer weeping. Her arms had come around him. She molded her body to his. The Kid soothingly stroked her slender back, her shiny white-blond hair. He allowed her to relax completely in his warm embrace.

When he heard her sigh and she sagged tiredly, contentedly against him, the Kid smiled and forcefully pushed her away. He turned her about and gave her bare bottom a hard, stinging swat with his open-palmed hand. She screamed as she again went sprawling.

Crossing to the door, the Kid said over his shoulder, "Take care of yourself, Honey."

Chapter 21

⟫⟫⟫ Shorty Jones took one last, long drag off the cigarette dangling from his lips before flicking it away into the darkness. He removed his sweat-stained gray Stetson, smoothed his short brown hair awkwardly, shoved the silver link chain and whistle down inside his white western shirt, and climbed the steep stone steps of Salt Lake City's Memorial Hospital.

He walked through the heavy double front doors, crossed an empty waiting room, and stepped into a wide, silent corridor. In the hall's center, directly before him, a plain but pleasant-looking woman who was almost as skinny as he sat at a small wooden desk. The thin young woman wore a nurse's starched white hat and uniform. She looked up as Shorty attempted to tiptoe past her.

"Ah, wait . . . hold it," she said, her voice as thin as her body. Rising to her feet, she asked, "Where do you think you're going, cowboy?"

Shorty stopped, gave her a sheepish grin, and said, "Thought I'd just look in on an old friend."

"I'm sorry, sir, but no visitors are allowed at this late hour," said Nurse Mitchell, pushing back her chair and circling the desk. "My goodness, don't you realize it's nearly midnight? I'm afraid you'll have to return tomorrow during regular visiting hours."

"He might not be here tomorrow," said Shorty, nervously twisting his hat in his hands and shifting his slight weight from one booted foot to the other. "I have to see him now."

"But surely if he's going home tomorrow, then you can—"

"Ma'am, I didn't say he was going home." Shorty looked straight into the woman's light eyes.

"Oh . . ." Nurse Mitchell nodded understandingly. Her reedy voice lowered and softened. "Who is it you've come to visit?"

"His name is Ancient Eyes. An elderly Ute Indian who—"

"Yes, I know the patient. He was admitted yesterday morning, wasn't he?" She automatically looked down the long corridor toward Ancient Eyes' room. "The poor old dear is still in a coma. . . ." She shook her head. "He won't know you're here."

Continuing to twist his Stetson, Shorty said, "How do you know he won't?"

"Why, because he . . . the doctor said . . . the patient doesn't respond to—to—" Nurse Mitchell stopped speaking, looked cautiously around, and whispered, "I see no harm in you looking in on your friend. But let me warn you, if you stay past midnight, it'll be at your own risk." Again she looked around, stepped even closer to Shorty, and said behind her hand, "That's when Nurse Spencer comes on duty." She lifted her eyebrows meaningfully.

Shorty shyly smiled, thanked the sympathetic Nurse Mitchell for the warning, turned, and tiptoed down the long, silent hallway. He paused outside Ancient Eyes' door, drew a deep breath, and stepped inside.

A lone lamp burned on a small white table across the room. The mellow light cast eerie shadows on the white ceiling and walls and on the still, seemingly lifeless form of the man in the bed.

Dropping his Stetson on an uncomfortable-looking straight-back chair, Shorty moved up close to his sick friend. Ancient Eyes' broad, ugly face was so gray and drawn he was hardly recognizable. His snow white hair lay limp and damp on the pillow, and his squat, massive body seemed to have already shrunk.

Shorty sadly examined the big, bare arms lying motionless atop the white sheet, arms which had remained firm and ropy with hard, powerful muscles long past Ancient Eyes' prime. Now they were the weak, useless arms of a helpless old man; the flesh hung loose and crepey from the bone. The massive hands were wrinkled and covered with age spots.

A deep sadness pressing down on him, Shorty cautiously picked up one of those hands, held it firmly in both of his own. And speaking past the lump in his throat, he addressed the unconscious man.

"Ancient Eyes, old friend, it's me. Shorty. I come on back as soon as I could get away." He looked at the Indian's face as he spoke. "I figured you'd want to know how it went and all." Shorty swallowed again. "Now I ain't gonna' lie and say we had a great turnout but . . ."

The skinny animal wrangler stood at the dying Indian's bedside and filled him in. Shorty told Ancient Eyes how the parade and opening Salt Lake City performance had gone off right on schedule that very afternoon. Said the Colonel had considered canceling the entire engagement, but Mrs. Buchannan had convinced him to go on with the show, said they couldn't disappoint the fans.

The wrangler stood in the nighttime silence and talked to the unconscious Indian about everyday things, like who was winning the chess games while he, the old master, was away. He told which Rough Rider had won the most money betting on the Ping-Pong tournaments that constantly went on between shows. Said the latest gossip was that Arto, the handsome young Mexican charro, was courting little Sue Crow Dog, old William Crow Dog's pretty daughter.

Shorty talked and talked, speaking of everything and anything, so long as it was nothing that might in any way upset the sick man. Shorty Jones had no idea whether or not the old Ute could hear him, but just in case he could, he kept his steady flow of conversation pleasant and light. He told how Texas Kate had hit fifty out of fifty thrown glass balls at the evening's performance. Said she had looked mighty pretty out there in the spotlight with her brown hair all curled and her cheeks rouged. Shorty smiled and admitted he'd been tempted just to step right up to her and plant a kiss on her smiling mouth.

"Course, I didn't do it," Shorty told Ancient Eyes. "Kate'd likely beat hell out of me if I'd tried it." He grinned, shook his head, and reached into his breast pocket for a cigarette. "What a woman. What a woman."

In time Shorty moved his hat from the chair and took a seat. He stayed there watching over his old friend through the long night, smoking one cigarette after another, recalling fondly all the years he and the old Ute had been with the troupe.

Shorty Jones was still there at dawn, worn out and worried. As the September sun began to spill through the hospital room's one tall window, Shorty was again at Ancient Eyes' bedside. This time he wasn't speaking; he was listening.

Ancient Eyes' lips were moving; he was struggling to speak. Shorty held his hand and leaned close, doing his best to understand the old Indian's murmuring.

"I'm here, my friend," Shorty assured him in quiet, soothing tones. "I'm listening. Tell me what you want. I'll get it for you."

Ancient Eyes' hand, clasped tightly in Shorty's, moved slightly. Shorty's gripping fingers loosened immediately. "What is it, Ancient Eyes?"

The Ute weakly pulled his hand from Shorty's. Feebly he reached up and patted at Shorty's white shirtfront. The weak, trembling fingers seemed to be searching for something as they tapped lightly on Shorty's bony, narrow chest.

"I don't know what you want, old friend," said Shorty, "I'm sorry . . . I . . ."

Those frail fingers slowly climbed to the open collar of Shorty's shirt, touched the silver link chain, and curled tenaciously around it. Shorty smiled and quickly hauled the silver whistle outside his shirt. Ancient Eyes' mutterings continued as he clutched at the silver chain as though he would never let it go.

"Yes," said the animal wrangler, "yes, old friend. Now you know it's me, Shorty. I'm here, I won't leave you. You can hear me, can't you?"

"Of course, he can't hear you!" boomed a loud, intrusive female voice from behind. Shorty looked sharply over his shoulder. A big, stocky nurse wearing a patronizing expression filled the doorway. "What are you doing in here?" she snapped irritably.

"Watching over my friend," Shorty replied resolutely.

"You're not allowed here at this hour!" She glanced past Shorty to Ancient Eyes. "That old Indian's the same as dead; you're wasting your time. Get out of here."

Ancient Eyes immediately stopped murmuring, his face drew up into a frown, and his hand fell away from Shorty's silver chain.

Horrified that a so-called angel of mercy could be so callous and uncaring, the distraught Shorty Jones, for the first time in twenty years, lost his temper. Now Shorty was still Shorty, so he didn't shout and raise a ruckus. He didn't curse and yell and wake up half the hospital.

The skinny little man simply looked the big, insensitive nurse in the eye and coolly said, "I'm going nowhere. *You* get out." His skinny body vibrated with anger and his eyes were murderous.

Taken aback, the startled nurse said, "You can't talk to me like that! You don't belong here."

"It's you who doesn't belong here, so leave." Shorty's voice was so cold and commanding the bullying, portly nurse winced and took a step backward. "It takes a lot more than a white uniform to make a nurse." said Shorty Jones, dismissing her, and turned back to the bed.

"Why, I've never been so insulted in my—"

"Get out. Now! I don't care where you go, so long as it's out of my sight."

Furious, talking to herself, the big, stocky woman backed out of the hospital room, turned, and waddled away. She never noticed the big, stocky woman standing just outside the door.

Texas Kate had arrived just in time to hear the entire exchange between Shorty and the nurse. Kate hadn't meant to eavesdrop, but she'd stopped short and listened intently, as surprised by Shorty's behavior as was the retreating nurse.

She had no idea that the skinny little animal wrangler could be so assertive. So commanding. She'd always thought of Shorty as a pleasant, kind, thoughtful man, a tame little lapdog who ran errands for her and assisted in her act.

Texas Kate's heart fluttered like a schoolgirl's. Never had she seen Shorty the way he had been just now. How different he was, how provocative.

How manly.

Kate straightened her skirts and patted at her curly brownish gray hair. She pinched her fleshy cheeks and bit her lips. She felt giddy and excited and like very much of a woman simply from being in the presence of such a man.

She stepped into the doorway. Shorty stood at Ancient Eyes' bedside, his back to her.

"Shorty," Kate softly called his name.

He turned to look at her, and Kate saw yet another side of Shorty Jones. Shorty's eyes were swimming in tears. His thin face was drawn and haggard. He looked as if his big, kind heart were breaking.

"Ah, Shorty, don't . . . don't . . . ." cooed Kate, crossing to him.

And her fleshy arms opened wide.

Chapter 22

🔹🔹🔹 By high noon they had ridden down out of the western foothills, having successfully crossed the awesome Front Range, going up and over America's backbone, the high, jagged Continental Divide.

In the early afternoon they rode across a flat, high mountain meadow, but another range of mountains loomed just ahead on the near eastern horizon.

Diane had been silent all morning.

She was angry. She was confused. She was afraid.

She was thoroughly disappointed in herself. This cool, handsome savage who spoke perfect English seemed able to control her as no man ever had and it mystified her.

She should have killed him. Instead she had kissed him.

Now she knew she would *never* kill him, no matter how many chances arose. She knew as well she would *always* kiss him, anytime his cruel, sensual lips closed over hers.

Diane involuntarily shivered at the recollection of that powerful, prolonged kiss.

"Cold, Beauty?" came the deep, monotonic voice from just above her ear.

Diane gave no verbal reply. Grateful he couldn't see her face flushing, she shrugged slender shoulders and hoped that would satisfy him.

"If you're chilly, I can unstrap a blanket from behind the cantle." She shrugged again, more pronouncedly. "Or you can lean back against me and I'll—"

"I am not cold!"

"I thought I detected a slight shiver."

"Well, you didn't." Her violet eyes on the mountains ahead, she asked, not really expecting an answer, "Tell me where you're taking me."

"To Wind River, Wyoming," came the calm, soft reply.

She twisted around to look at his face. "You're an Arapaho?"

"No." He bit out the word, and his stark features instantly hardened perceptibly. "The Arapahos are our oldest foes." Silent for a moment, he then added, "I'm Shoshoni."

"I see," she said, trying to recall if she'd ever known any Shoshonis. "And you want to go back and be among your own kind?"

"Something like that."

"But why take me?" He didn't answer. Sighing, she pointed. "Are those the Wind River Mountains in front of us?"

"Beauty, we're still in Colorado. That's the Ni-chebe-chii Range of the Rockies."

"Can you give that to me in English, Beast?"

"Literally translated, it means the Place of No Never Summer. The white man has shortened it to the Never Summers Range."

"Because it's always cold up there?"

"Not today. It will be warm enough for you to have a bath. We can make camp on a branch of the Cache la Poudre River or beside a mountain tarn and you can . . . wash yourself."

Diane said nothing. She hated the thought of taking off her clothes with him around, but she felt as though if she didn't have a bath soon, she'd scream. Her hair was dirty and tangled, and her skin was caked with dust and grime. Her purple dress was filthy and wrinkled. She was hot and dirty and miserable and knew she looked a mess.

She resented the Indian for habitually appearing clean and cool and comfortable and . . . and . . .

Suddenly it dawned on Diane that she had seen him shaving this morning! She remembered now. When they'd first awakened, there had been the dark shadow of a beard on his face. And when he had hotly kissed her, she'd felt the definite tickle of prickly whiskers against her cheeks.

Good Lord, she hadn't even thought about it then!

Now she puzzled over it. She'd been around Indians all her life. She'd seen Ancient Eyes and the other show Indians pluck the few scattered hairs from their bronzed faces with tweezers. They had never needed to shave. Why, then, did this Shoshoni have to shave?

There was only one way to find out, much as she hated talking to him. "Beast?"

"Yes, Beauty?"

"Why did you shave this morning?"

"I shave every morning."

"I know, but why? I thought Indians didn't have any hair on their— their—" Into her mind leaped the remembered glimpse of his almost exposed groin, and Diane's sentence was never finished.

"On their what?"

"Faces!"

"Most don't. Hair grows on this Indian's face." He paused, then added, "As well as on other parts of my body." He gave her his coldest black-eyed stare.

Diane stiffened, wondering if he'd read her thoughts. Wishing she had never mentioned it, she said nothing more on the subject.

The sun was still hot overhead when they rode into a high rocky gap up in the Never Summers Range. In deep shadow they rode between the twelve-thousand foot-high mounts Cirrus and Nimbus. Starkeeper expertly guided the stallion along the treacherous trail over Thunder Pass, and Diane's eyes widened when they came down out of the pass and she saw the small community spread out in the narrow valley below.

"LuLu City," he said, anticipating her question.

"Are we going there?"

"I am," he said. "You're not."

She turned anxiously to look at him. "Oh, please. I won't give you away, I promise. I'll pretend that we're—we're—"

"Married?"

She swallowed hard. "Yes. Yes, I'll say you're my husband and we're—"

"Look at yourself, Beauty. Then look at me." His tone was flat. "A pale-skinned white woman in a torn, dirty dress with a wild-looking Indian in breechcloth and chaps." He paused while she studied him appraisingly. "Would anyone believe *you* are married to *me?*" Diane's gaze met his, and there was something inexpressibly cold and savage in his eyes.

She shook her head. "No . . . no, I guess they wouldn't." She turned back around without considering the possibility that her answer had stung him.

Diane hated the Redman for having so little trust in her that he sat her down under a tall lodgepole pine on a forested slope directly above LuLu City and tied her arms around the tree's base.

She considered screaming. He shook his dark head and said, "It would do you no good. I'll be back within the hour."

He climbed on the stallion, rode down out of the stand of trees, and disappeared. He cantered into town, tied the stallion at a hitch rail in front of the Glory Hole Saloon, and boldly walked up and down the wooden sidewalks so the townspeople would see him.

Then he stepped quietly into a general store.

He returned to Diane in less than an hour, bringing with him soap, towels, food—even a bottle of red wine—taken from the LuLu City general store. He didn't pay for the items—he had no money—but he did leave his calling card in plain sight on the counter.

A brightly beaded square of leather.

Well before sundown they stopped for the night. Diane didn't attempt to hide her delight with the stolen food he laid out before her like a banquet. It was a wonderful treat to feast on bread and cheese and ham and fresh fruit. She even nodded yes to the offer of red wine, eagerly tipping the green bottle up to her lips again and again.

When the exquisite meal was over, Diane closed her eyes, leaned back on stiffened arms, and sighed with satisfaction. Staring intently at her, Starkeeper could hardly keep from smiling. At that particular moment she looked like a happy, dirty-faced little girl who'd been playing outdoors all day. Any minute her mother would call for her to come inside for her bath before bedtime.

When Diane opened her eyes, Starkeeper rose, walked over, and sat down in the shade of a thick-branched Engelmann spruce. He produced a long, thin cheroot from his stolen stash, put it between his lips, and leaned back against the trunk of the tree. He stretched out his long legs—bare of the chaps—and crossed them at the ankle. He struck a stolen match on a stone, lifted it to the cigar's tip, and puffed the cigar to life.

He blew a well-formed smoke ring in the still, thin mountain air. Then he said, "I brought you something even better than the food."

Diane squinted at him. "Nothing could be better."

"A bar of soap and a fresh white towel," he continued in that low, monotonic voice that so intrigued her. "The alpine pool you see below us is all yours, Beauty."

She looked at him, tempted yet skeptical. "You won't spy on me?"

His dark eyes hooded, he drew slowly on his cigar and blew out the smoke. "No. There's no need."

"What do you mean by that?"

Star was examining the nail of his index finger. He looked up. "Nothing. Go now while the sun's still up."

Ten minutes later Diane stood alone at the edge of a grass-bordered pool. It was a breathtakingly beautiful place. Ringed entirely by green and blue mountains, shadowed by the cottony white clouds hanging low over the jagged peaks, it was a pristine paradise. Rich green grass dotted with dainty yellow sunflowers grew right up to the water's edge. A scattering of large emerald leaves floating lazily on the pool's smooth surface looked as if they'd been carefully placed there by the master designer of this lush alpine Eden.

The water was so perfectly still it mirrored the pale gold leaves of a stately aspen grove rising majestically on the nearby bluff. A white-tailed ptarmigan winged gracefully down, landed a few feet away, and began to feed greedily on fallen willow buds.

Diane smiled, eagerly stripped off her dirty purple dress, and dropped it. She fell to her knees on the soft grassy bank of the clear alpine pool, bent over, and wet her long black hair. Happily she shampooed the tangled tresses with the sweet-scented soap, silently blessing the enigmatic Indian for stealing it.

When her hair was clean and rinsed and swept in long, wet locks down her back, Diane picked up the discarded purple dress and washed it. She then carefully spread it out in the sun to dry.

She looked cautiously around. All was quiet, peaceful, perfect. So she stripped off her lace-trimmed satin chemise and sat back on her heels wearing nothing but her daringly brief satin underpants.

Smiling she splashed cool, clear water all over herself, took up the bar of soap, and happily went about lathering her throat and arms and back and bare breasts, hardly realizing that she had begun to hum softly. She laid the soap aside and rinsed away all the suds. She then sat back on her heels, letting the hot sun kiss her tingling flesh, debating on whether she should strip off her underpants and have a real bath.

Diane closed her eyes, inhaled deeply of the sweet, clean mountain air, and tipped her face up to the sun. She hooked her thumbs into the waistband of her underpants. Eyes remaining closed, head thrown back, she leisurely, lazily, began shoving the satin underpants down over her flat belly and flaring hips.

And choked with fear, her eyes flying open, when a firm hand abruptly clamped over her mouth and an arm of steel came around her bare waist.

"Don't move," warned her Indian captor, his lips brushing her ear, his bare knees spread on either side of hers.

Frozen with fear, Diane felt her heart kicking against her naked breasts, felt his chest pressing insistently against her back. Wondering frantically how she could have been foolish enough to trust him, she sensed that this was to be a brutal sexual possession, without tenderness or mercy.

Kneeling behind her, he whispered, "Our mountain lion has been watching you. He grew curious, and now he's coming toward us. When I move my hand, don't make a sound. Don't move suddenly. Just try to relax."

His hand left her lips. Diane didn't dare even turn her head. She was at once greatly relieved and terrified. She heard the low, inquiring growl of the big cat and bit her lip to keep from making a sound.

"It's all right," whispered the Indian against her ear. "It's going to be okay. Stop holding your breath."

Diane drew a shallow breath and from the corner of her eye saw the big tawny cat edge warily closer. In seconds the cougar with the dark diamond throat reached them, and Diane trembled against Starkeeper when the big cat's golden eyes casually looked her over. She couldn't hold back a soft wince when the powerful beast walked right up and nudged her bare arm with a furry shoulder.

"Stay still," murmured Starkeeper, his arms clasping her protectively to him. "Do exactly as I tell you."

Diane tried to draw up into herself when the huge cat lowered his head and rubbed it back and forth on her bare thigh. The great head lifted. The cat turned and rubbed his side against hers, then walked around behind them, rubbing up against Starkeeper's bare back.

The cat appeared on Diane's other side and again rubbed himself on her. When he gently laid a paw up on her bare thigh, she thought she'd surely faint. And when he stepped up onto her trembling thighs with both front feet, she felt all the blood drain from her face.

The cat moved fully across her, placing his front paws on one side of her, back paws on the other. There he stayed. He pressed his sleek, warm body to hers. Against her bare breasts, Diane could feel the rapid, powerful heartbeat throbbing through his body. She turned her face to the side, seeking closeness and comfort from Starkeeper.

His lips now almost touching hers, Starkeeper said, "He's making you his, just the way a tame tabby does. Putting his scent on you, so you'll belong to him. If you let him do it, he won't hurt you."

Even Starkeeper was struck with fear when the cat, finally moving off Diane, turned slowly, looked at her, and opened his huge mouth, showing his sharp, dangerous canine teeth. But Starkeeper kept that fear from his voice when he said against Diane's open, trembling lips,

"If the cat takes your arm or hand in his mouth, don't jerk it away. Force it farther down into his mouth. Do that and he'll let go."

"Oh, God," she finally whispered brokenly against Starkeeper's bronzed jaw, "help me. I'm so scared."

Watching only the cat, Starkeeper said, "I have you. It's all right. Now he's going to take hold of your arm. Let him have it. Don't pull away."

The big tawny mountain lion growled loudly, advanced again. He lowered his head and clamped his teeth over Diane's forearm. It took superhuman control for her not to jerk it free. But she didn't because Starkeeper's warm lips were against her cold cheek, murmuring to her, instructing her, reassuring her. She obeyed Starkeeper. Diane looked into the cat's golden eyes and slowly shoved her arm farther down into his huge mouth, expecting to hear the crunch of bone, to see the arm bitten completely off.

The lion immediately released her.

For a moment he stood there staring at her, growling menacingly in the back of his throat. Then the growling stopped. He twisted his head and again rubbed it back and forth across her breasts and rib cage. Then, to Diane's shock, the big beast stretched out beside her and laid his big head down in her lap. He moaned softly as if begging her to pet him.

"Should I?" she whispered to Starkeeper.

"Yes," he instructed softly, his arms squeezing her encouragingly, "very slowly, very carefully."

Diane slowly lifted the arm that had been inside the lion's mouth. She tentatively laid her hand atop the cat's great head and gently stroked it, just the way she'd stroke a harmless house pet. The fierce lion responded just like his domestic counterpart.

He bowed his big head back, closed his golden eyes in ecstasy, and made purring sounds of unadulterated pleasure.

"Look," she whispered, smiling nervously. "Look at him."

"Yes, he loves it," murmured Starkeeper. "He knows you're his now, and he's enjoying the stroking."

Diane continued to pet the big tawny lion while he lay with his eyes closed, paws stretching, purrs growing deeper, louder. Then, just like a house cat, in time he grew tired of the attention, the confinement. Abruptly he lifted his head, bounded up, and shot away across the verdant grass and disappeared in the timber.

Diane let out a long, loud sigh of relief, sagged back against Starkeeper's solid chest, and said, "How do you know so much about cats?"

"I'm half cat myself," he replied with almost a smile in his voice.

"I believe it," she said, drained, waiting for her pulse to return to normal.

The danger past, Diane soon became aware of the position they were in, of their state of near-total undress. Suddenly self-conscious and uneasy by the sexual threat he posed, Diane lunged up and crossed her arms over her bare breasts.

She made a big mistake when she said insultingly to the man who had just saved her life, "Get away from me! Don't touch me! I won't allow you to take advantage of me just because—"

Her sentence was never finished.

Instantly Diane found herself flat on her back with both arms raised and pinned above her head in one of his hands. His dark, angry face was inches from hers, and his bare, broad chest was pressing against her bare breasts.

"You're a very foolish woman, Beauty," he said, cold fury darkening his eyes. His free hand captured her face, thumb and fingers biting into her cheeks. The pulse hammering in his temple, he lowered his sculpted lips so close to hers that Diane could feel his breath fanning her cheek.

He said in that unique voice, "You'd do well always to remember that men—even Indian men—are not all that different from cats."

Chapter 23

Diane was stunned by the quicksilver turn in her captor. ➤➤➤❥ Speechless, she looked up into his smoldering black eyes and felt their heat and hatred. Her arms remained pinioned above her head, and his thumb and fingers continued to grip her chin tightly. His broad bronzed chest pressed intimately down on her bare breasts, and a hard, muscular thigh was wedged between her legs.

She was trapped, unable to move.

The Indian's thinned, cruel-looking lips hovered inches from her own. Any second that ruthless mouth would capture and cover hers. Her breath coming in short pants, Diane anxiously anticipated the fierce invasion of that mean but masterful mouth, knowing she was helpless. She couldn't fight it.

The pulse hammered in her throat, and she trembled, realizing instinctively that if he even went further than the demanding possession of a kiss, she wouldn't be able to stop that either.

And wasn't really sure she wanted to.

Above her, Starkeeper looked down at her beautiful, frightened face, his heart pounding as forcefully as hers. His gaze riveted to her full, inviting lips, a terrible, dark, but alluring thought seized him.

His strength was far superior to this temptingly sensual woman beneath him. She wasn't able to move unless he allowed it. She was also nearly naked, as was he. She was intensely afraid of him; he could see it in those arresting violet eyes. She was physically attracted to him; he could see that as well.

She was subdued. Caught. Trapped.

Chained by fright and fascination.

And here in this high mountain Shangri-la they were miles from civilization. Totally alone. No one would stop him if he stripped away her flimsy satin underpants and kissed her all over her pale, silky body. No one would respond to her protests if he forcefully took her, burying himself deep within the sweet, hot flesh that so enticed him.

Starkeeper abruptly realized with alarm that he was almost as trapped as the defenseless Diane. Chains of desire imprisoned him, held him fast. The very scent and sight and feel of her, lying beneath him, so intoxicated him he felt weak and helpless. He knew he should let her go. He wasn't sure he could. Conscience warred with passion, and passion was winning as it never had before.

Starkeeper trembled violently.

Self-control had always been as much an integral part of him as his jet black hair, his tall, lean build. Never once in his thirty-five years had he so much as considered taking a woman by force. Such an act was totally abhorrent to him.

A fierce urgency was communicating itself from Starkeeper to Diane. She felt the thundering beating of his heart against her bare breast, read the raw desire flashing from his heavy-lidded eyes. He was on the verge of taking her in a primitive act of passion. She was powerless to stop him. She was powerless to stop herself as well.

Looking into those hot black eyes, Diane was seized with a terrible, dark, but alluring thought. They were alone here in this beautiful mountain paradise, she and the magnificent beast. No one for miles around. This harshly handsome Indian could make uninhibited love to her here this hidden alpine aerie and no one would know the difference.

And it wouldn't be *her* fault.

He was the male, the dominant one, the one to be held responsible. She had no chance against his greater strength, couldn't physically fight him off. And she had no will to fight the rapidly building desire she felt for him. The strong sexual magnetism that drew them together was too powerful and mysterious to conquer.

Starkeeper stared at Diane's mouth for a long time. Then his burning lips covered hers in a kiss of heated, unbridled lust. His tongue instantly broke the barrier of her teeth and plunged deep inside her mouth. His head turned to the side, and his blistering lips slanted across hers, seeking, taking what he wanted. The long, devouring kiss conveyed such frank sexual hunger that Diane quivered with a deep, reactive yearning.

Paradoxically it was Diane's surprising response to his kiss that saved —or cheated—her of his complete lovemaking.

Starkeeper was by nature a caring and sensitive lover. So when Diane didn't physically protest against his hard, brutal kiss, when instead she willingly molded her sweet, hot lips to his, Starkeeper's punishing mouth immediately eased its pressure, then lifted. In her kiss he had found much more than he'd hoped for.

Not surrender. Something so much better. Shared desire. A passion that matched his own. Starkeeper knew instinctively that she was now his for the taking. And for the giving.

Instantly repentant for his reckless, caveman behavior, he started over—at the very beginning. The hand that pinned her arms above her head released them, and the lips that then bent again to taste hers were cautiously warm and infinitely tender. His softened lips brushed gentle, featherlight kisses to Diane's open lips while his lean bronzed fingers cupped her face as if it were priceless porcelain.

Diane's breathing deepened as Starkeeper's smooth bronzed skin burned against hers. She sighed as his mouth—that marvelous mouth—played provocatively with hers, pressing the sweetest of kisses against her sensitive lips.

Teasing kisses. Caring kisses. Permission-seeking kisses.

The effect was overwhelming.

But sobering.

This powerfully sexual savage was much more than just a powerfully sexual savage. He was also cunning and clever. Intelligent and sensitive. He was not going to force her. Diane knew the reason. This wise Indian refused to allow her the guiltless luxury of "not being able to stop him." He was making it very clear that he wanted her, that his body yearned for hers. That he longed to make love to her, that he would make love to her. If she wanted it. But not unless she was totally willing. She did *not* have to submit to him. He was letting—making—her be the one to decide just how far this dangerously delightful love play would go. The choice was entirely hers.

Damn him to hell!

Diane sighed with frustration and turned her face away. Starkeeper kissed her flushed cheek, his lips sliding beguilingly to the sensitive spot just below her ear.

"No, don't. Stop," she murmured breathlessly, torn between meaning it and wishing he'd never, ever stop. "Please. Let me go, Beast." She said it with as much conviction as she could manage.

Starkeeper's moving lips stilled; his dark head lifted. Diane slowly turned her head to look at him. In his beautiful dark eyes was an appealing blend of passion and puzzlement.

Strangely a lump rose in Diane's throat. She wanted—needed—to cry. Why, she didn't know. Confused, she looked into those eyes and steeled herself against their magnetic power. Mentally reminding herself that those compelling eyes promised as much punishment as pleasure, she felt her frustration and anger returning.

And it was his fault. All his fault. He was beautiful and tender and dangerous all at the same time. So very appealing.

"You're nothing at all like the big cat," Diane said. She pushed at his smooth, sculpted shoulders, urging him to move.

"No, Beauty?" His tone was cool, but his breath was labored. He levered himself up, sat down on the grassy bank, and pulled her into a sitting position. He reached for her discarded satin chemise. She snatched it from him.

Anxiously placing it over her bare, hard-nippled breasts, Diane repeated, "No. No, you're not. I freed the big cat, and he was grateful. He remembered my kindness, so he didn't hurt me." She narrowed her violet eyes at him. "But you. I freed you when no one else would, and what thanks do I get? You kidnap me! You frighten me half to death. You carry me off to God knows where. Then—then you throw me down here and try to—to . . . You take advantage of—of . . . you kiss—kiss . . ." Her words trailed away.

"Beauty, I don't believe the man's been born who could take advantage of you," he said in that low, quiet monotone. He paused and added, "Don't worry. I won't touch you again."

Hopefully she asked, "Will you let me go?"

"Soon." He rose to his feet, looked down at her, a muscle working furiously in his bronzed jaw. "Soon you'll be free and back with your own people."

Diane nodded. But she suspected she would never be totally free again.

The journey continued.

Up and through Milner Pass they rode. Then down to follow the Canadian River northward, riding in the shadow of the Medicine Bow Mountains. Eventually they turned more westward, angling toward the emerald green Sierra Madre rising in the near distance.

Skirting the rugged foothills of the Sierras, they crossed over the Wyoming border, moved through Bridger Pass and down into the Great Divide Basin. Desolate, treeless, endless, the basin was a hot, semiarid desert of sagebrush and sun.

Dotted by an occasional lonely-looking ranch house, wide open rangelands stretched in every direction. Straight ahead in the distance, snow-draped mountain peaks rose to meet a blue Wyoming sky. Diane, staring up at those cool, inviting peaks from beneath the brim of the stolen Stetson, had no need to ask. She knew they had to be in the Wind River Range.

They were almost to their destination.

There had been little conversation and absolutely no physical contact between Diane and her enigmatic captor since the incident at the alpine pool. It seemed that his aloof behavior went a bit further than was needed to reassure her he had no intention of harming her.

He was distant, almost sullen, insisting they push on up the trail at a steady pace as if he couldn't wait to get her to the reservation. And out of his sight.

So Diane was thoroughly surprised when right in the middle of the hot afternoon he asked quietly, "How would you like to go for a swim?"

Diane answered without hesitation. "Lord, I'd love it."

Starkeeper said no more. He neck-reined the big stallion a little more westward, and in half an hour the hot, tired Diane felt as if she were surely seeing a mirage.

A large body of water cut through the bleak sage land, a wide stream with beautifully clear waters and wonderfully sandy beaches.

"The Green River," Starkeeper announced flatly, swung down off the horse, and reached for Diane.

Her wide violet eyes were on the tempting water lapping lazily at the smooth, sandy banks. She clutched at Starkeeper's wide, bare shoulders, and as soon as her feet touched the ground, she smiled up at him and said, "Are you as anxious as I am to feel that cold, clean water close over your head?"

He clung to her small waist a second longer. "I'm allowed to enjoy the water, too?"

Her eyes met his. "I'm not that big a bitch."

She stepped away from him, hurried toward the water, ripping off the Stetson as she ran. She wasn't the least bit uneasy when she pulled her purple dress up over her head. He'd said he wouldn't touch her, and she believed him. She dropped the dress, kicked off her shoes, and raced eagerly across the hot sand and out into the icy water, yipping and squealing like a delighted child.

On the sandy banks Starkeeper watched her with half-hooded eyes as he unstrapped the shotgun chaps at the back of his waist and behind his knees. He stepped out of his moccasins, dropped the sheathed knife, and headed to the water's edge. He waded out and stopped when the river's cold, bracing water lapped at his hard thighs.

Diane, treading water in the middle of the river, saw him hesitate and called to him. "What are you waiting for? It's wonderful! Come on in!"

Starkeeper looked straight at her, hooked a thumb under the thin leather string of his breechcloth, and said, "Your satin underwear will be dry ten minutes after you get out. It will take hours for this leather to dry."

Diane cocked her head thoughtfully. What he said was true. She was sympathetic to his predicament.

"Take it off," she called, and quickly turned away.

Starkeeper yanked at the leather string knotted atop his hip, pulled the tiny leather apron up and away from his body, and sailed it back to the sandy beach. He immediately dived under the river's surface and swam underwater with his eyes open until he reached Diane.

She was still turned away from him, her feet busily churning the water, her hands splashing on the top. He couldn't resist. He plunged down, reached out, and tugged playfully on a cute toe.

His tightly closed mouth stretched into a grin when he heard her squeal of laughter. Kicking fiercely, she spun about and peered down into the water. Starkeeper heard her shout of glee when she spotted him. She promptly grabbed double handfuls of his flowing black hair. Diane gave his hair a firm yank, pulling him up.

His dark head broke the surface a foot from her. Laughing, she released his hair, kicked at his wet smooth chest, intending to push rapidly away and swim backward. But when her foot touched his slippery chest, Starkeeper's quick fingers locked around her slender ankle.

Diane shrieked and giggled as he reeled her to him, capturing the other ankle despite her wild splashing and kicking. Starkeeper was still smiling as he effortlessly hauled her in to him, drew her long, slender legs around his waist, and pulled her close.

He locked his wrists firmly beneath her bottom and said, "Got you."

"No, you haven't," she said, struggling against him, unlocking her legs from around him, lowering her feet to dig her toes into his shins. "Hey, that silver bracelet is cutting into my—my . . . it's hurting me," she said.

His wrists came unlocked at once, and Diane hooted with laughter because he had fallen for the ruse. She hurriedly pushed him away, but he was swifter than she. Realizing she had tricked him, he wrapped a hand around the nape of her neck and jerked her back in place.

The amusing game soon came to an abrupt end.

They had laughed and played together in the water for only a brief, lovely moment before into their midst came an uninvited guest whose name was desire.

Her wet, tangled hair falling into her sparkling violet eyes, her gay laughter warming Starkeeper's heart, Diane squirmed and bucked and shimmied up and down his lean body in a fun-loving attempt to escape the powerful bronzed arms imprisoning her. He played along, enjoying the frolic as much as she.

The laughing Diane had managed to climb up Starkeeper's sleek body until her arms were wrapped around his dark head. His smiling face was pressed into the curve of her neck and shoulder. She was rocking against him in an attempt to break the locked wrists beneath her bottom.

Starkeeper's wrists did come unlocked, but he grabbed for her firm bottom, his long fingers spreading on the twin cheeks. His hands pressed her soft, wiggling body against his hard, ungiving frame. Diane's hugging arms forced his dark head against the bare swell of her breasts.

Diane's laughter died and Starkeeper's indulgent smile vanished simultaneously. For an instant more he pressed her body intimately close to him, all his muscles hard and straining. Diane, tightly pressing his dark head to her breasts, felt his lips against her wet flesh not an inch above her taut nipple.

His touch made her shiver and involuntarily take in air. Starkeeper's fingers reflexively tightened on her rounded buttocks; he urged her closer, then slowly slid her down his rigid body. Diane unwrapped her arms from around his head, her legs from around his body.

Her feet touched bottom; she avoided his eyes. Starkeeper released her, his tall, tensed body as still as a statue.

Overhead dark clouds suddenly obscured the sun.

Diane trembled from the cold and emotion. She turned and without a word swam away from him. Starkeeper stayed where he was, the hands that had cupped her satin-clad bottom balling into tight fists at his sides.

He waited until she was fully dressed and sitting on the sandy banks hugging her knees, facing away from him. He came out of the river as a bolt of heat lightning flashed over the distant Wind River Mountains.

The first large drops of rain peppered his bare back. A breeze kicked up from out of the east, blowing fine grains of sand against his wet, chilled body.

He stopped and, standing naked behind Diane, reached for his loincloth. Holding the tiny scrap of leather in his right hand, he said softly, "By nightfall we'll be at Wind River."

Her bare arms covered with gooseflesh, Diane said, "How can we be? It's starting to rain."

"A summer shower, nothing more." As anxious as she to get to the reservation, knowing it was highly dangerous for the two of them to be alone any longer, he added as he drew the leather apron over his nakedness, "We'll ride on through the rain." He paused and added, "We won't have to spend another night on the trail, Beauty."

Diane sighed with relief. "Thank God."

Chapter 24

➳➳➳➳ The summer shower was sporadic and brief. Minutes after the first drops started falling, the rain stopped and the dark, ominous clouds quickly dissipated. The sun came out again, higher and hotter than before.

The silent pair riding a stolen stallion steadily northward were not overly bothered by the hot, dry heat. They took little notice of the fierce Wyoming sun beating down with a vengeance. They were much too preoccupied with a heat of a different kind. A far more potent heat. A highly dangerous heat.

A heat that would not go away with the setting of the sun. The old earth would cool pleasantly with the coming of the night, but the all-encompassing heat torturing the solemn pair would not release its hold on them even in the darkest of midnights.

Starkeeper no longer kidded himself.

This beautiful pale-skinned, raven-haired woman was not safe alone with him. Or was it the other way around? *He* was not safe alone with *her*. Either way, something had to be done and soon before it became impossible to keep his hands off her.

Diane, clutching the saddle horn to avoid any physical contact with her unsmiling captor, gazed down at the firm fingers loosely holding the leather reins, noted the pull and play of muscles in Starkeeper's bronzed forearm. An icy heat swept over her as she confronted a terrible truth. She yearned for those strong arms to hold her fast. Longed to have those beautifully tapered fingers touching her. All over.

She was not safe alone with this strange dark man who was not conventionally handsome yet was extraordinarily attractive. Or was it the other way around? *He* wasn't safe with *her*. It made no difference. Something had to be done. And soon.

Late afternoon finally came and with it a spectacular view on the near western horizon. The Wind River Mountains were graced with puffs of white clouds in a pale blue sky and dramatically backlit by the setting summer sun. There were shades of pink and orange and gold, and the westering sun sent a shaft of brilliant white light through a break in the rugged range.

Awed by the vista, Diane stared at the changing shifts of light and shape, dazzled by nature's splendor. When she turned her attention back to the trail, she saw a scattering of buildings straight ahead.

"Is that the reservation?" she asked, speaking for the first time since Green River.

"No." Starkeeper's voice was low, soft. "That's Lander. We'll be stopping there. I need to pick up a few things."

"What about me? Do you plan to tie me—"

"You will come in with me."

Diane was more than a little surprised when they entered a large store on Lander's busy Main Street and the portly proprietor came forward to greet Starkeeper warmly. She was further surprised when Starkeeper introduced her, giving the storekeeper her real name. The stocky man smiled, nodded, and shook her hand.

It was clear that the shopowner knew nothing whatsoever of the kidnapping. A tingling of doubt rushed up Diane's spine. Surely the Colonel had immediately notified the authorities. Or had he?

Diane watched Starkeeper move swiftly about, going up and down the store's wide aisles, picking out items. She wasn't sure how to react when he chose a lovely, stylish white summer skirt and blouse from a rack of ladies' things, came over, held them up to her, and said, "See if these fit."

Fifteen minutes later Starkeeper said to the storekeeper, "Put everything on my bill, Edgar. I'll settle up with you in a day or two." He placed the last of the red beaded leather squares on the wide counter and added, "Anybody comes looking for me, tell them I'll be waiting at the reservation."

"I'll do it," said the stocky man. "Come back soon, miss."

They left the Lander store with Diane looking fresh and pretty in the white cotton eyelet skirt and blouse. Starkeeper wore an ice blue collarless pullover shirt, a pair of dark twill trousers, and shiny black boots. New leather saddlebags were draped over his left shoulder.

It was twilight when Starkeeper pulled the stallion up in a flat, wide meadow on the south bank of the Little Wind River. He pointed to the sprawl of tipi villages across the river.

"My home, Beauty. Wind River."

Diane nodded, staring. "Is all your family here?"

"Yes," he said flatly. "All the family I have lives here at Wind River."

Diane felt strangely tense and uneasy now that they had finally reached their destination. What would his people be like? Were they civilized? How would they treat her? Would she be safe among all these Indians?

Those questions danced through her mind as Starkeeper nudged the stallion into motion again. They forded the shallow Little Wind River and rode onto the huge Wind River reservation as dusk descended over the land. Starkeeper neck-reined the stallion past the agency buildings. Outside, several aged Indian men sat puffing on pipes. Starkeeper nodded and waved to the old-timers, then pulled up on the stallion outside a small post store.

"This won't take a minute," he said, dismounted, and went inside. Not five minutes later he walked out with two bottles of soda pop hooked between the fingers of his right hand. He opened the new leather saddlebags, carefully dropped the chilled bottles inside, and swung back up onto the horse.

On they rode through three separate large tipi villages. At a widely spread-out fourth village, Starkeeper halted the big stallion outside a tipi located at the very end of a long row. He sat for a moment looking at the old-fashioned tipi made of animal skins, then dismounted.

He turned, plucked Diane from the horse, and said, "My grandmother's name is Golden Star. She's the only family I have." They were standing very close to each other. Diane could see the muscles flex in his jaw before he added, "No matter what you think of me, you will treat Golden Star with all the respect she deserves."

"Of course, I will," she replied sharply, annoyed that a savage like him felt it necessary to tell her how to behave.

Starkeeper tossed the new saddlebags over his shoulder, put a hand to the small of Diane's back, and urged her forward.

Just outside the tipi's open triangular flap, Starkeeper called out, "Golden Star, are you there? It's Starkeeper. I've come home."

They waited.

Several long seconds passed before a slight, stooped form appeared in the shadowy tipi opening. A tiny, gaunt, aged Indian woman with silver gray hair pulled into a knot at the base of her head stood looking curiously up at them. She was sunbaked, her skin folded and carved like the arroyos of her native land. Her face was creased deeply with age, and her hands were disfigured by arthritis. She wore a cream-colored dress fashioned of soft, supple suede, its yoke heavily beaded in shades of gray and blue. On her feet were intricately beaded moccasins. From a heavy silver chain around her neck swung a large silver disk.

One arthritic hand outstretched toward the tall dark man smiling down at her; the old woman's shrewd black eyes immediately lighted with pleasure. She had a child's merry laugh when she looked up at the beloved face of her only grandson.

"Starkeeper!" she exclaimed with joy, reaching for him, then hesitating. Those shrewd black eyes darted from the tall dark man to the pale, slender woman at his side, then back again. Her wrinkled brow puckered, and she said doubtfully, "How do I know it is you? I don't see as good as I once did. If you are my grandson, prove it." Those black eyes snapped challengingly at him.

Diane, watching the exchange, felt her heart flutter wildly when an almost boyish grin softened the harshly handsome features of Starkeeper. He presented his right wrist to the old Indian woman. Puzzled, Diane observed as the woman's arthritic hands eagerly wrapped themselves around Starkeeper's wrist and drew it up close to her face. Those arthritic fingers were strong enough to pry apart the wide silver bracelet. Golden Star stared for a split second at the inside of his dark wrist, and then that child's merry laugh again.

"Grandson!" she exclaimed happily, drew his hand to her lips, and kissed it. "Starkeeper, my boy, my boy!"

"Yes, sweetheart," he said, freeing his hand from her tenacious grasp. His arms went around the spare little woman, and he lifted her from the ground while she laughed delightedly and hugged him.

"Starkeeper, Starkeeper," she repeated his name over and over. "You grow to be a big, tall man since last I see you."

He kissed her leathery cheek, and said, "No, Grandmother. You've just forgotten. I've been this height since I was fifteen years old." He carefully lowered her to the ground.

Her hands clung to his blue shirt sleeves. "Fifteen? You are quite a bit older than that now, are you not, Starkeeper?"

"A little," he said gently, that appealing, boyish smile curving his sensual lips. "I'm thirty-five."

The old woman laughed again and shook her gray head. "If you are that old, child, I must be fifty or more."

He affectionately cupped the back of her silver head in his hand. "Golden Star, you turned seventy-nine on your birthday last April."

Her eyes sparkling, Golden Star patted her tall grandson's chest. "Did I? Years slip away; I lose count." Those alert black eyes again shifted to Diane. "Starkeeper, who is this beautiful white girl? Have you married then? Is she your bride? Is she with child yet?"

"No, I—he—" Diane began.

"Forgive my bad manners, Grandmother. This is Miss Diane Buchannan. Miss Buchannan, my maternal grandmother, Golden Star."

"It's a pleasure to meet you, Golden Star," said Diane graciously.

"You are very pale, very pretty," observed Golden Star aloud, and her penetrating gaze moved over Diane's face to the bare shoulders and arms revealed in the low-cut white eyelet blouse. "You are from Nevada?"

"Nevada? I—"

"No, Grandmother," Starkeeper interrupted. Quickly changing the subject, he said, "I brought you something. Invite us in, and I'll give it to you."

"Coca-Cola?" the little woman asked hopefully, clapping her gnarled hands together excitedly. "Come in, come in!"

Inside, Diane sat with her feet curled to the side while the happy Golden Star thirstily drank the bottle of soda pop her grandson had brought her. Starkeeper politely inquired about his grandmother's health and asked after his friends on the reservation. Between long swigs of the fizzing Coca-Cola, Golden Star answered his questions. And oddly, to Diane's way of thinking, asked no questions of him. Which disappointed Diane. She was hoping to learn something of the enigmatic Starkeeper from a grandmother's typical questioning of her grandson.

Diane glanced around at the small but spotless dwelling. The light from a small fire at the tipi's center mingled with dancing shadows on the conical walls made of animal hides. She noticed that photographs of a young, handsome Starkeeper decorated one of the wide panels. Furniture was sparse: a chest made of cedar, a square table, a couple of fur pallets, on opposite sides of the tipi. Glancing first at one narrow bed, then the other, Diane couldn't help wondering about the sleeping arrangements.

She didn't have to wonder long.

Within an hour of their arrival at Wind River, Starkeeper said, "Grandmother, we have tired you. It is time you go to bed."

"No!" objected Golden Star, sounding very much like any white grandmother. "Grandson, you just got here. Open me another Coca-Cola, and let's visit!"

"Listen to me now," he addressed the little Indian woman in that quiet, monotonic voice, "I am going. Miss Buchannan will be staying here with you. She, too, is tired and needs rest. Show her your best Shoshoni hospitality." He kissed Golden Star's wrinkled temple and rose to his feet.

"Going? Where?" Diane quickly stood up to face him. "Where are you going?"

He didn't answer, and Diane felt immediately panicky. Did he plan to leave her here on the reservation while he went somewhere else? Anxiously she followed as he turned and ducked out of the tipi. Outside, she grabbed his shirt sleeve and lifted worried, questioning eyes up to his.

"You can't go. Please—please don't leave me here."

"Beauty, you'll be perfectly safe and comfortable with Golden Star."

"But . . . why aren't you staying? Where are you—"

"I have my own lodge a half mile from here." He added pointedly, "The Shoshonis are a very moral people. An unmarried woman never stays in the lodge of a man who lives alone. Good night, Beauty. Sleep well."

Without another word he picked up the stallion's trailing reins, turned, and led the weary mount down a wide corridor between the long rows of tipis. Her hand at her throat, Diane watched him walk away and was seized with the strong impulse to rush after him, to beg him to take her along.

"Yes, you, too," she murmured soundlessly. "Sleep well, Beast."

Feeling somewhat like a frightened small child who'd been left by her parents with a stranger, Diane sighed, turned, and ducked back inside the tipi.

Golden Star proved to be a gracious hostess. She placed a basin of water, a bar of soap, and a clean towel on a low wooden trunk beside one of the fur-covered pallets. She pulled a curtain across the tipi so that Diane would have total privacy for washing up and for sleeping. She did everything she could think of to make Diane's stay comfortable.

When her tasks were completed, Golden Star laid an arthritic hand on Diane's arm, smiled, and said, "My grandson is right. We are both tired, you and I. We will sleep now, and tomorrow we will get acquainted."

"Thank you for allowing me to share your home, Golden Star." Diane replied.

That child's merry laugh filled the tipi, then: "If you are as spoiled as my handsome grandson has become, then my humble home may be too primitive for your tastes."

"Oh, no," lied Diane, "it's—it's charming, really."

The old Indian's black eyes twinkled, but she was unconvinced. She said, "It will be for only a short time, I imagine." The flashing eyes turned wistful, and the old woman added, "My tall grandson never stays long at Wind River."

"He doesn't? Where does he—"

"Sleep now, pale, pretty one." The Indian woman raised her arthritic hand. "Talk tomorrow." She disappeared through the heavy curtains, and moments later Diane could hear her slow, even breathing as Golden Star slumbered.

Sleep didn't come that easily for Diane.

Stretched out in the darkness, she tossed and turned restlessly on the soft bed of furs. She was uncomfortably warm although she wore only her satin underwear. She sighed with frustration. Outside, there was a definite chill to the night air. She longed to get up, hurry out of the close tipi, and let the rising night winds stroke and cool the annoying heat from her overwarm body.

Miserable, she blamed her dark, erotic captor for this strange, unsettling warmth that kept her awake. Anger mingled with her discomfort as she envisioned him cool and comfortable in his lodge, sleeping soundly.

Starkeeper was not asleep.

Long after midnight had come and gone, he lay awake in the darkness of his silent lodge, smoking one of the thin aromatic cigars he'd bought in Lander. Naked on his soft bed of furs, his long, lean body was covered with a sheen of perspiration despite the chill night breeze that blew in under the rolled-up back panel of his large canvas tipi.

Annoyed, Starkeeper finally gave up, rose, and reached for his trousers. He ducked out of his darkened lodge and moved with long, determined strides toward his destination, his hands tight fists at his sides, his face set in hard lines of determination.

His heart was hammering with exertion when he reached the high rocky bluffs above the Wind River. He stripped and stood naked in the moonlight for a moment, then dived from the high jutting cliffs into the dark, icy waters of the river.

Starkeeper swam back and forth in the frigid waters until his long arms and legs were so tired they tingled and his bare body was so chilled his teeth chattered. And still he swam. Swam until he could no longer lift those tired, trembling arms and he was so cold he shivered inside as well as out.

Only then did he turn over and float toward the bank. He was so weary and so chilled to the bone he had to struggle to make it back up to the rocky cliffs to where he'd left his trousers. He didn't bother with putting the pants back on. Holding them wadded and clutched to his groin, he walked back to his tipi.

Wet, cold, and utterly exhausted, Starkeeper sank down to his bed of fur and fell into a deep, dreamless sleep.

Chapter 25

→→→→ They walked together under the rising sun of the new day, Golden Star and her grandson. Starkeeper respectfully adjusted his customary long-strided steps to the slow, short ones of his aged grandmother. Solicitously he held her arm, steadying her, but she was the one to choose their destination.

Stifling a yawn, the tall, sleepy man carefully hid his irritation at being awakened so early. The intrusion had been no surprise. He had expected as much.

At daybreak Starkeeper had come instantly awake when Golden Star softly called his name from just outside the closed flap of his canvas tipi. Agilely he had rolled up from his soft bed, hurriedly dressed, and come out to meet her.

"We will walk together, Grandson," Golden Star said as the first gray light of dawn delineated the eastern horizon.

Starkeeper nodded and took her arm, knowing what was in store for him, dreading it: a probing interrogation followed by a scathing lecture.

The pair made their sure, unhurried way to a spot on the river where they'd spent many golden hours together when Starkeeper was a child. It was a place of eye-pleasing beauty, and at this early-morning hour a mist rose from the placid waters. A few wild irises and sturdy cattails still graced the grassy banks. From somewhere nearby a sweet-voiced western mockingbird greeted the brand-new day. Golden Star and her grandson stood silent in the peaceful glade, she nostalgic, he impatient.

When she spoke, Golden Star said, "I remember the first summer we came here to this place. So long ago. When you were only eight—yesterday."

Starkeeper said nothing. He exhaled when finally she took his hand and pointed, indicating where she wished to sit. With his help she was finally settled comfortably on the ground, her brittle back resting against a smooth rise of rock which was decorated with crude carvings made by a small boy with his first hunting knife. Starkeeper dropped to the ground before her.

With no preamble, Golden Star said, "Who is this pale beauty? Why have you brought her here? What have you done, Grandson?"

Starkeeper's dark eyes squarely met the shrewdly alert ones of his aged inquisitor. He told Golden Star most of what had happened, omitting the fact that he had been beaten with an ax handle. Like any proud Shoshoni male, Starkeeper had, from the time he was a boy, instinctively concealed from others his personal hurts and disappointments.

So, leaving out the bodily injury done him, he started with the hot day he was prospecting alone in the Colorado mountains and saw the mountain lion being needlessly beaten. He concluded with last night, when he and his beautiful captive had ridden into Wind River.

The old Indian woman listened carefully, by turns nodding, frowning, gritting her teeth, and shaking her head in anger and despair. But when she spoke, it was not to offer sympathy to the grandson who had been trapped and chained by the white man.

"Starkeeper"—she addressed him with narrowed black eyes—"I am ashamed of you as I have never been before. Why did you seize the pale woman? You say she is the one who set you free. She offered you mercy, compassion. Why would you punish her for extending kindness, for turning you loose?"

"I haven't harmed her, Grandmother. She was frightened in the beginning, but that couldn't be helped." Shame nagged at him as he explained the reason for his less than sterling behavior. No one on this earth could make him feel quite as guilty as this tiny Shoshoni woman he loved and respected. "I took her as bait to draw out the man who caught and chained me. The pale beauty is his woman; he'll come after her. When he does—"

"I think not," Golden Star interrupted.

"Yes, he will. I know he'll—"

"That is not what I mean, Grandson." She again cut him short. "I believe there is another, far more selfish reason that you took her from that train."

Starkeeper shrugged wide shoulders. "What other reason could there possibly be?"

She said bluntly, "You want her for yourself."

Stung by the accusation, which was uncomfortably close to the truth, Starkeeper at last turned his head and looked away. "No, I don't," he said in that flat monotone. But his dark eyes held a trace of melancholy when he added, "She means nothing to me."

"If that is so," cautioned Golden Star, "then you must make it plain to her."

His head snapped around. "Jesus, I can't make it any clearer."

"Since when do you swear before your elders!" she snapped back at him. Then, softening, she smiled at the grandson she loved more than life itself. "A woman is a thing not to be understood," she told him with quiet authority. "While it is true that the pale beauty does not hold you in great esteem, she *is* attracted to you. She is, I am afraid, helplessly drawn to you."

Starkeeper's handsome face hardened. "Grandmother, the curiosity of beautiful white women is something I've been used to since my first week in college."

The old woman nodded. "So you have, so you have," she said thoughtfully. Her eyebrows lifted questioningly, and she touched her grandson's knee. "Perhaps this one is different?"

"No," he assured her with a bitter edge to his voice, "this pale beauty is exactly like all the others."

By noontime on that first day at the Wind River Reservation, Diane was aware that Starkeeper was purposely avoiding her. She knew as well that it was more for his sake than for hers. He had no real regard for her; that wasn't the reason he stayed away. It had nothing to do with honor and respect and a wish to keep her safe, even from himself.

No.

It was because of the fierce, undeniable physical attraction that existed between them. Diane reasoned that ironically, had the handsome, sensual Starkeeper been *less* attracted to her, more than likely he would have casually made love to her by now. Such a deduction might be a somewhat conceited view, but it was a correct one nonetheless. The reason she could see it so clearly was that she felt much the same way about him. The mutual attraction was so potent, so powerful it was unsafe for them to be alone together.

So Diane was relieved that Starkeeper apparently meant to stay away from her. At least she told herself she was relieved. But after she had been at Wind River for two full days without once seeing that tall, commanding lithe frame approaching her, or looking into those beautiful black eyes, or hearing that deep, intriguing voice, Diane realized, regretfully, that she missed him.

Her attempts at trying not to think about him were hopeless since Golden Star spoke of little else. From the talkative old woman Diane learned that Starkeeper had gone away to the Carlisle Indian School in far-off Pennsylvania when he was just thirteen. It was there that he had learned to speak English.

"My grandson is trilingual, you know," Golden Star told Diane, beaming with pride. "He speaks his native Shoshoni, English, and Spanish, all fluently. He's a very intelligent man."

"I'm sure he is."

"And a patient one!" That appealing child's merry laugh erupted from Golden Star's lips. "He taught me to speak English, and my head"—she touched her skull with an arthritic forefinger—"is very hard. I do not learn quickly. But never once did Starkeeper raise his voice," Golden Star mused, sighing. "Such a sweet young boy. Such a dear—"

As if she had been questioned, Golden Star told Diane that Starkeeper's father had been a mighty warrior chief. Chief Red Fox's Shoshoni tribe had lived in the Nevada Territory. "The chief had come one summer for a visit with his Wind River kinfolks." Golden Star paused, and her black eyes disappeared into folds of wrinkled flesh as she smiled in fond remembrance. "The chief was thirty years old and very strong and very handsome, and he had no wife. So all the winsome young Wind River maidens buzzed around him like bees after sweet pollen in the springtime." Her eyes opened, and she looked at Diane. "But Chief Red Fox saw the shy, beautiful sixteen-year-old Daughter-of-the-Stars—my precious only child—and fell immediately in love with her. The two of them were married within a week and Chief Red Fox took my daughter back to his Nevada village."

All traces of her smile disappeared as Golden Star went on to say that when Starkeeper was only three years old, Chief Red Fox was ambushed and killed by the hated Arapahos. The grieving Daughter-of-the-Stars brought her young son home to Wind River. Only twenty-two when she lost her husband, Daughter-of-the-Stars never married again. When Starkeeper was a happy, healthy boy of ten, Daughter-of-the-Stars fell ill with a fever and died.

Diane listened intently, fascinated, longing to solve some of the dark mystery that was Starkeeper. She was not surprised when Golden Star told her that her grandson had made such high marks at Carlisle he was accepted into the Colorado School of Mines when he was only sixteen and that he had earned a degree in geology by the time he turned twenty.

"My grandson is very bright," Golden Star again pointed out, "a brilliant man."

Diane knew instinctively that the way to learn the most about the enigmatic Starkeeper was to allow his grandmother to tell—without being prodded—those things about him which she wanted to reveal. So, with effort, Diane was patient when the aged woman lapsed into silence or lost her train of thought or skipped back and forth from present to past, leaving her waiting anxiously for an explanation that never came.

But she couldn't keep from asking one question. "Golden Star, when Starkeeper and I arrived at Wind River, you asked if I was from Nevada. Why would you think that?"

Those shrewd black eyes pinned Diane. "I did not know at the time the circumstances of your meeting. I thought . . . I hoped you were. . . . Nevada is my grandson's home."

"Oh? He lives there with his father's people?"

Golden Star shook her head. "All of Chief Red Fox's people have gone on to the Great Mystery." Almost immediately she preened and stated, "My grandson owns a big, fine mansion in Nevada. He is a very rich man."

"Is he?" Diane replied, hiding her skepticism. She seriously doubted that Starkeeper was wealthy. What pathetic definition of wealth could have had him alone up in the wilds of Colorado wearing breechcloth and moccasins? She waited, thinking Golden Star might elaborate, tell more about his Nevada home or how he made all his money.

But she didn't.

Distracted by other thoughts crowding into her mind, Golden Star forgot entirely that she had been talking about Starkeeper's home in Nevada. She got off on the topic of when he was a young man. Back when he had just passed his sixteenth birthday and gone away to college.

". . . and he had the most beautiful black braids," Golden Star said, smiling, "just like satin." Abruptly a veil seemed to fall over her wrinkled face, and her expression became cold. She turned glittery black eyes on Diane and said, "Do you know what happened to my grandson that first day he walked up the steps at the Colorado School of Mines?"

"No, Golden Star. What happened?"

The old woman's bottom lip began to tremble, and her eyes snapped with rage. "A gang of white boys held Starkeeper down and cut off those beautiful black braids."

Diane's expressive eyebrows drew together, and her violet eyes deepened to purple. "No!" she exclaimed, horrified. "Starkeeper told you they actually cut—"

"I see you know nothing about my proud grandson," Golden Star impatiently interrupted. "Starkeeper was not the one who told me. Starkeeper would *never* have told me about such a thing!"

Day three at Wind River.

Diane and Golden Star went down to the river at midmorning. Diane washed her long raven hair and let it dry in the sun while the aged Indian woman talked of the days gone by, of carefree, happy summers when she herself was young and pretty. Of long, cold winters when several friendly tribes would occupy the same stream and there was plenty of food and the big winter camp would be a place of constant rest and enjoyment.

But no matter where Golden Star's conversations began, they always returned to Starkeeper. Starkeeper swathed to the chin in his cradle, peering out at everything from his mother's back. Starkeeper as a young boy learning to become a tracker and hunter—essentials for becoming a good provider. Starkeeper learning skill, endurance, and daring. And, most important of all, the ability to withstand pain. Mental as well as physical.

With a chuckle Golden Star told of how the young, quick-witted Starkeeper had learned to gamble with the aged warriors who passed their days in games of chance, how he had won a prized pony in a gambling exercise when he was just eleven. Continuing to smile, she told of how the pretty maidens had begun to take notice of Starkeeper by the time he was twelve.

Golden Star's loud sigh filled the peaceful glade as she confided, "In the summer of his fifteenth year Starkeeper came home from Carlisle. He was as tall and strong as he is today and beautiful in the way only the very young and very innocent are beautiful." She paused, looked embarrassed, and bowed her head. "My grandson lost a great deal of his innocence that summer." Quickly she pointed out that he never misbehaved with any of the pretty unmarried girls of the village. He had been properly raised! He was never even alone with a maiden.

Diane was tempted to ask how he had lost his innocence if he wasn't allowed to court the young girls. She didn't dare. But, then, she didn't have to.

Suddenly Golden Star was amazingly frank. "In our village lived a lonely woman twice widowed. She was a Sioux by birth, tall, straight-backed, and as pretty as any woman I've ever seen. Her name was

After-the-Summer-Rain; she kept to herself much of the time and seemed not to care what gossip was spread about her."

Golden Star fell silent, closed her eyes, and Diane, dying to hear more, was tempted to shake her. Hardly daring to breathe, she waited, hoping Golden Star wouldn't forget what she was talking about.

The papery-thin lids remaining closed over the black eyes, Golden Star added, "Summer-Rain was twenty-seven at the time. Twelve years older than Starkeeper and knew better." Again she stopped speaking.

"Knew better?" Diane prompted.

"The Sioux woman lured Starkeeper to her tipi on his first night at home. After that they were together every night in her lodge." The old woman's eyes opened. "Summer-Rain fell in love with him, wanted to take him as her third husband."

Diane made a face. "When he was only fifteen?"

"Then. And after he became a man. And even now."

"After-the-Summer-Rain still lives here at Wind River?" Diane suddenly experienced a sharp jolt of jealousy.

Golden Star nodded. "The Sioux woman lives alone in the same lodge where Starkeeper so rapidly grew up that fifteenth summer."

Diane swallowed hard. "Do they—does Starkeeper—what I mean, is . . ." Her words trailed off.

The old woman shrugged narrow shoulders. "Who knows?"

Diane told herself she didn't care. Didn't give a fig if Starkeeper had gone straight to After-the-Summer-Rain's lodge and had been staying there the entire time they had been at Wind River. If he was spending his nights and days in bed with a woman forty-seven years old, then it was revolting testimony to what an overly sexual animal he was! Imagining the lean bronzed Starkeeper making love to an aging, unattractive gray-haired woman filled Diane with disgust.

She first blinked in confusion, then narrowed her violet eyes in resentment when, on their way back to the tipi, Golden Star pointed to a tall, strikingly attractive woman with silky black hair falling past her waist and voluptuous curves who stood laughing in the sun.

"Summer-Rain," said Golden Star.

Diane felt sick.

She quickly shook her head no when Golden Star asked if she'd like to meet the Sioux woman. Diane fretted all afternoon and wondered how any woman that old could look that young. Now it was all too easy to imagine Starkeeper and Summer-Rain together, and Diane was tortured with mental images of the beautiful Sioux woman and the handsome Shoshoni man.

Restless, troubled, Diane left Golden Star napping and went for a stroll in the middle of that hot afternoon. She had no destination in mind. In the distance, on an open quadrangle beside the agency buildings, she saw a small crowd gathered. There were women among the men, and they were laughing and talking, so Diane sauntered forward to investigate.

When she was approximately thirty yards away, she saw that a handful of men were engaged in a tomahawk-throwing contest. A large bull's-eye was painted on the side of an agency building. Several contestants had already had their turn. A tall, lean man stepped into position to have a go, and Diane's heart skipped a beat, then raced.

Starkeeper stood before the admiring crowd, a sharp tomahawk in his right hand. He wore a pair of snow white leggings that clung to his lean flanks and long legs like a second skin. His naked torso and deeply clefted back and long, leanly muscled arms had been well oiled and shone like bronze satin in the sunlight. His silver-streaked raven hair was plaited in two shiny braids, the braids' tips bound with soft white leather strips that brushed his shoulders. The wide silver bracelet flashed on his right wrist.

All eyes clung to the tall, magnificent man as he lifted the hatchet and threw it with perfect precision and power, hitting the bull's-eye dead center. While the crowd of admirers, including the pretty Summer-Rain, clapped and called his name, Starkeeper stood there godlike in the brilliant sunlight. Diane was so awed by his masculine beauty she felt something akin to worship. Felt as if she should fall to her knees before such a supreme being.

When she could again breathe and think and move, she whirled and hurried away. But she couldn't get the vision of him out of her mind. All afternoon and on into the late evening she kept seeing that gleaming naked torso, those long legs encased in white leather, that sure, skilled hand wielding the sharp-bladed tomahawk.

What had seemed so spiritual at the time became more worldly as Diane continued to think about Starkeeper. He was not a beautiful, untouchable god. He was a handsome, accessible man.

"I think I'll take a walk," Diane casually announced to Golden Star at sunset.

She looked the village over for Starkeeper and couldn't find him. But she felt a great sense of relief when she spotted After-the-Summer-Rain talking with other women of the village on the agency porch.

Diane turned and headed directly to Starkeeper's tipi. She had never been there, but she knew where it was. She hurried, anxious to get there, feeling she couldn't wait one more second to see him. The last traces of pastel light remained behind the peaks of the Wind River

Range when Diane reached Starkeeper's lodge. She stood before the closed flap of his tipi.

Diane didn't call out to him. She was afraid he wouldn't invite her inside. And she had to see him. She pulled back the lowered flap, ducked in, and let it fall back into place. A flickering fire burned at the tipi's center.

Starkeeper lay stretched out on his bed across the tipi, his hands folded beneath his head. He still wore the tight white leather leggings. His smooth bronzed chest still gleamed with oil. His raven hair was still braided and dressed with white leather bindings.

He slowly turned his head and looked at her. In his dark eyes was a strange, unsettling expression, one she'd seen before in the eyes of the Redman. He appeared both dangerous and vulnerable. The combination was overpowering.

Starkeeper looked at the incredibly beautiful young woman standing there staring at him, the white eyelet blouse falling off one pale, delicate shoulder, her raven hair shimmering in the firelight. He knew exactly what was going through her mind. She was curious, just like all the other beautiful white women he had known. That's why she had come here. She was wondering how would it be to make love with an oiled, hatchet-throwing savage.

He wanted her. Wanted her so badly he was almost ill with desire, but still, he hoped that she would prove him wrong. That she would turn him down. Prayed she would say no.

Starkeeper's flat voice was soft when he said, "Go now, Beauty. You still have not learned who I am. Go back to Golden Star. You're not safe here with me this night."

Diane felt her knees go weak. The pulse in her bare throat throbbed. It was unforgivable, it was foolish, it was wrong, but she was overwhelmingly attracted to this paradoxical man.

Nervously she said, "What if I don't want to be safe this night?"

"Then come here."

Chapter 26

➼➼➼➼ For a minute Diane didn't move.
She couldn't.

She began to shiver, although it was so warm inside the firelit lodge Starkeeper had rolled up the tipi's back panel to admit the cool fresh air.

It wasn't the chill of the night that caused Diane to tremble.

It was emotion. Powerful, potent emotion.

Her fear of and fascination with the dark, lean man lying in the fire-light was so compelling Diane felt numb, incapacitated. She couldn't go to him, but neither could she retreat. Paralyzed by an odd mixture of anxiety and anticipation, she stood there transfixed. Trembling.

Starkeeper silently stared at her.

As intense as the physical attraction was between them and as much as he wanted to make love to her, he already felt a sad sense of loss. The pale beauty standing across the tipi from him was about to become interchangeable with dozens of other restless, spoiled, thrill-seeking white women he'd held in his arms.

How naïve he still was. How childlike. How incredibly foolish he'd been to hold out any hope that she might be different.

Starkeeper was annoyed by the painful squeezing of his heart. How absurd he was to feel a sense of loss over something he'd never had. Could never have.

His chiseled face abruptly hardened, and so did his heart.

The dark eyes that were fixed on Diane changed as well. Beneath the lazy lids those eyes began to smolder with sexual heat as he languidly examined the lush, slender curves appealingly outlined beneath the white blouse and skirt.

This ivory-skinned beauty wanted a naked savage to make fierce love to her. Well, so be it. He was her man. He'd give her what she'd come for. And more. By the time she sneaked from out of his tipi in the wee hours of the morning, she would feel both contentedly satiated and brutally violated.

Exactly what she wanted.

"Beauty," Starkeeper said, continuing to lie there stretched out on his back, "come here. Come to me."

"Yes . . . I . . . all right," Diane managed, and was relieved to find that her legs would work, that she could walk after all.

That short walk seemed like a very long one to Diane as she made her way across the firelit tipi to the dark, reclining man. Finally she reached him. She swallowed with great difficulty and stood there above, unsure what to do next. Uneasily but eagerly she waited for him to rise. She expected him to leap to his feet and take her forcefully in his arms. Felt certain that those cruel, sensual lips would cover hers in a kiss of ruthless passion.

It didn't happen.

Starkeeper stayed just as he was, lying there below her, his sultry dark eyes touching her with a force so powerful she could feel her skin flushing with warmth. At last his left hand leisurely came out from beneath his head and moved to the hem of her white eyelet skirt.

Diane held her breath as he casually reached up under the skirt, wrapping his long tanned fingers possessively around her slender ankle.

"Beauty, I'm not clean," he said in that low, flat voice as his hand glided up over the curve of her shapely calf to the dimpled back of her knee. "I haven't bathed or washed up since you saw me this afternoon at the tomahawk throwing."

Diane foolishly felt the need to deny she'd been there. "Tomahawk-throwing contest?" Her voice sounded unusually shrill. "I have no idea what you're—"

"Yes, you do," he coolly interrupted. "You were there this afternoon. You saw me throw the hatchet. Saw me split the bull's-eye. You heard the crowd applaud me." His hand tightened its grip on the back of her knee. "That's when you decided to come to me."

Those black, burning eyes challenged her to contradict him. She didn't. It was the truth. He had stood there in the sunlight in those tight white leggings with his bronzed chest and back and long arms gleam-

ing with oil, and his overpowering maleness had been her final undoing.

"Yes," she admitted, facing the truth for the first time. "I knew then. I
watched you, and I knew I would come here."

"I knew as well," he said with calm authority. "I should have cleaned
up for you. If you'll wait, I'll go wash. . . ."

"No," she murmured, helplessly beguiled by the sight of his bare
bronzed chest and long, muscled arms gleaming with the residue of oil.
"It doesn't matter. I don't care if you're not clean."

His fingers stroking the sensitive bend of her knee, Starkeeper finally
rolled up into a sitting position. He turned slightly, and his right hand
joined his left beneath her white skirt. Diane sighed when she felt the
coolness of his wide silver bracelet graze the bare flesh of her leg.

With both hands wrapped around the backs of her knees, Starkeeper
tipped his head back, looked up at her, and said softly, "Beauty, if I
make love to you, then you'll be dirty, too. Are you sure you want that?"

He waited, supposing that the beautiful but equally astute woman
would immediately grasp the double meaning of his question.
Starkeeper wasn't speaking merely of the sweat and oil and semen his
body would leave on hers, in hers. He was asking her if afterward she
would feel unclean for making love to him.

For making love with an Indian.

He hoped she would say no, hoped she would assure him that his
loving wouldn't make her dirty. That neither of them was or would be
dirty. That there was nothing the least bit profane about the two of them
making love.

Unfortunately Diane was much too nervous and excited to comprehend his meaning. She knew only that she was tingling with the sweet
anticipation of being in his arms and she didn't care about the oil and
perspiration that covered those arms, that smooth bronzed chest. She
knew nothing else but that she wanted to be held and loved by him.
She wanted to know nothing else.

"I don't care," she murmured throatily, "how dirty you are. I don't
care how dirty you make me."

After she said those words to him, Diane's violet eyes dreamily darkened to purple, and her heavily lashed lids slipped closed. So she didn't
see the expression of hurt that fleetingly clouded Starkeeper's dark eyes
or the flash of cold fury that replaced it.

Starkeeper's fingers aggressively tightened on her flesh, and he
roughly jerked her down to her knees before him. Diane's eyes flew
open, and her breath caught in her throat. That ever-present mingling
of fear and fascination was so strong her heart raced as she shyly,

nervously smiled at him. His hands abruptly released her and Diane cautiously sat back on her heels.

Starkeeper braced his weight on a stiffened bare arm and looked into her half-frightened purple eyes. "Take your hair down for me, Beauty," he commanded.

Diane immediately complied. Lifting tense arms, she anxiously removed a smooth silver clasp, laid it aside, and shook her head so that the long, unbound tresses would fall around her shoulders and down her back. She waited for him to speak, but he said nothing.

"We—we have hair of the same color," she said inanely, so nervous and expectant she hardly knew what she was saying.

Starkeeper's right hand shot out. He touched a long, silky lock that lay atop her smooth shoulder and said, "But not skin of the same color, eh, Beauty?" He released her hair, his eyes locked with hers.

"No," she said without hesitation, her purple eyes lowering from his compelling gaze to inspect his naked torso and sculpted shoulders shamelessly. "No. You're so dark, and I—I'm so—"

"—so white," he finished for her, his black eyes cold, distant. "So flawlessly, untouchably, chastely white."

Diane's eyes lifted to meet his. She started to speak but stopped as his right hand suddenly gripped the midriff of her white eyelet blouse. Swiftly he pulled the blouse free of her skirt's tight waistband. His fingers immediately went to the white buttons going down the center of the low-necked blouse.

The blood started to pound in Diane's ears as Starkeeper began deftly to unbutton her blouse, telling her as he did so, of the ways he wanted to make love to her. She thrilled to the sound of that low, monotonic voice as the lean, handsome Indian spoke of all the shocking, forbidden things they would do. Her face flushed when he told her he meant to see, to smell, to touch, to taste every unblemished inch of her silky white flesh. She tingled from head to toe as he warned her that before this night was over, his dark-skinned savage's body would possess hers totally.

"This oiled, dirty dark body of mine will be on you," he said, his lean fingers pushing the tiny buttons through the buttonholes, "all over you" —he flipped open the last button—"and in you, Beauty. I'll be buried deep inside you." He swept the opened white blouse apart.

Starkeeper's eyes lifted to hers. In his dark, penetrating gaze Diane saw a confusing blend of passion and hatred. Tenderness was there in his dark glance, but so was cruelty. Touching adoration as well as menacing hostility.

It was clear that this dark, irresistible Indian who was going to make heated love to her here in this firelit tipi on the vast Wind River Indian Reservation didn't like her. He desired her, but he didn't admire her.

Diane didn't care.

It didn't seem to matter at that moment. It didn't matter that the things he said to her had nothing to do with love or respect or even a fondness for her. From the first minute she'd seen him that hot Denver twilight straining against the bars of his cage, she'd been shamefully curious and attracted by the sexual mystery he exuded.

She wanted him. It was that elemental. She had wanted him then; she wanted him now. Her body wanted his body with a powerful animal hunger that she could neither understand nor control. And she couldn't —wouldn't—stop wanting him until he'd taken her.

"Having second thoughts, my Beauty?" Starkeeper asked, his warm hand spreading on her throat.

"No," she said decisively, "no second thoughts, my Beast."

His lean fingers skimmed up and down the bare column of her throat. "What is it you want from me? Tell me, Beauty. Say it for me."

"I want you to make love to me," she told him. "And I want to make love with you as well."

A flash of new heat leaped into his dark eyes at her confession. In that low, flat voice, he said, "My God, you *are* exquisite, Beauty. Exquisite. I have wanted to touch you like this since the first time I laid eyes on you." His warm fingertips stroked the sides of her throat, his middle finger locating the throbbing pulse point. "Do you remember the first time I saw you?"

"Yes," she murmured breathlessly, feeling his fingers spreading fire as he pushed the open blouse off her shoulders.

"You came to my cage alone in the dusk. You were dressed in a white blouse, tight buckskins, and moccasins, and your hair was loose like it is now. I reached out for you, and you screamed in fear."

Starkeeper's hand moved down to the swell of Diane's breasts. He flattened his palm against the soft ivory flesh exposed above the lacy trim of her satin chemise.

"I know," she whispered, her breath short and rapid.

"But you kept coming back to me," he said in that low, resonant voice. "Why?"

"Because I—I couldn't stay away," she breathlessly admitted.

"You tortured me, Beauty," he went on, speaking slowly, absently caressing the rise of her swelling left breast. "You even came to torment me one night in your nightgown."

"I wore a robe," she said, defending herself.

"I could clearly see the outline of your pale body through your nightgown." He looked into her eyes. "The bars on my cage saved you that night."

"I know," she said, vividly remembering the night in question. "I thought you were sleeping, but all along you were watching me."

"Yes, I was," he lazily admitted as his fingers continued to caress her, touching her with gentleness. "I can still see you with the wind in your hair and that blue nightgown pressing against your—your . . ." His words trailed away. His handsome face abruptly hardened. "You cruelly taunted me when you came with your lover and I—"

"No," Diane interrupted, protesting, "you have it all wrong. I—"

"Kiss me, Beauty," he commanded, his dark eyes gone icy-hot, his stroking fingers no longer slow and gentle.

Diane's breath came out in a rush when he impatiently cupped his hand around the back of her neck and pulled her forcefully to him. He leaned up and captured her mouth with his sensual lips. His kiss was one of such quick, total possession that Diane felt as if her lips would be forever branded by the imprint of his.

Without preliminary, he forced her mouth to open wide to him. His tongue immediately thrust inside to meet and mate with hers. An explosion of heat swept through her as Starkeeper's masterful tongue did incredibly seductive things to the sensitive insides of her mouth.

He came up to a kneeling position, bringing her up with him. He raised his left knee from the pallet and put his bare foot flat on the floor. He pulled her still closer, urging her back against his raised knee. His hand moved up from her neck to cradle the back of her head as they knelt in the firelight.

His invasive seeking kiss continued, and the fire that burned through her was so swift and sudden it was unlike anything Diane had ever known.

Her head fell back as her whole body arched into his fierce embrace, and her eyes went half shut in unashamed pleasure.

Chapter 27

➤➤➤ Diane was breathless and weak when finally Starkeeper's searing lips released hers. Her head sagged back against his supporting arm and her eyes nervously fluttered open. She looked up at the dark, handsome man who had just kissed her as no other ever had and saw a pair of beautiful black eyes blazing with savage sexual heat.

For a long, tension-filled minute Starkeeper looked directly into her eyes, and Diane was struck anew by the compelling blend of promised pleasure and potential danger this strange man embodied. Hypnotized by those hot dark eyes, she knew she courted peril by being here but didn't care.

Diane sighed softly when Starkeeper slowly bent his dark head and kissed her again. A kiss totally different from his first forceful caress. His lips were no longer hard and punishing. They were soft and warm, and they brushed gently back and forth across hers until Diane strained to him, yearning to have that commanding mouth settle more firmly on hers.

As if he had read her mind, Starkeeper's lips closed fully over hers in an incredibly pleasing kiss which was midway between teasing invitation and total possession.

It was a kiss of such heart-stopping sweetness that Diane hardly realized that while Starkeeper's mouth was pressed to hers, his hands were sliding the open white eyelet blouse down her arms and off. Her lips clung to his as his lean fingers went to the lacy chemise straps atop her shoulders.

The honeyed kiss continued while Starkeeper effortlessly peeled the satin chemise down to Diane's waist. His mouth remained melded to hers as a dark hand came up to cup her upturned face tenderly. His other arm went around her. Diane felt his fingertips caressing her cheek and the cool, solid metal of his bracelet against the sensitive skin of her back.

Then his palm flattened just above her waist and he drew her flush against him. Diane sighed with joy when her bare, swelling breasts touched his broad, naked chest. She arched her back, pressing herself as close to his warmth as possible, her nipples tightening into hard, sensitive points of sensation at the minute of contact. Breathless, she tore her lips from his.

"Beast, Beast," she gasped excitedly, and her arms stole anxiously up around his neck to draw him closer. "Hold me. Hold me tight."

"Yes, Beauty," he responded in that appealingly flat, unexcitable voice, "I'll hold you. For as long as you want."

It was glorious.

The feel of Starkeeper's oiled smooth chest pressing so intimately against her tingling breasts was wonderful. It became even more wonderful when his sensual lips again covered hers and Starkeeper kissed her with a disturbing kind of barely controlled heat and hunger. A kiss designed to draw from Diane exactly the response she gave him.

Diane squirmed and rubbed herself erotically against Starkeeper's slippery chest and sucked anxiously at the arousing tongue that kept tormenting her by sliding into and then withdrawing from her eagerly seeking mouth.

If Diane was vitally aware that they both were naked to the waist, so was the man kissing her. The diamond-hard nipples of her pale, bare breasts pressing against his chest and the sweet, responsive mouth clinging to his lips had Starkeeper so aroused he was tempted to shove her skirts up out of his way, hastily unlace his leggings, and come into her just as they were, kneeling in the firelight. What sweet relief it would be to wait no longer, quickly, greedily to take what he wanted without any thought or concern for her pleasure, then send her on her way.

Starkeeper didn't do it.

He deepened his kiss and caressed her silky back, stroking her gently, molding her to him, touching her in a slow, possessive way he knew she would like. He patiently took his time.

While this beautiful white woman might foolishly suppose that to be swiftly, roughly taken by an untamed savage would be exciting and satisfying, Starkeeper knew better. She would derive no pleasure from the act if he came into her now. She was not yet ready. He would wait until she was. He would make her ready.

More than ready.

Starkeeper's lips at last left Diane's but remained on her feverish face. His mouth moved across her flushed cheek to her right ear. He gently bit the dainty ivory lobe, then the sensitive spot just below it. His open lips moved down the side of her swanlike neck, his sharp teeth teasingly nipping a path to her collarbone; then his lips slid around to the center of her throat.

His dark head turned to the side and he placed a warm, moist kiss in the hollow of her throat, the tip of his tongue tracing the delicate configuration of bone beneath the pale flesh. As he kissed her throat, one of his black braids fell onto Diane's bare breast. While his tongue stroked her throat, the white leather strip binding the end of his fallen braid tickled her taut nipple.

Diane's head fell back. Her passion-glazed eyes closed, and she drew a short, shallow breath through her mouth. She let her arms fall limply at her sides.

Starkeeper's mouth left her throat. He raised his dark head. Diane's eyes came open. She looked at him. He purposely held her gaze as he slowly sat back on his heels, his hands sliding up her sides to her underarms. He held her there kneeling before him. His black eyes leisurely lowered to her pale, bare breasts. Diane felt her aching nipples immediately respond to the heat of his glance. She held her breath and waited. Every nerve in her awakened body was screaming and straining against her flesh. *Please,* she silently begged, *oh, please.*

Starkeeper's hands gripped her firmly just under her arms while his eyes caressed her breasts. His were sensitive hands. He could feel on his palms the dewy perspiration of her rising sexual excitement. To touch the hot dampness of her velvety underarms was highly arousing to Starkeeper, the unique titillating kind of thing a woman wouldn't understand. Only a man would find it exciting. It was sweetly erotic to Starkeeper, and as his hands appreciatively pressed against that silky dewiness, he felt his growing erection surge and strain against his tight white leggings.

"Beauty, sweet Beauty," he murmured, and drew her closer as he leaned up to meet her.

He pressed a gentle kiss to the soft undercurve of her left breast, and then Diane's breath exploded in a loud rush when Starkeeper's hot, open mouth enclosed the throbbing nipple.

"God . . . oh, God," she whispered mindlessly as her hands came up to his dark head.

Diane's pale fingers curled around the back of his neck. Her other hand tenaciously gripped a leather-trimmed black braid. She moaned and sighed as Starkeeper kissed and licked and sucked on her breast. Her eyes opening and closing with pleasure, Diane decided then and there that what he was doing to her now—this very minute—was all she wanted. They need go no further. This was sheer ecstasy. There could be no greater ecstasy. If, for just this one night, she could hold his dark, handsome head to her breasts and feel that marvelous mouth hotly enclosing her like this, she'd ask for nothing more.

Ever, ever.

"Yes, oh, yes," she whispered, bending to him, lowering her face to kiss the gleaming hair of the dark head bent to her. "Oh, Beast, it feels good . . . sooooo good. . . ." She spoke softly, her lips pressed into the shimmering blue-black locks that smelled so clean. "I like to feel your teeth," she murmured as he very carefully, gently bit her nipple, then raked his teeth back and forth over it.

From that point on it was all like a beautiful erotic dream to Diane. Her skin was aglow with warmth; her eyes were shining with passion. She was more than willing to allow her commanding lover to take charge fully and lead her. To guide her wherever he wanted to take her. To do whatever he pleased to her, with her.

She felt absolutely no compunction when his loving mouth released her wet, budding nipple, and he said against her breast, "Beauty, I want the rest of your clothes off so I can love you properly."

Forgetting that only seconds earlier she had determined that his kissing her breasts was all she wanted or needed, Diane quickly replied, "You'll help me undress?"

"I'll undress you," he assured her, gave her breast one last kiss, and raised his head.

Diane looked into his eyes while his amazingly adept hands found the tiny buttons at the waistband of her skirt, the tape of her petticoats. Pushing both down to the flare of her hips, Starkeeper gripped her narrow waist and urged her to her feet.

He stayed on his knees before her. His hands left her waist, returned to the loosened skirt and petticoats. Diane closed her eyes, but he ordered her to open them.

"Look at me, Beauty," his deep, monotonic voice instructed. "Open your eyes and watch me undress you."

Diane obeyed and found the experience highly enjoyable and exciting. She stood there in the cozy tipi's flickering firelight while the most scarily handsome man she'd ever known knelt before her and slowly, expertly stripped her naked.

Starkeeper unhurriedly peeled away her white skirt, her full petticoats, and finally her lace-trimmed underpants. Soon the discarded garments lay pooled around her feet and Diane was as bare as the day she came into the world. And as unashamed.

Starkeeper sat back on his heels and openly admired her pale, naked beauty. Diane enjoyed his fierce scrutiny as much as he. Her slender form was firm and fit. She was proud of her body. She was in perfect health, had the long, graceful legs of a dancer, and kept herself as trim and well toned as an athlete.

Starkeeper saw neither dancer nor athlete as he looked at the beautiful woman standing proudly naked before him. He saw the palest, softest, most luscious embodiment of fragile femininity he'd ever laid eyes on. He saw a lovely raven-haired, ivory-skinned angel of love of which he was unworthy.

She was far too perfect to touch, to take. He should stay on his knees and worship her, not make love to her. She was so pale and lovely he felt the foolish need to protect her, even from himself. At the same time she was so innately sensual, so earthy and tempting he could hardly wait to get her in his bed.

"Exquisite," he said, as he had earlier. It was the one word that best fit. "Beauty, you are the most exquisite work of art I've ever—"

"No work of art," Diane softly interrupted. She reached for his hand, drew it up to her bare midriff. "Touch me," she said. "Touch me and see for yourself." Starkeeper's hand moved down over the luminous flesh; his palm spread on her bare belly. "See. No cold sculpted stone," she said, "but a woman. A flesh-and-blood woman. A woman on fire for you. Only for you."

"Mine. My woman," he said softly, the blood beginning to pound in his ears. "You're mine, Beauty. Only mine."

Starkeeper knew it wasn't true but was too aroused to care. His hands gripped Diane's narrow waist. He drew her close and kissed her ribs, her navel, her flat stomach. Diane gloried in the feel of his hot lips on her tingling skin. She was so caught up in the pleasure of his kisses she hardly knew when Starkeeper picked her up and laid her on his bed.

She stretched out on a soft bed of luxuriant furs and Starkeeper lay beside her. The sleek fur felt wonderful against her naked skin, and the dark, long-fingered hand stroking her sensitive flesh felt even better.

"I want you to stay here with me all night." Starkeeper's voice was low-pitched, very soft. He lay on his side, looking down at her, his weight supported on an elbow.

Diane looked up into his eyes. "Yes," she told him. "Of course, I'll stay all night. I'll stay with you forever."

He leaned over her face and kissed her. And while he kissed her, his hand caressed her breast, the thumb rubbing back and forth across the wet nipple. The long, drugging kiss continued, and when finally it ended, Starkeeper's hand was no longer fondling her breast; it was stroking her bare belly.

Tingling from head to toe, Diane wondered when he was going to take off his tight white leggings and make love to her. She asked, and his answer was an enigmatic smile, and then Diane watched as he deliberately smeared his fingers with the residue of oil covering his bronzed chest.

When his fingers were well greased, he said, "Beauty, first let me love you with my pants on."

And he promptly did so. Looking down into her dreamy purple eyes, Starkeeper raked his hand through the crisp raven curls between her legs, cupped her possessively, and whispered, "Give it to me, Beauty. Move your legs apart."

She did as he asked, mesmerized by those compelling black eyes staring into hers. He held her gaze while his oiled fingers slipped between her thighs to touch her intimately. Diane's breath caught in her throat when his middle finger settled onto that ultra-sensitive button of female flesh.

Starkeeper's well-placed middle finger touched and stroked and circled that highly responsive little bud with infinite care and gentleness. And while he caressed her, he continued to look directly into her eyes.

Diane had never known such intense pleasure. There was fire in the tips of Starkeeper's oiled fingers and fire in the black eyes locked with hers. The fire in his eyes held her in thrall; she couldn't turn away, couldn't keep from looking at him. The fire in his fingers held her captive; her body surged against that magical molding hand of her handsome conqueror.

She wanted this rapture to last forever. She wanted this torment to cease immediately. She was growing hotter and hotter, and she felt as if she were going to explode.

And so she did.

The glorious ecstasy-agony built to a great crescendo. And then that sweet eruption. Diane's purple eyes widened in disbelief. She cried out and dug her sharp nails into Starkeeper's shoulder as he lifted her to frightening heights of joy. Her eyes slid closed as she finally went limp against the soft bed of furs. She didn't see the pleased expression that softened Starkeeper's hard-featured face.

After only a few soothing, gentling kisses to her flushed face, Starkeeper rose to his feet and swiftly stripped off his white leggings.

Sated, blissful, Diane unabashedly rolled onto her side and watched as he undressed. Smiling foolishly, she admired his magnificent physique: the broad, powerful chest; the trim waist; the long, lean legs; the tight, firm buttocks. His bronze body was a study in male perfection, fierce strength emanating from every beautiful contour.

Naturally what most intrigued her about his splendid anatomy was that part she'd never before seen. Her eyes went to the pulsing masculinity rising from the dense growth of blue-black curls covering his groin. She was immediately awed and half afraid.

Then he was back beside her, kissing her, touching her gently, and Diane found herself growing warm and excited again. Starkeeper held her close, stroked the length of her back and rounded buttocks, deliberately letting her feel the hardness of his erection throbbing against her bare belly.

When he moved between her parted legs and touched her, he found there was no need for oil this time. She was silky wet and burning hot. He came up on his knees and pushed her pale thighs farther apart with his dark, strong hands. Diane's eyes closed. He asked her to open them. She did.

They looked at each other as he entered her. And when he was inside her, Starkeeper stayed perfectly still and stared at the beautiful woman, realizing he wanted her with a primitive need to possess her totally, to make her his own forever. Diane looked up at the harshly handsome man who was buried deep inside her and realized he truly was dangerous, a proud, primal male who held a frightening power over her.

Both felt the need to hold something of themselves back from the other. Neither was capable of doing it. Starkeeper began the slow, sensual movements of lovemaking, and Diane instinctively lifted her pelvis to meet his deep thrusts. They moved together in perfect carnal harmony, as though each knew the other's body well.

Diane clung to the hard biceps of her experienced lover and gave herself wholly to him. The electrifying sensations touched off in her by this bronzed god's artful lovemaking were frightening in their intensity. She realized she wanted him to be hers, and only hers. She longed to cry out to him that she belonged to him, and he belonged to her, and he must stay inside her forever.

Starkeeper supported his weight on his flattened palms and thrust rhythmically into her, sliding deeply inside, then withdrawing almost completely. He fully intended to keep the pace of his lovemaking slow and easy. He meant to bring his beautiful lover to climax again and again before he sought his own release. He wanted to show this lovely white goddess that he was no uncivilized savage who climaxed the minute he fell between a woman's legs.

But the hot tightness so sweetly gripping him was swiftly threatening the self-control he had always taken for granted. He couldn't believe it. He felt that rigid control slipping. He was in danger of losing it, of going over the edge.

Starkeeper quickly averted his eyes from that glowingly beautiful face, refused to look into those remarkable purple eyes. He bit the inside of his jaw with sharp, punishing teeth. He silently recited the words of a lengthy Shoshoni song he had learned as a boy.

Nothing worked. His climax was coming, and there was nothing he could do to stop it.

Diane knew what was happening to him and felt a glorious surge of female power. She kept her eyes open wide while his closed helplessly in ecstasy. Eagerly she accommodated his deep, powerful thrusts, speeding her movements to match his. She watched his handsome face grimace, saw the veins stand out on his high forehead and bronzed throat, heard his great groan of satisfaction.

She then affectionately cradled his dark head on her breast when he collapsed against her. He panted heavily, sweat and oil rolling off his lean body, heartbeat rapid and heavy against her bare breasts.

Starkeeper was ashamed. And angry. And frightened. He was ashamed of himself. He was angry with her for so easily shattering his control. Most of all, he was frightened of her and of the power she held over him.

Diane stroked his deeply clefted back and pressed kisses to his jaw, and soon Starkeeper raised his head. She smiled at him and gently pushed on his chest. He didn't smile back at her.

"No," he said, "let me stay inside you. Let me grow aroused again so that I can give you pleasure."

"But you did give me pleasure," she murmured, and again attempted to wiggle free.

He wouldn't allow it. He kissed her, forcing her to mold her lips to his. He kept kissing her until both began to grow excited.

This time Starkeeper made practiced, skillful love to Diane, slowing down each time she neared her release, then speeding up each time she began to calm, until at last she was begging him loudly, biting frantically on the slick flesh of his shoulder, very near to sexual hysterics.

And so he gave it to her.

Her climax was deep and earth-shattering. She screamed out and clung to him and cried, tears of wonder and joy spilling down her hot cheeks. Starkeeper kissed her and soothed her and murmured endearments until she stopped jerking in his arms. Gently he eased out of her, lay down beside her on the furs, and tenderly enfolded her in his arms.

After a sweet interlude of silent bliss Diane said against his throat, "Should I go now?"

Eyes closed, he answered lazily, "Sweetheart, the night is new. We've only begun to make love."

"Mmm," she sighed, and snuggled closer. In minutes both were fast asleep.

Diane awakened sometime hours later. She turned her head and saw Starkeeper asleep beside her. She was immediately overwhelmed by the recollection of what they had done. Of what she had done. She had shared with this handsome Indian the deepest intimacy possible between two human beings. Already she was sorry and ashamed.

Not that it wasn't wonderful. It was. Too wonderful. Far more wonderful than she'd ever imagined. Her violet eyes ran slowly down the length of the sleeping naked man, and Diane was filled with regret. She now intimately knew his splendidly beautiful body but knew nothing of the man himself.

Other than what Golden Star had revealed and that he was a Shoshoni Indian and he had coldly kidnapped her.

Diane cautiously moved away from him, being careful not to disturb him. Hastily she dressed, anxiously pulling her clothes on over her nakedness, mindless of the oil smudges his body had left on hers.

As soon as she was dressed, she ducked out of Starkeeper's tipi. There was only one thing on her mind. Escape. She had to get away from this dark, masterful man now before it was everlastingly too late.

Diane ran through the silent village in search of a horse. She would ride away, now, tonight, and forget that any of this had ever happened.

Starkeeper slowly awakened, smiled, stretched, and reached for Diane. His eyes came open. He sat up, looked anxiously around, then ground his even white teeth. She was even worse than the others. Once her curiosity had been satisfied, she couldn't bear the thought of actually having slept with an Indian.

Hoping he was wrong, that she had only gone back to his grandmother's for the sake of propriety, Starkeeper rose and pulled on the white leggings. He started toward his grandmother's lodge but stopped short when he caught sight of Diane mounting a paint pony.

She *was* like all the others! Like every white woman he'd ever known. Seeking thrills by lying in his arms, enjoying the titillating danger of making love with a savage. Forbidden fruit. A vein throbbed on his forehead, and Starkeeper started toward her.

Diane saw Starkeeper bearing down on her, his expression mean.

Immediately frightened, she attempted to ride him down. When she was upon him, he sidestepped at the last second, his arm shot out, he grabbed the paint's bridle and jerked the big pony to a halt. Roughly he dragged Diane down off the horse.

"A little late in the day for a ride, isn't it, Beauty?" he asked, angry and hurt.

Confused, frightened, she said, "Let me go! I want to leave! I don't want this. . . . You're not taking me back to your tipi! I won't allow you to—to . . ." She faltered before those accusing dark eyes and hung her head.

He grabbed her arm and angrily escorted her back to his grand-mother's tipi.

Just outside Golden Star's lodge, he stepped closer, captured Diane's chin, lifted it, and said coldly, "If you're ever in my arms again, just one word will do it.

"The word is *no. No.* That's all you have to say. *No.* If you mean it, say it. *No.* And I will stop."

Chapter 28

"No!"

 "Yes."

Their eyes clashed.

"No." Then, more firmly: "No, I don't, I won't."

"Yes. Yes, it's true, I—"

"No." The tall blond man repeated and again lifted the small square of red beaded leather held between gloved thumb and forefinger and studied it. "No, I don't believe you. You do know more about this. Now tell me." His green eyes were narrowed. His lips were pulled into a tight line amid the heavy growth of dark blond hair covering his tanned jaws and chin.

He lowered the small red beaded square, pushed his Stetson back on his blond head, and leaned over until his bearded face was only inches from the nervous little man behind the counter. He reached out, gripped the yoke of the store clerk's white apron, and pulled him even closer.

"I'm saying it one last time." The Cherokee Kid spoke angrily to the jittery proprietor of the LuLu City general store. "Is there anything you haven't told me? This beaded square came from the neckband he was wearing. You surely saw him that day. Maybe even waited on them. Where were they headed? Where did they go when he left your store?"

Beads of sweat popping out on his thin upper lip, the store owner shook his balding head. "No. I've told you all I know. *I* didn't see the savage or the woman. We all heard that a tall, fierce-looking Indian in breechcloth and chaps was walking up and down the sidewalks that day the merchandise was stolen from my store. I found the beaded square of leather here on the counter. That's it. That's all I know. Please . . . let me go!"

Exasperated, the Kid released him with a shove. "Let's get out of here," he said to the two huge toughs flanking him. "Maybe down at the saloon somebody will have a better memory." He stuck the beaded square into his shirt pocket, turned, and walked away.

Miners and cowboys anxiously got out of their way as the three big, dirty, rough men strode down the wooden sidewalks of LuLu City, Colorado. Whispers of speculation followed the dangerous-looking trio. Nervous glances were cast after their departing backs. The decent women of LuLu City cringed and quickly crossed the street.

At the Glory Hole Saloon the Cherokee Kid stopped. He gripped the winged double doors with both gloved hands and swung them inward. Then stood there holding the louvered doors open, the sunlight at his back, his booted feet wide apart. When every eye had turned to settle on him, he stepped inside. The brawny Leatherwoods followed the Kid to the long wooden bar at the back of the room.

The Kid hooked a bootheel over the bar's brass foot runner, peeled off his gloves, dropped them on the bar, and ordered a bourbon.

A ruddy-faced barkeep poured a shot glass full to the brim and shoved it across the polished bar. The Kid's right hand shot out and gripped the bartender's bony wrist.

"Leave the bottle," he ordered.

The Kid downed the whiskey, wiped his mouth on a muscular forearm, then slowly turned to lean back against the bar. His green eyes scanned the shadowy, smoke-filled room as drinkers, poker players, and prostitutes fell silent to stare at him.

"I'm the Cherokee Kid," he said, his leveled gaze sweeping over the sea of faces turned on him. "I'm trailing a no-good Indian that kidnapped a helpless white woman from *Colonel Buck Buchannan's Wild West Show*'s troupe train just outside Denver. They came through LuLu City a few days ago." He paused, hooked his thumbs in his low-riding gun belt, and added, "I'm waiting to buy drinks for the man who can tell me anything about the redskin and the woman."

The silent room erupted into dozens of spirited conversations. Chair legs scraped over the wooden planked floor. Thirsty miners and gamblers crowded up to the bar, ready to tell of seeing a tall, mean Indian in their little mining town. Without turning, the Kid lifted a muscular arm and snapped his fingers for the barkeep to start pouring.

After more than an hour of buying rounds and asking questions and listening to stories, the Kid knew little more than before. Many of those present had seen the Indian, but none was sure of his tribe. Since the redskin was this far north, they doubted he was a Ute. The best guess would be that he was Arapaho or Cheyenne. But then he could be Paiute. Or maybe even Shoshoni.

"When he left, I saw him aheadin' north, pardner." A grizzled old sourdough tugged on the Kid's shirt sleeve. "My guess'd be they was aheadin' for Wyoming's Wind River Indian Reservation."

His arm around a big-bosomed woman with powdered cheeks and wide painted lips, the Kid tossed off one last whiskey and told Davey and Danny Leatherwood to go on across the street and engage a couple of rooms at the LuLu City Hotel. They'd spend the night in town, then get back on the trail early in the morning, ride on up to Wyoming.

"Sure thing, boss." Davey nodded. "You coming?"

"Later," said the Kid, and turned his full attention on the smiling, curvaceous woman clinging possessively to his shirtfront. To her he said, "Well what about it, darlin'? Think you can show me a good time?"

The broad-bottomed blonde giggled and led him up the stairs, casting triumphant glances at the other six women employed at the Glory Hole. Upstairs the blonde eagerly wiggled out of her gaudy red satin outfit while the Kid undressed and got into bed.

Wondering how she had managed to get so lucky, the blonde was giggling happily when she came to the bed, sat down on its edge, and said, "Handsome, I'm gonna make you a happy man."

"You'd better, blondie," said the Kid. "I get downright nasty when a woman displeases me."

The blonde displeased him.

She tried very hard to make him happy. She made an all-out attempt to pleasure the big, good-looking stranger. But the more she tried, the more nasty-tempered he became.

"What is it? What's wrong, cowboy?" she asked, lying stretched out beside him, walking her short, plump fingers through the thick hair of his chest.

"You're what's wrong," the Kid said. He pushed her away and sat up.

"No, wait." She came up on her knees and threw her arms around his neck. "Give me another chance." She tried to kiss him on the mouth.

He evasively turned his head. He tore her arms from his neck and shoved them behind her back, clasping her wrists together in one of his hands.

"Put your clothes on and get out of here right now," he said, his eyes cold. "I want that slim, dark-haired girl. What's her name?"

"No. No, you don't want her. I'll show you a much better time than Lonnie. Come on, big boy, let me stay."

"You're leaving," he said, and threw her off the bed.

"Ohh!" she moaned when she hit the floor. Dazed, her ribs hurting, she lay there for a moment, unable to get up.

The Kid rose from the bed. He stood above her. "Get up and get out," he ordered.

Hurt and angry, the blonde scrambled to her feet and was going for his face when the Kid backhanded her with a force so strong it turned her completely around, staggering her. The naked blonde lunged anxiously for the door. The Kid came after her. With the full weight of his big body, he pressed the blonde's face against the heavy door. He kept her pinned there for several minutes, rhythmically slamming her against it, enjoying the sounds of her groans and curses.

"I want that pretty brunette," he said above her ear. "I'm tired of your giggles. I'm tired of you. If you don't want to get hurt, dress quickly and get out. And send me Lonnie. It's Lonnie I want, not you."

He stepped back then, freeing her at last.

She whirled around. Sniffling and eyeing him nervously, the blonde wiggled hurriedly into her discarded red satin gown. She was furious when she left the Kid sprawled naked on a rumpled pink bed and came stomping back down the stairs. Her lip rouge smeared, her nose shiny, blond hair askew, she marched over to a laughing woman in green satin seated on a gambler's knee.

"Lonnie, the Kid wants you to come up," said the miffed blonde, inclining her head.

"I knew you weren't enough woman for him," Lonnie taunted laughingly, and was off the poker player's knee quick as a wink.

Smoothing her green satin skirts, she hurried up the stairs to the big, bearded stranger.

The Kid liked Lonnie. She was slim, pale-skinned, and smart and had long dark hair that fell down around her face to tickle him pleasantly. She wasted no time proving that she could love him more satisfactorily than the banished blonde.

Midnight found the Kid still with Lonnie. Naked, he was propped up on a mound of pink pillows shoved against the bed's pink headboard. Idly he twirled a small square piece of red beaded leather in his fingers. The beaded square was identical to three others he'd found along the trail.

His green eyes riveted to the shiny red beads, he told the naked, lolling Lonnie all the things he carefully kept hidden from the people who knew him—or thought they knew him.

"I was even a husband once. Left after her daddy cut her off of the money." He stared intently at the red, intricately beaded leather square. "Hell, the old bastard should have been glad to get his homely daughter married but—"

The Kid told how he'd met his wife when he signed on as a drover at her daddy's half-million-acre spread down in West Texas. He had patiently courted the skinny, sallow-looking girl over her father's objections. He'd had no trouble persuading little Betty Lou to elope. After the marriage he'd moved into the sprawling headquarters ranch house with his bride, and there he'd stayed for two long, miserable years! Working as hard as the lowliest hired hand, making love to the skinny, whining Betty Lou every night, determined to produce an heir to her ailing old daddy's fortune.

Shaking his head, the Kid said, "She never got pregnant, but her daddy finally died. Trouble was, the vindictive old bastard had quietly cut his daughter right out of the will the minute he heard we'd gotten married." The Kid laughed bitterly.

He left Texas immediately, he told the attentive Lonnie, drifted up into New Mexico, and got into a little trouble there. Flat broke, he'd held up a stage with a couple of clumsy Mexicans. They were caught, he got away with the money, but the law was after him for a year. He moved around, never staying in one place long. Lived with a variety of women, found and lost several jobs. Never had any luck until he hooked up with *Colonel Buck Buchannan's Wild West Show.*

"Right from the start, I knew this was my chance," the Kid said, rubbing a calloused thumb over the shiny red beads. "The Colonel took to me immediately, so I made up a past for myself that would suit him— the last survivor of a fine old Virginia family. Convinced him I'm educated, intelligent, dependable, honest, and completely trustworthy."

"And none of it was true?" Lonnie asked.

The kid threw back his head and laughed. "Honey, I've never been to Virginia. And mine was not your typical fine old family. My daddy was a . . ." He paused. "Never mind all that. I may not be educated, dependable, and trustworthy, but I'm smart and good-looking." He flashed a smile at Lonnie. "The Colonel's granddaughter doesn't stand a chance. By the time I find her, she'll be ready to fall right into my waiting arms."

Lonnie giggled and clapped her hands. "Good for you."

"Yes, good for me." The Kid laid the red beaded square on the night table. "I may never be big rich, but I'll have a beautiful woman for my wife." His green eyes danced, and he absently rubbed his bare belly. "And soon as I take over the wild west show, I'll get rid of half the hangers-on and deadwood the softhearted old Colonel keeps on the payroll. I'll make the show turn a tidy profit, and it'll all belong to me." He reached for Lonnie.

Still giggling, Lonnie lifted a hand to toy with the thick mat of hair covering his broad, bare chest. "You're ambitious. I like that in a man."

"Know what I like in a woman?"

"Tell me," she said, smiling.

He lifted a hand, traced her full, parted lips with his little finger. "A wet, wide mouth like yours."

The Kid pulled her close and whispered into her left ear. Told her just what he'd like her to do with that wide, wet mouth.

Lonnie laughed.

Then wasted no time in pleasing him.

Chapter 29

"I will never forget," said Golden Star, "the speech our mighty chief made back in 'fifty-nine when the white man opened Lander Road across our hunting grounds."

The old Indian woman took another long swig from her ice-cold bottle of Coca-Cola, her papery-thin eyelids lowering with a combination of pleasure and thoughtfulness.

Golden Star loved the taste of sweet, fizzing Coca-Cola more than any child did. If she had a chilled bottle of frothy soda pop in her gnarled right hand, she was content. And when she was content, she liked to talk of the days gone by, to tell anyone who would listen of the things she felt should be remembered about her beloved Shoshoni people.

It was the morning after Diane had impulsively gone to Starkeeper's lodge. Had loved, then left him. Golden Star was ignorant of their night-time tryst, knew nothing of the young woman's inner turmoil. She'd been fast asleep when, deep in the night, Starkeeper had angrily thrust Diane back inside her darkened lodge.

Golden Star hadn't awakened. She hadn't seen Diane slip into her side of the tipi, strip off her soiled white dress, and anxiously bathe away all traces of Starkeeper. She hadn't heard the choking sobs, smothered into her pillow, that Diane couldn't control. Was totally unaware that the pale young woman had not slept a wink all night.

"Yes, I can still recall every word of the speech Chief Washakie made that long-ago day," said Golden Star. She took the last drink of her

Coca-Cola, swished it around in her mouth, and swallowed. "Would you like to hear a part of his speech, Pale One?"

"Yes. Yes, of course," Diane lied. She gave Golden Star a weak smile. "Tell me what he said."

Golden Star turned up her empty soda pop bottle, hoping that maybe a couple of drops remained. None did. She made a face, set the empty bottle aside, and leaned back against her lazy board.

"It was a beautiful day, but Chief Washakie looked unhappy, greatly troubled. He stood before us all and said, 'I am not only your chief but an old man and your leader. It therefore becomes my duty to advise you. I know how hard it is for youth to listen to the voice of age. The old blood creeps like a snail, but the young blood leaps like a torrent. Once I was young, my sons, and thought as you do now. Then my people were strong, and my voice was ever for war. . . . You must not fight the whites. I not only advise against it, but forbid it.' "

Golden Star was silent.

Diane stared at the aged Indian woman. "Golden Star, you amaze me. You've remembered your chief's exact words all these years?"

"I don't believe you understand, Pale One. Chief Washakie is like a god to his people. We all—"

"*Is?* You mean the chief is still alive?"

"He is not much older than I," Golden Star said. Then her black eyes suddenly twinkled, and she asked, "Would you like to meet the chief?"

"Yes," said Diane truthfully, "I would."

"I will have Starkeeper summoned to take you there this afternoon," said Golden Star.

Diane's face drained of what little color was there. "Oh, no, I—I didn't mean today . . . please." She shook her head violently. "Perhaps another time."

"What is wrong? You have better things to do today?"

"No. No, I . . . it's just . . . I washed my white blouse and skirt this morning. They aren't dry, and the purple one is—"

An arthritic hand reached out, clamped over Diane's forearm. "Help me up, Pale One. I will find you something to wear."

Diane managed a smile and again shook her head. "Golden Star, one of your dresses would barely cover my . . . it wouldn't. . . ." Her words trailed away.

"Help me up," the Indian woman repeated. "I have kept a dress that belonged to Starkeeper's mother, Daughter-of-the-Stars. She was about your height and slender, just like you."

Diane eased Golden Star up but protested. "I couldn't wear something that means so much to you."

Golden Star paid no attention. She ambled over to a wooden chest beside her fur pallet, motioned Diane over to lift the heavy lid. From the cedar-lined chest Golden Star drew a carefully wrapped garment. She peeled away the protective tissue paper and held up a soft doeskin dress of pale yellow. The yoke was decorated with beads of blue; the skirt was trimmed with fringe.

Golden Star lovingly fingered the blue beads. "The color of beads chosen to decorate a garment has sp-sp-spe-ci—"

"Specific?"

"Yes! That is the word I hunt. Specific. The color of beads has specific meaning."

Admiring the pretty, perfectly preserved dress, Diane nodded.

"Sky blue—like these on my daughter's dress—can represent a body of water in which the sky is reflected. They can also mean the sky itself. Or the distant mountains as they turn to blue at night." She smiled and added, "Or all of these things."

"The dress is beautiful," said Diane. "Far too beautiful for me to—"

Golden Star forcefully shoved the dress at her. "You *will* wear it! If you are to visit our chief, you must go dressed properly." She scowled, her black eyes flashing. "Our people are just like yours, Pale One. We wear our finest clothing to call on a respected leader!"

Trapped, Diane said, "Golden Star, I really hate for you to ask Starkeeper to—"

Golden Star waved a dismissive hand in the air. "It is no bother. Starkeeper will be glad to take you there."

He wasn't, but his grandmother never knew.

When, at precisely two o'clock, Starkeeper ducked in out of the bright sunlight into Golden Star's lodge, Diane's breath caught in her throat. He was all Indian in soft fringed leggings and matching shirt. His hair was dressed in neat braids with the front forelock fashioned into the shiny pompadour favored by the Shoshoni. A lone eagle feather was the beautifully braided hair's only decoration.

After he greeted his aged grandmother, Starkeeper's dark gaze turned on Diane. She saw his firm jaw clench, saw the fury flash in his eyes. She could read his thoughts. He deeply resented seeing her in his mother's dress. She wasn't worthy of wearing it. Her cheeks burned as vivid images of last night's intimacy rose to torture and shame her.

Starkeeper nodded almost imperceptibly to Diane. She felt his pointed coldness like a chill wind blowing through her.

"Grandson, remove the eagle feather from your hair," requested Golden Star. "I want to show it to the Pale One." The old woman never noticed his slight grimace as he took the feather from his hair. Golden

Star held the eagle feather out to Diane, "You see these lines of red beads going around the quill? They depict the number of battles in which the warrior who owns the feather took part."

Diane could only nod and smile, afraid to try to speak, afraid new tears would come.

"This feather belonged to Starkeeper's father, the brave Chief Red Fox." Golden Star handed it back to her tall grandson.

Replacing it in his silver-streaked black hair, Starkeeper said impatiently, "It's time we go. Better wear a hat, Grandmother. The afternoon sun is fierce."

The old woman smiled like one who knows a delicious secret and laid an arthritic hand on his chest. "I need no hat, Starkeeper. I am not going."

"Not going?" Starkeeper and Diane said the words in unison.

That child's merry laugh bubbled from old Golden Star's lips. "I can visit the chief anytime. I feel like a nap. You two go on without me."

They had no choice.

So it was a sullen, uncommunicative Starkeeper who reluctantly escorted an equally withdrawn Diane to Chief Washakie's cabin down beside the Little Wind River. On the twenty-minute walk neither spoke a word.

When Chief Washakie stepped into the front door of his cabin, Diane and Starkeeper smiled warmly. Raised to respect their elders, both put aside, for the length of the visit, the hostility that existed between them.

Diane was surprised to meet a still-vigorous, proud old man with a cascade of silvery hair falling to his shoulders. He seemed delighted by their visit, shook Diane's hand warmly when she was introduced, and hugged Starkeeper tightly, telling Starkeeper how good it was to see him again.

Inside, the walls of the chief's spotlessly clean cabin were covered with pictures of himself painted on oilskins. He beamed with pride when Diane asked him to tell her what each one meant. His thick shoulders straightened as the old Shoshoni chieftain pointed out pictures showing scenes of his hunts, his many buffalo chases, his triumphs as a young warrior.

Concluding, he grinned sheepishly and said, "I must sound like a foolish old man to you, Pale One." Before she could answer, he turned to Starkeeper. "Been long time since pretty young woman come see me." He laughed then, and they laughed with him. Starkeeper's easy smile remained in place when Washakie asked, "You come for my blessing to marry? You have it!" The silver head went up and down. "I like Pale One already."

"I like her, too," said Starkeeper, his voice calm, revealing no trace of sarcasm, "but we're just friends, nothing more."

"Too bad," said Washakie. "Thought maybe you two—"

"Show the pale one your special saddle," Starkeeper smoothly interjected.

"I not show you yet?" he asked Diane.

"No, not yet. I'd certainly like to see it."

"Come." The old chief took hold of her upper arm with amazingly strong fingers and propelled her into the room where he slept each night. There on a sawhorse, directly beside his bed, was a handsome well-oiled saddle embellished with silver trimming. The chief's hand dropped away from Diane's arm. He moved forward and touched the saddle.

Patting it almost reverently, the chief said, "Your Great White Father President Ulysses Grant sent to me this saddle long ago."

From the doorway Starkeeper elaborated. "The President honored the chief for his services to the U.S. Army. For unfailingly being a friend of the white man."

Nodding his silver head, Chief Washakie added, "The Great White Father changed name of Camp Brown to Fort Washakie." He looked at Diane and stabbed a blunt finger into his broad chest. "Name it after me."

"Such an honor and so well deserved," said Diane. "You must have been very proud."

Leaning a muscular shoulder against the doorframe, Starkeeper said, "Tell her about the formal ceremony, Chief. The day the saddle was presented to you."

Black eyes flashing with joyous recollection, Chief Washakie said excitedly, "Big, big ceremony. Hundreds of people present, white and red. Military men march, and a band played music and—and . . . speeches, many speeches."

Diane smiled warmly at the chief. "I'll bet you gave the best speech of all."

Chief Washakie shyly grinned and said nothing.

"He did." Starkeeper pushed away from the door, came to stand beside the shorter man, draped a long arm around his shoulder. "Remember what you said that day, Chief?"

Chief Washakie's black eyes disappeared into laugh lines. "No. Too long ago."

Addressing Diane, Starkeeper said, "He's being modest. He remembers everything."

"Enough about that day," the chief said abruptly. "Come, we go sit now. Talk of you and what you do since I last see you."

After they had been there an hour, the chief began to tire; his eyelids began to droop with drowsiness. Diane and Starkeeper noticed it at the same time. It was she who said it was time they leave. The old man protested politely, then made both promise to return. He was dozing in his chair by the time they stepped outside.

They'd gone only a few steps from his cabin when Diane asked, "What did the chief say the day he was presented with the saddle? Please tell me."

"Grandmother recalls that he stood through the ceremony with his arms folded, silent and deeply touched. When it came time for him to speak, he was at a loss for words. He stood there before the waiting crowd, all eyes turned on him. Then finally he said only this, 'Do a kindness to a white man, he feels it in his head and his tongue speaks. Do a kindness to an Indian, he feels it in his heart. The heart has no tongue.' "

"That's sweet. Beautiful," Diane said softly, "so very touching."

"Yes, well, you know us Indians," Starkeeper coldly replied, his handsome face growing hard, "like children, foolishly trusting and overly sentimental."

"I didn't mean—"

"Never mind what you meant," he cut her off. "Let's get back to Golden Star's."

He walked away from her, his strides long, quick. Diane stood for a minute, looking after him, gritting her teeth. When he disappeared around a timbered bluff at a bend in the river, she hurried to catch up. Just as she reached him, she made a misstep and lost her balance. Starkeeper instinctively reached out and caught her before she fell.

His arms were tight around her. Her hands clutched at his chest. Their bodies were pressed together. Fire instantly flashed through them both, now hotter than those torrid times back on the trail, all because of last night's ecstasy.

They were in a secluded clearing by the river. They looked into each other's tortured eyes. Neither said a word. Starkeeper groaned helplessly as his dark head bent to her and his lips covered hers. It was the intimate, probing kiss of a lover, and Diane eagerly responded. The kiss lasted for a long, long time, and when at last their lips separated, both gasped for air, changed positions slightly, and kissed again.

They kissed and kissed until finally, too weak, too aroused to stand, they sank to their knees on the grass. Starkeeper's hands slid down

Diane's waist and around to cup the cheeks of her bottom. He pulled closer, and Diane sighed into his mouth.

But when his hands began anxiously to urge the soft doeskin dress up over her thighs, Diane tore her flaming lips from his and softly, breathlessly murmured, "No."

As good as his word, Starkeeper immediately released her.

Chapter 30

❊❊❊❊ At sunset that day Starkeeper sat alone on a high bluff above the Little Wind River. Every muscle in his lean body was tense; he felt as if he were about to jump out of his skin. Grim-faced, he wished for the thousandth time that he had never taken Diane Buchannan from the train. He wished it more than ever now.

He stared straight into the setting sun until a quick flash of movement in the trees across the river drew his attention. Starkeeper watched as the big diamond-throated cat leaped over a silvery willow and up onto a large jutting rock. The tawny cougar stood silhouetted against the dying sun. He raised his great head and gave a low, plaintive growl, then sat back on his haunches and moved no more. Starkeeper looked at the big solitary beast and smiled wistfully.

They were two of a kind, he and the cat.

Starkeeper's chest tightened. After just one night of lovemaking, the fierce attraction between Diane and him was more potent and undeniable than before. Now he wanted her with an all-consuming passion. Felt as if he couldn't make it through this long, lonely night without holding her in his arms.

Starkeeper silently cursed himself. He cursed Diane. He disliked her, but he desired her. He couldn't stay away from her. He was aching this very minute to go to his grandmother's lodge so he could see the violet-eyed beauty.

Starkeeper stayed where he was.

He would *not* go there now, or tomorrow or the next day. He had never been anybody's fool; he wouldn't be Diane Buchannan's. Nor, on the other hand, would he back away should she come to him again. It *could* happen. It had happened before. A curious white woman intending to be with an Indian just one time, then coming back for more. Again and again.

It could be that way with the haughty Miss Diane Buchannan. She had come very close this afternoon by the river. She had wanted him almost as much as he wanted her. Had they been alone in his lodge . . .

Starkeeper came to his feet.

It had been at this very hour last evening when Diane had stepped into his tipi. Starkeeper's heart kicked against his ribs. Hopeful anticipation sprang up and quickly grew. He leaped down off the bluff and began to run. He ran swiftly, his long legs taking great strides.

The wind caused his eyes to sting and his now-loose black hair to flow out behind him. Starkeeper raced eagerly toward his secluded canvas tipi, his heart pumping furiously, his breath coming fast.

In minutes he reached his lodge, relieved to have beaten her there. He dashed inside, reached behind his head, grabbed his shirt, and yanked it up and off in one fluid motion.

Starkeeper washed up, shaved, brushed his hair, put on fresh clothes, and then waited, pacing restlessly back and forth outside his tipi.

But Diane never came.

She wanted to.

While Starkeeper waited impatiently, Diane sat alone outside Golden Star's lodge, watching the stars come out. Her arms wrapped around her knees, her head thrown back, she looked up at the heavens as one by one stars twinkled to brilliant life in the black night sky.

She smiled when she caught sight of the luminous Milky Way. Golden Star had told her that Shoshoni law was responsible for the glittering trail of stars. Diane couldn't recall all of the legend. Something to do with a banished black bear climbing above the timberline, then rising up to the Heavenly Hunting Ground, shaking the snow crystals off his feet, leaving a silvery trail behind him.

Golden Star's voice had dropped low when she told Diane earnestly, "The white crystals will always be there in the sky on clear nights to light the way to the Land of the Souls, and all people will call it the Milky Way."

Diane sighed and lowered her eyes. How could she look at those mystical, mesmerizing stars and not be reminded of the mystical, mesmerizing Starkeeper? She leaned her forehead on her raised knees. Guilt, misery, and passion overwhelmed her. Especially passion. She felt terribly guilty for what she had done last night, and she was miserable over it. But, oh, how she longed to be in Starkeeper's strong arms again.

She raised her head. It was all she could do to keep still. She felt almost physically ill with desire for the handsome Shoshoni. Was tempted to give in to base passion, to race through the village to Starkeeper's lodge. To throw herself into his arms and beg him to make love to her.

Diane stayed as she was.

She would *not* go there tonight, or tomorrow night or the next. She would never go there again. She had never been anybody's fool; she wouldn't be Starkeeper's. On the other hand, since it was too late to change what had happened, there wasn't much point in turning him down should he want her again. And she knew he would. He did. The way he'd kissed her down by the river this afternoon; why, if they had been alone in his lodge . . .

Diane came to her feet.

It was at almost this very hour last evening when she had gone to him. Was he remembering, too? Was he wanting her as she wanted him? Would he come here for her tonight? Show up any minute, hoping she would now say yes?

Diane hurried into the tipi, anxiously pulled the borrowed doeskin dress up over her head and off. She washed up, brushed her long raven hair, put on her freshly laundered white skirt and blouse, and went back outside to wait expectantly.

But Starkeeper never came.

The following days at Wind River were a paradoxical blend of simple joys and growing misery. For Diane. And for Starkeeper.

The more Diane saw the unfailingly kind and likable Starkeeper among his people, the more she respected and admired him. It was pleasurable to quietly observe him when he didn't realize her eyes were on him.

Like the warm afternoons when he sat in the sun with the old men before the agency buildings, listening intently while they spoke of days gone by. So respectful and totally focused he never noticed her pass by on her regular trips to the camp store to buy cold Coca-Cola for Golden Star. Or the bright, sunny mornings when he played games of ball with the village's rowdy youngsters, laughing and looking almost as boyish and carefree as the happy children.

If Diane took silent pleasure from quietly watching Starkeeper, so it was with him. He was pleased by the deference and consideration she always showed his aged grandmother and Golden Star's many friends. More than once he watched a wrinkled old Shoshoni face light up as Diane bent to give a warm hug or pat a stooped back or inquire after someone's health.

He caught himself helplessly smiling as he stopped to watch a laughing, barefoot Diane playing chase with a giggling gang of little Indian girls. She looked like a little girl herself. And acted like one. She squealed and raced across the grass, the skirt of her white dress flying up around her knees, her unbound hair flowing out behind her.

But the role of child was immediately discarded for that of caring parent when a tiny, chubby girl fell, bumped her head, and began to cry. In mid-flight Diane stopped, whirled about, and raced back to the fallen child. She fell to her knees on the grass, plucked the crying little girl up from the ground, and cradled her close, murmuring and pressing healing kisses on the bumped forehead.

As he watched the touching scene, it was far too easy to imagine the beautiful young woman with her own child in her arms. With his child in her arms. Their child.

Starkeeper ground his teeth and turned away.

Four days had passed since that night in Starkeeper's lodge.

It was late afternoon. Golden Star, Diane, and Starkeeper stood in Wind River's Shoshoni cemetery. Diane and Starkeeper were quiet while Golden Star pointed out graves of those who had gone before.

Golden Star's husband, Running Elk, rested there. And Daughter-of-the-Stars. The beloved Sacagawea. Many others. Diane listened as Golden Star pointed out family and friends whose graves overlooked the beautiful Little Wind River valley.

"When it is time for me to go to the Great Mystery, I will lie here beside Running Elk," Golden Star said, standing above his final resting place. She raised her head, smiled, and added softly, "Old Sacagawea believed the white flowers that grow up here at the snow line are the spirits of little children who have gone away but return each spring to gladden the pathway of those still living." Abruptly she turned away. "I am tired. I must go."

Starkeeper saw them back to Golden Star's lodge but didn't come inside. Diane helped the old woman prepare for her afternoon nap, and when Golden Star was stretched out on her bed of furs, she took Diane's hand and said, "There is a legend, Pale One, of a lake north of here. It is said that there are times a beautiful Indian princess who drowned in the lake rises from its mists. Those who live nearby say the princess's false lover forever calls out to her in the moaning voice of the wind."

"That's sad and beautiful," said Diane. "Who was she, this beautiful princess?"

"My mother," said Golden Star. "Stardust."

"But I—"

"A handsome fur trapper stole Stardust's love from my father and from me."

Shocked, Diane said, "Oh, Golden Star, I'm sorry."

"Ah, child, when we are young, all is clouded by desire—as fire by smoke or mirror by dust."

"Yes," Diane admitted, "that's true, I'm afraid."

"If we could know why one person selects another from the multitudes, all things would be possible." The old Shoshoni woman smiled wanly. "But we cannot help loving whom we love." Her black eyes, fixed on Diane, held a knowing expression, as if she were waiting for what she knew Diane was about to say.

"I *must* talk to you, Golden Star," Diane blurted out anxiously.

"I know, child. I know."

"You do?"

"Yes. You desire my grandson."

"I do. Oh, I do." Diane lowered her eyes, embarrassed. "I mean, I care for him the way a woman cares for a man and . . . you must think me terrible." She felt her face flush.

The old woman smiled and said, "We're all taught that love can only grow out of a long and lasting friendship." Her child's merry laugh, and then came an honest confession. "It is not true, Pale One. I fell in love with Running Elk the first time I saw him ride into my village, so straight and tall and handsome. The only thing I knew about him was that I wanted to be held in his arms." Still smiling, she said, "Friendship and love grew as our years together passed, but first there was desire."

"Golden Star, you're so understanding, so wise." Diane's voice was soft. "I'm falling in love with Starkeeper, and it's so foolish of me."

"I don't think it's foolish."

"Oh, but it is. Starkeeper has very little use for white women. The two of us . . . there could never be a future. Never." Her eyes glistened with unshed tears. "What must I do, Golden Star? I love your grandson, and I know it's hopeless."

Golden Star smiled. "Perhaps not as hopeless as you think." Her black eyes twinkled mischievously. "Starkeeper is a white man born."

Chapter 31

Diane stared at the smiling old Shoshoni woman, thinking she must surely have misunderstood. Starkeeper *not* an Indian? No. No, that couldn't be true.

Her face screwing up into a frown, Diane said, "What are you telling me, Golden Star? You can't possibly mean that—"

"Starkeeper is white. As white as you. His blood mother and father were both white." The black eyes twinkled at the confused Diane. "But," Golden Star added, "he is *my* grandson. Has always been, will always be." The smiling old woman then instructed, "Make yourself more comfortable, child. I'll tell you all about Starkeeper."

Diane sat flat down on the floor beside Golden Star's bed, curling her legs to the side. There she stayed for the next half hour, listening intently, asking dozens of questions.

The Indian woman told her of Starkeeper's true heritage. Told how Chief Red Fox had saved a white baby from the fire that killed his parents. The rescue had come shortly after Daughter-of-the-Stars had lost her newborn son. The chief brought the orphaned baby to his grieving young princess, and the tiny boy saved Daughter-of-the-Stars' life. She took the child as her own son and loved him as much as if she had borne him.

Golden Star told Diane of the scar concealed by Starkeeper's silver bracelet and of its meaning. Said Starkeeper had been raised as a Shoshoni, but now he lived as a white man. He was known in that other world as Ben Star. He was a wealthy, successful man who had amassed a fortune from prospecting.

"Starkeeper has many rich gold and silver mines in California and Nevada," Golden Star said with pride. "He lives in a fine mansion in Nevada, and he owns a tall office building in San Francisco—it touches the sky."

"Is he . . . married?" Diane asked. Golden Star shook her head no. Feeling a great sense of relief, Diane pressed on. "Was he? Has he ever been married?" Again the old woman shook her head. "Why?" Diane wanted to know. "There must surely have been women who—"

"Wanted to be his wife?" Golden Star finished her sentence. Nodding, she said, "I understand wealthy, handsome men are much prized in your world. The white world."

Diane admitted it was true. "So why has Starkeeper never married?"

"Appe?" Golden Star said, and it was more a question than a statement. "Perhaps it was the work of Appe." She smiled at Diane's look of puzzlement. "Appe is the creator of the universe and all that is in it. Who knows? Maybe Appe created you for Starkeeper." She smiled up at Diane and patted her hand. "I hope it is so. I would like to have a great-grandchild before I go on to the Great Mystery." She yawned then and said, "A boy, I think. A sweet little boy like—like . . ." Her papery eyelids closed.

Golden Star was asleep.

Diane sat there for a minute longer, digesting all the old Shoshoni woman had told her. Then she silently rose to her feet. She left Golden Star, went directly to Starkeeper's lodge. She called his name loudly as soon as she reached his remote tipi. No answer. Determined to speak with him, she ducked inside, still calling his name. The lodge was silent and empty.

Disappointed, she stepped back outside and jumped, startled.

A mounted rider was there right before her. Waiting. The silvery-haired old Chief Washakie, astride a big paint pony, looked down at Diane and extended his hand.

"Come, Pale One. I will show you where he is."

Diane didn't question how the old chief had known she was looking for Starkeeper or how he knew where Starkeeper would be. She nodded, took the revered chieftain's outstretched hand, and agilely swung up behind him.

Chief Washakie wheeled the big paint about and cantered out of camp. He immediately turned the mount up toward the jagged mountain peaks and began climbing to a higher elevation. In minutes they'd ascended well above the valley floor.

Over his shoulder Chief Washakie said, "There is a place in these mountains where Starkeeper goes when he is troubled. It is the home of Tamapah, the Sun Father. Starkeeper comes up here alone to communicate with Tamapah."

Her slender arms around the old chief's thickened waist, Diane said, "Will he be angry with me for interrupting that communication? If he is troubled—"

"*You* are Starkeeper's trouble." The chief pulled up the snorting paint. He turned his silvery head and looked at her. "Time you two communicate." He motioned for Diane to dismount. Nodding, she slid to the ground and looked quizzically up at him. He raised his arm and pointed the way out to her. Then silently he backed his big paint away and left her.

Diane stood there alone, high above the scattered Indian villages, the only sound that of the wind sighing through the pines. And the pounding of her heart. She hesitated, considered leaving without seeking out Starkeeper. Squared her slender shoulders and turned toward the vast, towering pillar of rock pointed out by the old chief.

Up and over a narrow, treacherous pathway she climbed into an eerily quiet and shadowy crevice. Breath labored, at last she rounded the massive fluted granite column and stopped short.

Twenty yards away Starkeeper was seated on a flat ridge of stone. The entire canyon was in deep shadow. But he was not. A shaft of bright sunshine poured down through a gap in the higher peaks above, bathing Starkeeper in brilliant white light.

A hand went to her tight throat. Diane was awed by the sight of the silent, unmoving man seated there on the rock, awash in white-hot sunshine when all else was in shadow. His dark, handsome face was turned up, his eyes staring unblinkingly into the sun.

Softly Diane spoke his name. Starkeeper seemed to come out of a trance. Slowly he turned his head and looked at her. He said nothing. She cautiously approached him, not quite sure what she was going to say.

After she'd ascended the stone steps to him and stood just above, she said from the covering shadows, "May I sit?"

"If you like," was his cool reply. His hooded gaze swung away from her, returned to the sun.

Diane took a shallow breath, stepped from the deep, cool shade, and sat down in the harsh sunlight beside him. Blinking in the brightness, she said, "Look at me, Starkeeper." He slowly exhaled, turned, and looked directly at her. His eyes held that now-familiar mixture of heat and cold. "I have finally learned," she said softly, "who you are."

"Have you?"

"Yes. You're an impostor. You're as white as I am."

His stern lips lifted into a smile that didn't reach his eyes. He placed his dark forearm next to her pale one, so close his sun-heated skin touched hers. "Not quite."

"I'm not speaking of the color of your skin," she said.

"Nor am I." He moved his arm away. "Being Indian is not a matter of color. I'm more Indian than white, and I always will be." His tone was dismissive.

"Oh, really? Then why, I wonder, don't you live here with your—"

"And do what?" he interrupted. "Sit on the agency porch all day with the other idle men?" His eyes flashed.

"No, but—"

"Look around you. What was once our kingdom has become our cage," he said sadly. He lifted a hand, swept it about in a wide, encompassing arc. "Not long ago this whole country—all America—belonged to the redman. There was room for all tribes and they were happy and they were free." A muscle danced in his tanned jaw. "But then the white man came, drove them out, killed them, herded them onto reservations. Like this one."

"I know all that, Starkeeper," she said, tempted to point out that he selfishly left his sweet, aged grandmother here in the place he called a cage. Why didn't he care enough about her welfare to allow her to live with him in his fine Nevada mansion? "I know."

"Do you now? Do you know that all his life old Chief Washakie has befriended the white man? That he willingly allowed them to cross his sacred hunting grounds, indeed, helped guide them safely across it? Never raised a hand against them?"

"No. No, I didn't know that."

"It's true. But guess what? It made no difference. He, like the others, was cornered into one little spot of the earth, cornered like a prisoner and watched by men with guns."

"I'm sorry." Diane said, and meant it. "I'm truly sorry. But, Starkeeper, I'm not the one responsible."

"I know that," he admitted. "What I'm telling you is I'm Indian. These people are my people. I've seen them suffer and lose the will to live, and it breaks my heart." He shook his head sadly. "You and all your white friends believe that the Indian is by nature a stoic and impassive race. That's not true. But after years of being endlessly ridiculed and tortured, many a happy-go-lucky Indian has become stoic and silently endures the white man's humiliation."

Diane said, "Like you when they cut off your braids at the university?"

He turned flashing black eyes on her. "No. Like me when you and your lover taunted and tormented me while I was chained in that damned animal cage."

"I deserve that," she said. "I was cruel and unkind, and I'm sorry."

He laughed bitterly. "So *now* you're sorry? Could it be because you've since found out I'm supposedly one of you?"

"No," she said, "I'm sorry because I treated another human being so shabbily. I felt guilty about it when it happened, I still do. I'm asking you to forgive me."

"You're forgiven." His tone was flippant. "Now your conscience is clear, so why don't you run along and—"

"I want to stay here with you," she said with frankness and honesty. "I want to stay here as long as you stay. And then, when you leave here, I want to go with you back to your lodge. I want to stay there with you. Never to leave unless you leave. I want to . . . love you, Starkeeper."

"What for?" His dark eyes narrowed. "Where would the thrill be for you now? I'm white, remember?"

Diane's slender shoulders sagged. "What happened between us meant a great deal more than a passing thrill. At least it did for me."

"That a fact?"

"Yes. Yes, it is." Her violet eyes held a soft, loving expression as she gazed at his dark, sullen face.

"Sure. It meant so much you couldn't wait to run out on me afterward." His face, lighted by the shaft of sunlight, was as hard as granite. "It's all right. I understand. You were ashamed, and who can blame you? Who wouldn't feel bad about making love to a filthy savage? An uncivilized beast?"

"That isn't fair, Starkeeper." She felt tears stinging the backs of her eyes. "I never—"

"Please, Beauty," he interrupted. "Your memory can't be so short that you've forgotten calling me savage and animal and Beast and—"

"But I was afraid of you! You're the one with a short memory. Maybe you've forgotten you kidnapped me! My God, I was terrified. Hardly responsible for the foolish things I said. And yes, before you say it, let me assure you, if a 'white man' had kidnapped me, I would have been just as scared!"

His stern mouth softened slightly. "I doubt that. But it doesn't matter." He sighed heavily and added, "My behavior was inexcusable, and I'm sorry. I'd undo it all if I could."

She reached out, touched his arm. "But you can't. And I can't." She smiled hopefully at him. "So let's go on from here."

He didn't return her smile. "Why did you come here? What is it you want from me, Beauty?"

"I don't want anything from you, Starkeeper." His dark eyes flickered as she spoke his name. "I want to give you something."

"There's nothing you can give me, Beauty."

"Yes, I can. I can give you friendship and affection and respect and—and . . . love."

She saw the fabric of his pale blue shirt pull across the flat muscles of his chest as he took a deep breath. Saw his beautiful eyes change expressions. Her simple declaration was having an effect, and Diane felt suddenly lighthearted and hopeful. If only he'd give her the opportunity, she'd show him that she cared for him as a human being, as a person, as a man.

Scarred by the past, distrustful, Starkeeper remained unconvinced, unreachable. Unwilling to risk being hurt, he said sarcastically, "Ah, Beauty, Beauty. I know you better than you know yourself."

"You don't know me at all," was her firm reply.

"Yes, I do." His tone was accusing. "I know you all too well, have known dozens just like you."

"No, you haven't, damn you!" Diane said, anger flaring. "There is no one else just like me!" She glared at him. "If you don't believe me, give me a chance and I'll prove it!"

He looked into her angry eyes and thought she was surely God's most endearing creation. Had they met under different circumstances, there might be a chance for the two of them. But they hadn't. And there wasn't. And if she had temporarily forgotten about the big blond Cherokee Kid, he had not.

Starkeeper said, "I'll see you back to Golden Star's lodge now, before it grows dark."

"No! I can find my way alone." She shot to her feet.

He nodded and without looking at her said, "Tomorrow we leave Wind River."

Diane's heart sank. "Leave Wind River? But I thought you wanted to wait until . . . wait for—"

"Your lover to catch up with us? I did, but—"

"He is not my lover!"

Starkeeper shrugged wide shoulders and ignored her statement. "I've changed my mind about waiting. It's time you were back safely with your family. There's a morning train from Lander which makes connections in Salt Lake City for San Francisco. I'll escort you as far as Virginia City."

"To your Nevada home?"

"Yes, I'm going home. Now please leave me. Go back to the village before the sun sets."

"What—what time tomorrow?"

"We'll leave Wind River shortly after sunup. Be ready."

No longer trusting her voice, Diane nodded. But Starkeeper was again looking into the lowering orange sun.

She had promised herself that she wouldn't cry.

But now, as she stood outside Golden Star's lodge and watched—for the last time—the sun rise over Wind River, Diane felt that familiar lump rise to her throat and her eyes burn.

Golden Star stepped out of the tipi, came to Diane, and wrapped both arthritic hands around Diane's slender arm. Diane looked at her, swallowed hard, and tried to smile.

The old Shoshoni woman fondly pressed her gray head to Diane's shoulder and said softly, "Do not give up so easily, child. The ride to Virginia City is a long one. Who knows what will happen? You are a persuasive young woman."

Diane patted the gnarled hands that were clamped around her arm but said nothing.

There was that merry child's laugh from Golden Star. Then she said confidentially: "For centuries woman has changed man's mind. Change Starkeeper's mind about you."

"But how?" Diane spoke at last.

"Why, the same way women have always done it." She looked up at Diane and winked.

Before Diane could reply, Starkeeper appeared. "Ready?" he asked, his tone flat, cool.

Diane squared her slender shoulders, smiled brightly, and said, "More than ready. Are you?"

Starkeeper didn't respond. He turned to his grandmother, draped a long arm around her shoulders, and said, "I don't suppose it would do any good to ask one more time if you'll come with me."

Golden Star smiled broadly, patted his chest, and shook her head. To Diane she said, "My grandson is a stubborn man. Each time he comes to Wind River, he asks me to leave my home. Wants me to come to Nevada and live with him."

Surprised, Diane looked from Starkeeper to Golden Star. She'd been thinking how ungrateful and selfish he was not to allow his grand-mother to live with him when all along it was Golden Star who refused.

"Why don't you?" she said to the smiling Shoshoni woman. "I'm sure he would take good care of you and—"

"I take care of myself," said the independent Golden Star. Then she softened and added with a barely perceptible sigh, "We have had our day, Chief Washakie and I and the rest of the old ones—just like the buffalo. The future belongs to you, Pale One. And to my grandson, Keeper of the Stars." She smiled then and added, "This is my home. Up here is the air the angels breathe. I could never leave this place."

"You've left out one of your reasons," Starkeeper gently prompted.

"If I go away from here"—Golden Star soberly addressed Diane—"I could not see the moccasin prints in the sky to guide me to the Great Mystery." She looked up at her tall grandson. "I do not wish to lose my way."

"I know, sweetheart," he said, bent and kissed her wrinkled temple affectionately, and pressed her gray head to his chest.

She hugged him tightly and said into his shirtfront, "You will come again to see me?"

"Count on it," he murmured, and released her.

The old woman turned immediately to Diane. When Diane hugged her, Golden Star said, "You will come see me again?"

"Count on it," Diane whispered with a confidence she wished she really felt.

Diane released her. Golden Star quickly turned away. Her slumped shoulders shook. She was crying.

When the silent pair rode out of the Wind River Reservation, Diane felt certain she would never see it—or Golden Star—again. It was noon when they boarded the train in Lander. Seated by the window, Diane looked back at the snow-capped Wind River Range rising to meet a cloudless Wyoming sky.

She laid her forehead against the cool train window and watched the mighty mountains growing steadily more distant.

Diane's head shot up as something streaking closely by the train captured her attention. She leaned forward, peered out, and saw the diamond-throated cat racing the moving train. A small smile lifted the corners of her lips. She watched the cat, thinking he was the most beautiful beast of them all, with perfect conformation and a grace of movement that was unique. The tawny mountain lion ran with a fluid motion through the dense tangle of sagebrush without ever breaking his stride.

And then disappeared.

Diane pressed two fingers first to her lips, then to the window in a silent salute and good-bye. She turned to look at Starkeeper, but his dark eyes were shut, arms crossed over his chest.

The locomotive's whistle blew loudly at a railroad crossing. Diane sighed, leaned back in her seat, and closed her eyes. All was silent save the rhythmic clickity-clack of the train's steel wheels on the tracks.

The wheels of a train which was rapidly speeding her westward.

Chapter 32

⊰⊰⊰⊰ The train rolled into the station just as the fog rolled in over the bay.

It was early afternoon when Boz, the engineer, poked his head out the train's window. His striped railroad cap pushed way back, his dust-covered goggles shoved up on his wrinkled forehead, Boz blinked and squinted, his eyes locked on the swinging red signal light guiding him safely through the dense fog and into the Oakland, California, switching yard.

When the tricky maneuver had been successfully accomplished and the troupe train had come to a complete stop at its siding, Boz wiped his perspiring face with his red bandanna and addressed his locomotive as if it were a person.

"Whew!" he said aloud, mopping his face. "That was danged tricky, old girl, but we made it." He grinned, congratulating himself and his faithful, aging locomotive.

Boz tried not to think about the fact that this could be his last time to guide the "old girl" into one of America's busy train terminals. He *wouldn't* think about it. Something would happen. Something would save the show. And the train.

Boz swung down out of the locomotive's cab and shook hands with the lantern-swinging signalman. Their attention was drawn to a pair of white-uniformed men standing on the platform in the thickening fog.

The white-clad pair quickly boarded the train. Short minutes later they carried a stretcher bearing Ancient Eyes off the train, across the tracks, and to a waiting ambulance. Shorty Jones, a cigarette dangling from his lips, hands nervously twisting his battered Stetson, was right on their heels.

"Watch it now, boys," Shorty warned when they reached the horse-drawn ambulance. "Be mighty careful loading him." Shorty glanced down at Ancient Eyes' weathered face and said, "Don't you worry, Chief. I'm going with you. See they treat you right and all."

A faint smile touched the old Ute's lips. "With me," he managed, and Shorty grinned, nodding reassuringly.

"You bet," said the skinny animal wrangler, hopeful that in time the Indian would fully recover from the heart attack and stroke that had almost taken his life.

Ancient Eyes had come out of his deep coma back in Salt Lake, and now he was even able to say a few words, to comprehend some of what was going on around him. But he remembered nothing of the day he was stricken or of the events and circumstances leading up to it.

They all waited until Ancient Eyes had been taken off the train. When he was on his way to the Oakland General Hospital, the rest of the tired troupe poured off the train, pushing trunks and carrying valises. Shorty's boys began the unloading of the animal cages, preparing them for transport to nearby holding pens.

The performers tried their best to be keep their spirits up, to be optimistic about their future and the future of the show. It was far from easy.

Colonel Buck Buchannan hadn't been his old jolly self since his beautiful granddaughter had been kidnapped and Ancient Eyes had fallen ill. A trouper to the bitter end, the Colonel kept a stiff upper lip. He'd discharged his duties and played to the sparse crowds that attended the Salt Lake and Sacramento performances, but the customary twinkle was missing from his expressive blue eyes, and those who knew him best doubted it would ever return.

The thick fog blanketing the coastal city on that chilly September afternoon added to the feeling of gloom. Texas Kate's raucous laugh didn't ring out through the high-ceilinged train station as usual. Kate didn't feel like laughing. She didn't feel like talking either.

With several other show people she boarded an omnibus for the short ride to the troupe's winter quarters. From the bus's window, she looked out at the bay, which she could barely see through the fog.

Texas Kate knew it was time she started thinking about the uncertainty of her future. She knew *Colonel Buck Buchannan's Wild West Show* was on the verge of collapse. Ruth Buchannan had confided that unless the Colonel could manage to obtain substantial financing before the spring season rolled around, there would no longer be a show.

Texas Kate felt a shudder surge through her stocky body.

If there was to be no show, what would she do? Go back home to Texas? The prospect of returning to that lonely little ranch made her shudder again. For the first time, realization struck Kate. She didn't want to go home to Texas. Ever. This was her home! This traveling wild west show was her home, her only home. These people were her family. These talented, remarkable show people who smiled no matter how blue they were, who performed no matter how sick, who loved and lived for the thrill of performing. Kind, loyal, gritty folks whose lives would be considered hard and unrewarding by ordinary people.

Well, civilians just didn't know! No, sirree, they had no idea how it felt to claim the spotlight. To step out there before thousands of awed, anxious fans and bring them screaming to their feet! Those who'd never experienced it couldn't possibly know how it warmed a body's heart to be greeted and cheered and loved by admiring throngs!

Dear Jesus, Kate suddenly offered up a silent prayer, *please don't let the Colonel lose this show! Don't let me lose it! It's the only home I have!*

The long caravan of taxis and omnibuses carrying the Colonel's troupe began arriving, one by one, before the four-story rooming house that was to be their home for the winter season.

It was not the kind of lodging they'd been used to in the past. Back in the glory days they would have boarded a ferry as soon as they got off the train. They'd have crossed the choppy bay and checked into the fine hotels found in exciting, glittering San Francisco.

Not this year.

This year they were lucky to have a roof over their heads. There was nothing grand or imposing about the big wooden building which was sadly in need of paint. Nor was the address impressive, located only a few blocks from the train switching yards, loud saloons, a smelly wholesale fish market, a smithy's, a furniture maker's shop, and other run-down rooming houses. The street was narrow and noisy. Vagrants in threadbare jackets loitered under lampposts lining the sidewalks.

A heavy suitcase in each hand, Texas Kate stepped into the dim, sparsely furnished room assigned to her. The one window across the room was tightly shut, the worn lace curtains closed. Kate dropped her baggage, charged across the room, yanked back the curtains—coughing when dust flew—and raised the window.

She poked her head out. There was nothing to see but the rear of another building, a brick one less than fifteen feet away across a narrow alley. Kate sighed and turned back to look at the shadowy third-floor room: an iron bedstead, a lamp table and lamp with a smoked globe, a battered chest, and two straight-backed chairs.

Kate told herself there was nothing whatsoever wrong with the room. It just seemed a bit dreary because of the fog. Why, soon as she unpacked, spiffed the place up with a few personal belongings, and the sun came out, this would be a right pleasant room.

Kate sighed again.

She didn't feel like unpacking. She didn't even feel like lighting the lone lamp. She trudged tiredly over to the bed. And frowned. A big double bed instead of her usual single one. Its size gave it a lonely appearance. It was meant to be shared. Meant for two, not one. Kate sat down on the edge of the double bed, heard the springs squeak under her weight, and the sound was somehow forlorn.

Texas Kate felt a strange tightness in her chest, a worrisome lump rising to her throat. Her fleshy chin drooped low; she bowed her head. She hadn't wept in almost thirty years, but on this dim, foggy, depressing afternoon, she felt like bawling.

A loud knock on her door snapped her out of it. Before she could respond, Shorty's unmistakable voice called through the door, "Open up, Kate. It's Shorty. We have to talk."

Texas Kate blinked, swallowed, and jumped up from the bed. She ran blunt fingers through her gray-brown curls, shoved the loose tails of her blouse down inside her waistband, straightened her wrinkled brown skirts, and went to the door.

As soon as she turned the doorknob, Shorty pushed the door open wide, stepped inside, and closed it behind him. Kate's eyes widened when he threw the bolt, locking the door.

"Kate, sit down," Shorty commanded, taking off his Stetson and dropping it atop the scarred chest.

"Why? Is something—"

"Woman, I said, 'Sit down.' " Shorty pointed to one of the straight-backed chairs.

Mouth gaping in shock, Kate backed away from him, turned, and hurried to the chair. When she was seated with her hands folded in her lap, Shorty walked over to the night table, snuffed out his half-smoked cigarette in a tin ashtray, then came to stand directly before Kate. Booted feet apart, he held her gaze as he hitched up his faded Levi's and then hooked his thumbs into his leather cowboy belt.

Wondering what on earth he was up to, Kate felt a sense of unease and expectancy.

"Kate, I've had enough of your nonsense," Shorty said with cool authority.

"Nonsense?" Texas Kate echoed, her eyes wide.

"That's right. It's time I put a stop to it, and that's just what I mean to do." Shorty's eyes were narrowed, his jaw firm.

"Well," said Texas Kate, "it appears to me you're just gettin' a mite too overbearing." She started to rise.

Quick as a flash he reached out, clamped his hand atop her shoulder, and shoved her back down into the chair. "I said for you to sit down."

Texas Kate gasped, flabbergasted. But then she smiled nervously. Nodding, she murmured, "Yes, sir. Okay, Shorty, if that's what you want."

"It is," he assured her, his hand still atop her shoulder. "I got something to say, and you're going to listen." He abruptly released her shoulder. "I don't want you interrupting, you hear me?"

"I hear you."

"Good." Shorty coughed needlessly, cleared his throat, and plunged ahead. "I know you loved Teddy Ray Worthington, and I know there ain't no man could ever take Worthington's place. But, Katie, the man's dead. Your husband is dead. He'd been dead for over thirty years and nothing—"

"I guess—"

"Be quiet. I'm not finished. Worthington was killed in the War Between the States. If he hadn't been killed, why, he'd a come home to Texas and you as soon as it was over. No man would have stayed away from you. But he didn't come back, and he's not ever coming back. And that's the God's truth, Kate."

"Yes . . . I know. I guess I've known for a long time." Kate was surprised at herself. It didn't make her feel sad to say it. Teddy Ray Worthington, the sweet, gentle boy she'd married when she was little more than a girl, was dead. Had been dead for over thirty years. And now she couldn't even remember exactly what he had looked like. "Teddy Ray died in the War. I know that, Shorty."

Shorty reached out, touched her cheek with calloused fingers. "Honey, he's dead, but you're not. And I'm not." He cupped her cheek tenderly in his hand. "I love you, Kate Worthington. I've loved you for an awful long time. You're my first love, and you're my last love. I can't wait much longer." His eyes and his voice softened when he added, "Ah, honey, don't you see, we ain't kids. We don't have that many good years left to us. Let's don't waste any more of 'em."

"Shorty, I—"

"I know, honey, I know. You need a little time to think it over. I understand that. You can't bury one man in the afternoon and marry another that same night." He smiled at her. "You start saying good-bye to Teddy Ray now, my sweet Katie. And when you've said that final good-bye, why, I'll come for you and we'll just take ourselves on down to the parson and get ourselves married." Still smiling, he leaned down and kissed her. Kissed her right on the mouth.

"If you had any idea how many times I've wanted to do that," Shorty said, his eyes warm with feeling. Still reeling from that unexpected kiss, Texas Kate was shocked to the roots of her grayish brown hair when Shorty suddenly winked at her, inclined his head, and added, "Marry me, honey, and I'll show you there's more to life than shooting glass balls out of the air."

"Why, Shorty Jones!" Kate blushed hotly, and butterflies took wing in her stomach. "Is that any way to talk before a woman?"

"It's the way for *me* to talk before *my* woman," he said. Then: "I'll make you a good husband, Katie. I can't promise the road ahead will be easy. We both know the show's in trouble, but whatever comes, it'll be easier if we face it together."

Nodding, Texas Kate smiled while tears glistened in her eyes. Flustered, happy, excited, she said, "Yes, we'll face it together. The two of us. Together." She smiled shyly then and asked, "Shorty, can I get up now?"

Shorty laughed. "Darlin' girl, you can do anything you please." He drew her to her feet, wrapped his wiry arms around her thick waist, and squeezed her so tightly she dissolved into giggles of embarrassed pleasure.

Texas Kate looped her arms around Shorty's neck, and the pair danced happily around the room like a couple of carefree kids. When they finally grew dizzy and sagged against the wall to catch their breath, Kate realized that the gloomy afternoon fog had cleared away. Her third-floor room was flooded with bright, cheery sunshine.

And so was her heart.

Chapter 33

✦✦✦✦ Starkeeper's dark face in profile against the distant redwoods seemed somehow sadly fitting. Perfectly framed there in the train's window, his harshly sculpted features appeared as hard as the solid wood of those faraway giant sequoias.

Pretending to doze in the seat beside him, Diane silently studied the sharply cut contours of his set, handsome face. He had remained distant and unreachable throughout the long train trip. He had sat in the seat beside her—so close she could reach out and touch him—the entire time. All the way down from the mountains of Wyoming, across the rugged canyon lands of Utah and through the high country deserts of Nevada.

In all that time, through all those countless hours of crisp, chilly mornings and bright, hot afternoons and dark, starry nights, Starkeeper had been polite but aloof. Solicitous yet detached. Civil but cool.

So near yet so far away—like a star.

Golden Star's advice came back to Diane. When she asked the old Shoshoni woman how to change Starkeeper's mind, Golden Star's eyes had twinkled mischievously, and she'd said, "Why, the same way women have always done it," and she had winked.

Diane knew exactly what Golden Star had meant. The wise, understanding old woman knew that Diane's only chance was first to make Starkeeper desire her. To make him want her so badly he couldn't resist taking her in his arms. And when she was in his arms, when his defenses were down, maybe then she'd be able to make him realize that she really cared, that she loved him.

Diane experienced a terrible sinking feeling. She was not going to get the opportunity.

The sagebrush-dotted desert lands had been left behind, and they were now well up into the Sierras. A violent afternoon rainstorm had ended a half hour ago. The sun was out again, shining down from a clear blue sky. But the air was cool and thin, their elevation high. Bristlecone pines grew down to the railroad right-of-way, and the train's locomotive and several cars were out of sight around a mountainous curve.

They were nearing their final destination. Her time with Starkeeper was rapidly running out. Or had it already run out? Was the station just around the bend? Were there only a precious few minutes left before—

The moving train suddenly lurched. The screeching sound of the heavy wheels grinding to a sudden stop on the slick steel tracks was almost deafening. Startled passengers, jolted in their seats, looked about in confusion. Nervous chatter erupted.

Diane lunged up, looked anxiously out the window, and saw men on foot up ahead, madly waving their arms. Puzzled, she turned questioning eyes on Starkeeper. He shrugged but rose from his seat, stepping past her when the train pitched to a final stop.

"Stay here," he ordered, and moved down the narrow aisle.

After hurriedly scooting over into his vacated seat, Diane threw open the window, leaned out, and watched Starkeeper as he walked along beside the halted train, moving forward at a leisurely pace, seemingly in no particular hurry. Other curious passengers poured from the coaches and joined him in the trek toward the front of the train.

In minutes Diane saw Starkeeper coming back toward her. Flanked by two shorter men who both were excitedly talking at once, he appeared to be unruffled. He reboarded the train, came down the aisle, dropped down into the seat beside her.

"A rockslide," he said flatly. "The thunderstorm dislodged a number of huge boulders on the higher cliffs above. The loosened rocks came crashing down across the tracks. Looks as if it just happened."

"Then we're lucky we weren't hit."

"Yes, lucky," he said, not sounding as if he thought they were lucky. "A couple of those rocks are as big as this coach and must weigh several tons each."

"Good heavens, that's frightening," she said.

Then it occurred to her, if rocks weighing tons were covering the railroad tracks, how would the train be able to move? How could they get to the depot? Maybe that's why Starkeeper had begun to scowl.

"How far are you able to walk?" His question surprised her.

"I'm not really sure. How far away are we from—"

"Too far," he said, shaking his dark head.

"Then why ask me?"

He exhaled. "It's going to be morning before the tracks will be cleared. We could possibly get a ride into town, but it wouldn't do much good."

"It wouldn't?"

"No. You still couldn't get out of Virginia City until these tracks are clear and this train comes through."

Her eyes clinging to his hard, handsome face, Diane asked, "Then what will we do? Stay here on the train?"

He said, "You look pale and tired. You need a good night's rest. My home is not that far from here. Five miles at the most. If you feel up to walking it, we can stay the night there and—"

"Yes!" Diane could hardly hide her excitement. "Let's do that. Let's spend the night at your place. I think—I'm sure I can walk five miles." A reprieve! Another chance! *Oh, thank you, God, thank you!*

"Let's go then," he said, his irritation barely concealed.

If Diane was thrilled about the unexpected delay, Starkeeper was not. He had suffered through every hour of the long train ride with her beside him. He had gritted his teeth each time her dark head had sagged tiredly against his supporting shoulder. He'd kept his eyes off her pale, beautiful face and slender, lissome body as much as he possibly could. He'd felt that even idle conversation was dangerous, so he had assiduously avoided it. Just the sound of her voice speaking his name—his real name, Starkeeper, instead of Beast—made his heart race.

And just when he thought the torture was finally coming to an end, a damned rockslide had halted the train. Jesus, if the fallen rocks could have held on to the mountainside for another ten minutes, the train would have been safely past. And then within the hour he'd have stood watching from the Virginia City platform as the train pulled away from the station. With her on board. Taking her once and forever out of his sight. Getting her out of his hair.

And out of his heart.

Damn his rotten luck to hell!

By the time they walked a couple of miles, Diane was breathing hard and her heartbeat was rapid. Walking in the mountains was not easy.

They climbed up and over the rugged terrain, and the air was so thin she felt as if her lungs might explode.

"You okay?" Starkeeper cast a glance at her as she struggled up a rocky draw.

"Fi—fine," she assured him, feeling as if she couldn't go one more yard. "Just fine."

Silently cursing him for taking long strides, making it almost impossible for her to keep up, she followed him over rock-strewn hillsides and through forests of thick, fragrant evergreens and tall pines. Besides, he had on boots and trousers while she was dressed in her white blouse and skirt and wore only thin leather slippers on her feet.

Using her hands to help pull herself up an incline, she saw Starkeeper poised at the top. With effort, she managed to scramble the rest of the way up to where he stood. He pointed across a verdant valley to a massive mountain which appeared to be solid rock. Diane stared intently at the soaring peak and almost missed the lone dwelling located far up on its southern face, a huge structure which was the exact same hue as the rock to which it clung.

"Sun Mountain," Starkeeper pointed to the mountain's rocky summit.

Diane pointed, too. But she pointed at the curious earth-colored edifice clinging to the mountainside. "What is that?"

Casually Starkeeper replied, "My home."

As she held her side where a painful stitch plagued her, Diane's eyes were fixed on Star's house. It was easy to imagine the home's big porcelain bathtubs and clean, soft beds. But she was so tired she wasn't certain she could make it all the way down into the valley and then up the steep face of Sun Mountain.

Diane's head snapped around when Starkeeper moved closer, looked down into her upturned face, and said, "You can't make it, can you?"

"I most certainly can, I—"

She stopped speaking when he swept her up into his powerful arms and started off down the hill, carrying her as if she were as light as a feather.

Diane sighed with grateful relief, wrapped her arms around his neck, and said, "Thank you, Star."

"You're welcome, Diane."

Diane smiled, confident he could and would safely take her all the way up to his mountainside home. Cautiously she laid her head on his shoulder and was grateful that he didn't seem to mind. She closed her eyes for a few minutes and rested. When she opened them, they had crossed the smooth valley floor and were climbing swiftly up the southern face of the soaring Sun Mountain.

Star's home had momentarily disappeared. They climbed higher, and Diane could again see the stucco mansion above. It sat alone in solitary splendor, so secluded and private it was as if there were no one else in the world.

Diane was about to comment on that fact when her attention was drawn to a big, sleek cat poised on a craggy ledge a few yards ahead. Alarmed at first, she spotted the dark diamond patch of fur beneath the lion's throat and immediately relaxed. She couldn't believe her eyes. The *same* big cat. He was here in Nevada. He'd followed them all the way from Wind River.

Diane blinked when a smaller, even more beautiful cat moved out of the trees and up alongside the big diamond-throated lion.

"Star!" she exclaimed. "Look! The cat. He followed us from Wyoming, and he's found a companion."

With her in his arms, Star turned and looked up as the big tawny lion lowered its great head and gently nuzzled the smaller cat.

Star said, "That's a female with him. He's found a mate." Diane saw Star's dark eyes turn wistful, almost sad. His voice was low and flat when he softly added, "It is said they sometimes mate for life."

Diane smiled dreamily.

A wonderful sense of well-being enveloped her as Star carried her the rest of the way up to his home.

Chapter 34

Star lowered Diane to her feet.

»»»» They stood beneath a high natural arch of rock which served as the entranceway to Star's mountain estate. Fifty yards ahead loomed the stucco mansion, even larger than Diane had imagined. And more handsome.

"The staff is not on duty." Starkeeper began apologizing as they started up the graveled drive.

"Doesn't matter."

"Not a single servant inside. No one to prepare a meal."

"I can cook."

"Good. I'm starving."

"Leave it all to me," she said, not wanting to admit—at least not right this minute—that she had never actually cooked a meal in her life.

The mansion's massive front double doors were of intricately carved cedar. The doorknobs were gleaming Nevada silver. Inside the cool, silent foyer Diane turned about in a slow circle, then asked, "May I look around?"

Star shrugged. "Why not?"

Beyond the spacious slate-floored foyer, a curving cedar staircase with wide marble steps led to a balcony, off which were many rooms. Diane curiously looked into each, and when she stepped inside a huge, airy skylighted room with leather-bound books from floor to ceiling and tall French windows looking out on the higher reaches of Sun Mountain and the rugged ranges beyond, she clasped her hands together.

"This is truly grand," she said excitedly, "I'll bet it's where you spend all your time." She turned and smiled at the tall, dark man who had followed her up the stairs.

Star glanced at the long leather sofa where he'd taken many an afternoon nap, then at the heavy desk where he often worked far into the night.

"I've whiled away a few hours here," he said noncommittally.

Impressed with his excellent taste, Diane hurried from room to room, eagerly exploring Star's large, comfortable home. This man amazed her. He was so nonchalant about the impressive mountainside dwelling. Star was casual in the extreme, as if this mansion, the priceless antiques, and the fine furnishings were really of no account.

Secretly Star was pleased by Diane's obvious approval. Almost shyly he closely trailed her as she examined and admired the paintings and furniture and special objects that meant so much to him.

A smile of delight lit Diane's face as she explored the many rooms. This was a man's house. Masculine in every way. From the dark polished woodwork to the stone walk-in fireplaces to the oversize cedar beds. The entire house and everything in it had been tailored to Star's individual tastes.

Diane loved it. Everything about this remote mountain mansion was dark and graceful and handsome, just like the man who lived here.

Back down in the large kitchen, Diane decided to confess.

"Star."

"Yes?"

"I don't actually know how to cook." She smiled nervously at him. "Do you?"

"No. No, I don't," he said. "You forget, I'm Indian. Indian women do the cooking at camp."

"We're not at camp," Diane reminded him, moving closer. "And you're not Indian."

Star took a step back, reached out, and clasped Diane's upper arms to stop her advance.

"I *am* Indian, Diane. A white woman gave birth to me, but I'm Indian, even to the blood." He held his right hand up between them. With thumb and forefinger he pried the wide silver bracelet apart to show her the scar. "Didn't Golden Star explain the scar?"

Her violet eyes on the perfect white *X* adorning his dark right wrist, Diane said softly. "Yes. She told me."

His hands fell back to his sides. "I am Indian," he repeated. "I will always be Indian." That cold Shoshoni mask settled over his handsome features.

Diane nodded. She knew what he meant. He was stating unequivo-
cally that they had no future together. As far as he was concerned, he
was Indian, she was white, and that was that. He wouldn't accept her or
her love.

"I understand, Star."

And she did. But she was not willing to give up so easily. Until Star
put her on that westbound train, there was the slim chance she might
be able change his mind. She intended to do everything in her power to
do just that.

"First, let me fire up the boiler, and then I'll see if I can't find something to eat that doesn't require much preparation." Star said, his expression softening.

Diane clapped her hands when he brought in a cured ham from the
smokehouse, a couple of large Irish potatoes, a half dozen apples from
the cellar, and a bottle of vintage bubbly from the wine cellar.

"Think you can peel potatoes, Miss Buchannan?"

"Why, Mr. Star, what a foolish question."

Diane laughed. Star smiled. Together they busied themselves fixing a
meal of sorts as the sun slowly set behind Sun Mountain.

Diane carefully peeled the potatoes. Star expertly cored the apples,
seasoning them with cinnamon and brown sugar. He scored the ham
with a sharp carving knife and poured thick, sweet honey over it, hardly
conscious of the fact that he was whistling.

But Diane was. She was acutely aware of his whistling, and the sound
made her heart sing. It was so easy to imagine that the two of them
lived here happily together. To pretend that the dark, handsome man
wielding the sharp carving knife and idly whistling a mellow tune was
her husband.

When the potatoes were simmering on the stove and the apples and
ham were baking in the oven, Star said, "I'd like to clean up for dinner.
What about you?"

"I'd love to, thanks."

Star showed Diane to a spacious guest room directly across the hall
from his own.

"I believe you'll find everything you need," he said, crossing to light a
pair of matching lamps on either side of the bed and pull the heavy
curtains against the night.

"I'm sure I will." She looked around at the immaculate bedroom. Not
one speck of dust. Nothing out of place. "How long has it been since
you last were here?"

"A couple of months. Maybe longer," he said. "When I'm not in
residence, a couple of the servants come in from Virginia City one day a

week to clean and keep the house ready should I come home unexpectedly."

"Ah." She nodded. "I wondered. They must have been here today."

"Could be," he said, and left, closing the door behind him.

Diane immediately kicked off her shoes, peeled the worn stockings down her legs, and sighed when she curled her bare toes into the plush beige carpet. Yanking the tails of her white eyelet blouse from the tight waistband of her skirt, she ventured into the big bath adjoining the bedroom.

There, right out of her dreams, sat a huge porcelain tub supported by fancy silver claw feet. She bent, twirled both gleaming swan-necked silver faucets, and jumped back laughing when a rush of steaming hot water poured forcefully into the deep tub.

Various kinds of soap and oils lined a silver and glass cabinet directly above the tub. Not one but three different size silver-handled brushes hung on silver pegs by the cabinet. Dozens of snowy white towels and washcloths filled floor-to-ceiling shelves along one entire wall of the spacious bath. Thrown over an armless beige velvet chair near the tub was a black silk robe.

Diane had never undressed so quickly in her life. In seconds her soiled clothes lay in a discarded heap on the floor and she was splashing into the hot, steamy bath. She stayed there for the next half hour, humming the same tune Star had been absently whistling in the kitchen.

After a luxurious soak in the oversize tub, Diane came down the stairs wearing Star's too-large black silk robe. Her feet were bare. Her coal black hair, falling down her back, was still damp from her shampoo.

She found Star in the kitchen, carving the honey-baked ham. Her bare feet had made no sound. He didn't hear her enter. He didn't turn around. Diane stood in the doorway for a moment, silently watching him, fascinated with the play and pull of muscles in his back, the slipping and sliding of his shoulder blades beneath the fabric of his snowy white shirt. How well she remembered the feel of that long, perfect back when it was bare. The glorious texture of the smooth, hot flesh. The strain and stretch of powerful muscle and sinew beneath her fingertips.

Softly Diane spoke Star's name. Sharp-bladed knife in hand, he turned, and Diane felt her heartbeat quicken alarmingly. His tanned face was smoothly shaven. His silver-winged raven hair, tied back with a black leather string was, like hers, still damp from his bath. The white shirt that pulled so appealingly across his back was open midway down his bronzed chest. Beige, perfectly tailored trousers were snug around his trim hips and down his long legs. On his feet were beaded moccasins.

Star's dark eyes widened, then narrowed as he looked at Diane. Never had he seen her look more adorable. Clean. Cute. Young. His first impulse was to smile at her and tell her how clean and cute and young she looked. But he didn't do it. He knew that she would interpret any gentleness or kindness on his part as a sign of weakness. It was crucial that he hold her at arm's length so she'd know that none of her feminine wiles would work.

"The food smells wonderful." Diane ignored the cool expression on Star's handsome face. Slowly she advanced on him, her watchful violet eyes searching for any telling signal that might betray him. With the unerring instinct of a predator closely watching its prey for some sign of weakness, she moved toward him, her long pale legs winking in and out of the black robe's front opening.

"Everything's ready." His voice was low, level.

His hard face and dark eyes gave nothing away. But Diane caught the minute expanding of his broad chest against the white linen of his shirt, the involuntary contracting of his flat belly below his ribs. Heartened, she moved in closer.

When she stood so close she had to tip her head back to look up at him, she said, "I borrowed your robe. I hope you don't mind."

Star backed away and shook his head. "That's what it's there for."

Diane nodded. "My clothes were all soiled. I couldn't bear the thought of putting them back on. So I didn't. How do I look?"

She held her arms out and spun in a circle. The robe was much too large. It reached almost to her slender ankles. She'd rolled the sleeves up over her hands. The tasseled sash was tied tightly around her narrow waist, but the swell of her pale breasts was visible between the parted lapels. Star swallowed hard. He had the sinking feeling that beneath that black silk robe she wore nothing at all.

"Well?" Diane, smiling, turned back to face him.

Everything about her curved in feline invitation. Her remarkable violet bedroom eyes. The lines of her high, classic cheekbones. The upturned corners of her full-lipped mouth. The lush feminine curves beneath the shiny black silk. Just looking at her had such an erotic impact on Star that he felt his knees buckle.

Quickly turning back to carving the ham, he said over his shoulder, "You look fine. If you'll spoon those baked apples onto a couple of plates, we'll be ready to dine."

In the large, tasteful dining room where gaslit crystal chandeliers cast a warm, mellow glow over everything, Diane sat across from Star at a long mahogany table covered with a pristine white cloth.

She complimented him on the succulent ham and delicious baked apples. He commended her on the fluffy potatoes. They sipped fine wine from sparkling tulip-shaped glasses, and Diane made light, pleasant dinner conversation.

The food was appetizing. The wine was superb. The atmosphere was relaxing. Slowly, skillfully Diane began to draw out Star by first talking about herself.

She began by relating an incident that happened when she was a little girl, then went on to tell him about losing her mother and father at an early age. She didn't really remember them at all. Nodding, Star said he'd lost his father, Chief Red Fox, when he was three, so he knew exactly what she meant. He couldn't remember the chief. Couldn't recall how he looked.

"But you remember your mother, I'm sure." Diane prompted.

"Yes." A pensive smile lifted the corners of Star's sculpted lips. "I was ten when Daughter-of-the-Stars died of a fever. I remember her well. I loved her very much. She was so soft-spoken, so gentle, and so pretty. She had the most beautiful shiny black hair I've ever seen." His eyes held a wistful look. "I used to brush her long, heavy hair by the hour while she told me stories about my father. I wish I could have known him. My mother said that he—" Abruptly Star quit speaking. He cleared his throat. "Listen to me. I must sound like a—"

"No, Star. No, you don't." Diane's tone was one of warm understanding. "Please. Tell me more. What did your mother tell you about your father?"

They lingered at the table long after they'd finished their meal and the dishes had been cleared away. Uncorking a second bottle of the excellent wine, they talked quietly in the comfort of the dining room, as two old friends might. Unobtrusively Diane asked Star questions about his childhood, about his present life in Nevada. And she listened intently as he spoke of the happy times at Wind River, of the loneliness he'd felt when he first left the reservation and went away to school.

He spoke of the four years he spent at the Colorado School of Mines. He was telling her how valuable those years were, how much he had learned there, when Diane, abruptly interrupting, said, "Star, tell the truth, was it awful for you there? How did you feel that first day at college when those white students held you down and cut off your black braids?"

Star looked steadily into her arresting violet eyes. "Naked," he said flippantly, still unwilling to share his personal hurts and disappointments with her or anyone.

"Oh, Star," she said softly, "you *were* hurt. Of course, you were, and I'm sorry." Diane longed to reach out and touch him, but it was not the time to do so. "I'm so sorry."

Star shrugged, poured more wine into her glass, smiled, and said, "I looked much better without the braids."

Then, hardly realizing he was doing it, Star sat there across from the beautiful violet-eyed woman and revealed to her a great deal more about himself than he'd ever told anyone else. And he listened as Diane told him about herself, her life on the road when she was a girl. The political position in Washington, D.C., she'd left to help her grandfather's failing troupe. She spoke candidly of her regrets, her hopes, her dreams.

She shared with Star her growing worry over the Colonel's financially troubled show. Said she didn't blame Star for hating the Colonel, but the aging showman was her grandfather and she adored him, faults and all.

"I'm so afraid," she confided, "that Pawnee Bill is going to make good on this threat to take over the show. If he does, it will kill the Colonel."

Star listened attentively, his dark eyes never leaving Diane's lovely, expressive face as she disclosed how deeply in debt her grandfather's traveling wild west show was and that if something didn't happen soon, he would surely lose it.

The hour grew late.

Diane had become charmingly tipsy from the wine. Star was enchanted by the appealing young woman in his black silk robe. So enchanted he didn't pull away when she suddenly stopped in mid-sentence, rose up to her knees on her padded, high-backed chair, leaned across the table, and curled her fingers around the wide silver bracelet on his wrist.

"Tell me about the scar," she said, slurring her words slightly.

Lounging comfortably back in his chair, Star said gently, "Now, Diane, you know all about the scar. Golden Star surely told you."

"I want *you* to tell me." Diane released her hold on the bracelet, placed both elbows on the table, and put her face in her hands.

Star smiled. "Strange as it seems, I don't remember a thing about it."

Diane laughed. "Gosh, I'm surprised." Then: "Daughter-of-the-Stars surely told you everything. So you tell me. Please, Star. Please."

Star raised his wineglass and took a drink. "I'll tell you, but then it's time you go up to bed. Agreed?"

"Agreed," she quickly assured him.

Face cupped in her supporting hands, elbows on the dining table, Diane knelt there in her chair like a child, eagerly waiting. Star began to speak in that low, flat voice she found so irresistible.

"It was thirty-five years ago. A hot, windy July night in 1860. I was one week old and asleep in my crib in a small frame house which sat on the banks of the Nevada's Carson River."

Diane's wide-eyed gaze was riveted to Star's dark face as he spoke of the long-ago night which had so drastically altered his life.

His black-sapphire eyes half hooded, Star took a drink of wine, swallowed slowly, and said, "Deep in the night a fire erupted in the valley. It swiftly spread across the rain-starved plain and moved toward the house where I slept beside my parents' bed.

"Just before the deadly flames reached us, a mighty Shoshoni chieftain and a small band of his braves rode out of the trees on the mountain high above. Chief Red Fox spotted the frame house in harm's way. The chief immediately kicked his big paint and came plunging down the mountainside, his warriors following. Before they could reach the house, it was fully engulfed in flames."

Diane's face was now screwed up into a worried frown. Her wide eyes had darkened to deep purple. Engrossed, she stared at Star, waiting, listening intently.

"The heat was fierce." His voice dropped, was barely above a whisper. "The roar of fire, the breaking of glass, and the creaking of burning timber were almost deafening. But Chief Red Fox felt drawn to the blaze. As if a powerful voice from the Spirit World were telling him he must go inside.

"The brave chief kneed his terrified mount closer, so close his face was punished by the blistering heat and his eyes stung. Undaunted, Chief Red Fox moved closer. And closer. Until he heard the faint, unmistakable sound of a baby crying."

Star fell silent. Diane swallowed anxiously.

"It was you. You were crying. You were the crying baby trapped in the burning house," she said breathlessly.

"Yes," Star calmly replied. "The chief leaped off his horse and ran straight into the burning house. He found me crying in my crib beside my dead parents. He snatched me up, wrapped me in a blanket, and crashed through a window to safety just as the roof collapsed."

Star told Diane all he had learned of that fateful night when the Shoshoni chieftain had saved him from the fire. He was a master storyteller, and his soft, low narration was filled with colorful details and exciting drama. Diane felt as if the events were taking place before her very eyes.

She listened enraptured as Starkeeper led up to the climax of the
fascinating and true tale.

"It was nearing dawn when Chief Red Fox rode back into his High
Sierra stronghold with me in his arms. He dismounted and ducked into
his lodge, ordering everyone out. Hopefully he laid me beside his distraught young wife, who had lost their firstborn son only days before.

"Daughter-of-the-Stars regained her lost strength the minute she saw
me. The beautiful Indian princess's black eyes flashed with angry denial
when the chief told her I was the white man's son."

Again Star paused. Seconds passed before he spoke again. A hint of a
smile touched his sensual lips as he looked back into the past.

"Daughter-of-the-Stars boldly grabbed the sharp hunting knife from
Red Fox's waist scabbard, took my right wrist, slashed an X on the
inside, bent, and kissed the blood away. She pricked the tip of her
finger, stuck it into my mouth, and I automatically sucked on it. Then
my beautiful Shoshoni mother possessively clutched me to her breasts
and defiantly announced to the chieftain, 'Now we are same blood! My
son. Mine!' "

His story told, Star concluded by saying, "So you see, I do have
Shoshoni blood. I'm Indian, Diane."

Diane said nothing.

She looked into his beautiful navy blue eyes, and her hands again
went to the wide silver bracelet on his right wrist. Gently she turned his
dark hand over atop the white tablecloth. She carefully pried the wide
bracelet apart, slipped it off, and laid it aside.

For a long moment she held his hand in both of her own and studied
the perfect white X adorning the inside of his dark wrist.

"Yes, Star," she murmured, "you are Indian. My darling Indian, my
love."

And Diane bent her head and pressed her open lips to his wrist,
lovingly kissing the telltale white scar.

Chapter 35

Diane's silky tongue was like liquid fire on Star's flesh, and the words she'd softly spoken rang loudly in his ears. "My darling Indian, my love . . . my darling Indian, my love . . . my love . . . my love . . ."

Diane felt the tendons in Star's dark wrist constrict beneath her lips. She pressed the tip of her tongue to the center of the white *X*, then slowly lifted her head. Their eyes met. Hers dreamy, adoring. His narrowed, skeptical.

Star drew his hand free. He pushed back his chair and stood up. He hesitated a moment, then leaned across the table, reaching for Diane. He plucked her out of the chair and lifted her up onto the table with such swift ease it took her breath away.

Diane sat back on her heels atop the white-clothed dining table, expectancy shining out of her darkening violet eyes. Her pulse quickened alarmingly as Star's right hand went into her hair, his lean fingers tangling in the heavy raven locks. He looked at her mouth for a long time.

Diane's heart began to pound with sweet anticipation. Honed muscles curved beneath Star's perfectly tailored white shirt, and his handsome face betrayed all the emotions he was fighting so hard to conceal.

"Star," she said, placing a splayed hand on his chest, "my beautiful Indian. My love."

Star groaned aloud.

And then . . . their long-delayed embrace, full of emotion and past any misunderstanding. His lips on hers were eager, urgent, wildly exciting. Diane thrilled to the mastery of his kiss and to the lean, deft hand that moved between them to yank decisively at the tied sash of her black silk robe.

When finally their lips separated, their hearts were beating wildly, their blood was running swiftly, hotly through their veins.

"Sweetheart," Star muttered hoarsely, "I'm sorry. I'm sorry for all the—"

"Don't, darling. It doesn't matter. I love you," she whispered breathlessly. "I do, Star, I do."

"Diane . . . ah, baby . . ."

Both knew the idea of waiting until they climbed the stairs to his bed was out of the question. They couldn't wait. The burning need they shared could not be denied nor delayed. They wanted each other.

Right now. Right here.

Star climbed up onto the table with Diane, dropping on one knee to kneel before her. "God, I want you," he told her hoarsely. "Sweetheart, I have to have you."

"I'm yours, Star," she assured him, realizing sadly that he hadn't said he loved her. "Yours, whenever or wherever you want me. I love you, my darling."

And then all manner of civility and restraint disappeared as pent-up passions were swiftly unleashed. Both were so anxious they began frantically undressing each other right where they were.

Whispering his name like a litany over and over, Diane clawed at the buttons of Star's white shirt. Murmuring tender endearments to her, Star snatched the untied sash from Diane's robe and tossed it away. Her violet eyes darkening to purple with growing arousal, Diane rose fully up on her knees, frantically tugging the long tails of Star's shirt from his tight beige trousers. His dark eyes gleaming with fierce sexual heat, Star swept Diane's robe apart, pushed it to her shoulders. Heart fluttering in her naked breasts, Diane's searching fingers went to Star's belt buckle and then to the buttons of his beige trousers.

They anxiously kissed and intimately caressed and wildly wrestled halfway out of their clothing, so hot and impatient for each other they were incapable of waiting until they were totally undressed.

When their yearning bodies came eagerly together, one leg of Star's beige trousers was still twisted stubbornly around his ankle, snagged and caught on the moccasin that remained on his right foot. A bunched-up sleeve of Diane's black robe was tangled around the elbow of her left arm, the robe itself swirled out and draped over the table's edge.

It didn't matter.

Lying flat on her back on the long dining table with the darkly handsome Star looming over her, Diane felt pleasure swamping her. She thought she would surely faint when Star came swiftly into her, the heat and hardness of him awesome. Wondrous. Her head was leaning back into his cupped hand, neither of them kissing, but their mouths were very close, her lips full and parted.

As soon as Star thrust fully, deeply into Diane, he drew her long, slender legs up around his back, leaned down, and kissed her parted lips. Diane moaned into his mouth, tightened her strong thighs around his waist, and arched up to him, wanting to feel him move within her. Star wanted the same thing.

He slid his hands up her delicate ribs to her underarms. He rose onto his knees, bringing Diane up with him. His hot, hungry mouth remaining fused with hers, he sat back on his heels, spread his knees wide, and settled Diane astride his hard thighs.

Diane finally tore her burning lips from his. Her breath was loud and rapid, her face awash with color. She wrapped her arms around Star's neck and trembled with pleasure when he lowered his head to her breast, the hot tip of his tongue flicking out to sear her aching nipples. She inhaled the fragrance of his clean raven hair and forcefully ground her pelvis down on the hard, pulsing flesh rapidly expanding inside her.

Star raised his head. He drew a deep, ragged breath and said with appealing honesty, "God, you're good. You're loving me so good, baby. So damned good."

Diane smiled, pleased, clasped her hands behind his dark head, stiffened her arms, and leaned back to look into his sultry dark eyes. Star's strong hands were at her waist, urging, guiding, bringing her to him. For a few lovely seconds the pair enjoyed the incredible thrill of watching each other closely as they engaged in the age-old act of lovemaking.

It was fleeting joy that had no equal. Diane observed and savored the changing expressions on Star's handsome face. The love shining out of his beautiful dark eyes. The laying open of his heart and soul to her. Star experienced the same intense thrill watching her.

It was electrifying.

Their pleasure swiftly escalated, and too soon the initial tingles and spasms of their shared climax began. Both in excellent health with perfectly toned bodies which moved together like well-oiled machines, the excited pair made very energetic, highly physical love. While the chandelier above their heads cast honeyed light over their moving, surging bodies and a strong night breeze ruffled the heavy curtains at the room's open windows yet did nothing to cool their ardor, Diane and Star wildly, shamelessly mated atop that cloth-draped dining table.

"Star . . . Star . . ." Diane gasped as the muscles across her flat stomach constricted in an erotic spasm.

"Yes, sweetheart, yes," Star said, his hands filled with the rounded cheeks of her bare bottom, drawing her to him, his driving strokes becoming faster, deeper.

Diane gasped again, arching against him. She could feel the thrusting vibrations coming up through her. Her hands curled around the nape of his neck, her purple eyes widened, and she cried out as together they climaxed, the rapture so intense it was frightening.

When finally the fierce explosion had passed, Diane's face was flushed, her hair damp at the temples. Her head sagged to Star's shoulder, and she pressed her palms against his sweaty chest. They stayed like that for a time, locked together, panting, resting, regaining their lost breaths.

His hands gently stroking Diane's slender back, Star sighed heavily and began to smile against her tousled dark hair. Her face pressed into the curve of his neck and shoulder, Diane, moaning softly and kissing his slick flesh, began to smile as well. Star locked his wrists behind Diane's waist. His body began to shake with laughter. Her smile broadening, Diane raised her head, looked at his handsome, laughing face, and she, too, began to laugh.

The gloriously sated pair laughed at the absurdity of the situation. Suddenly it seemed hilarious that the two of them were naked on their knees atop a white-clothed table in a formal dining room. So they laughed. They laughed at themselves. They laughed at each other. They laughed with pure, unadulterated joy.

Faces hot, tears rolling down their cheeks, they fell tiredly over onto the table. And continued to laugh. They laughed until their stomachs hurt. They laughed because they were together, because they were happy, because they were in love. They laughed because they *could* laugh. Because there was no one to hear them, no one to see them, no one to think they'd gone quite mad. They laughed because here in this delightfully remote mountain mansion they were free to laugh and to make love on the dining table. Or on the living-room floor. Or outside on the balcony if they wished.

So they lay sprawled there on the table, their naked bodies entangled, laughing and kissing and shaking their heads, enjoying to the fullest the frolic and fun and the freedom that was theirs.

At last Star coughed, cleared his throat, and said, "Think we can make it up to my bedroom now?"

"We can give it a try," said Diane, not at all certain she could.

Star rolled up into a sitting position and reached for Diane. She sat up beside him and pushed her heavy hair out of her eyes. Then promptly went into fits of new laughter when she saw that Star had on one moccasin and that a twisted leg of his beige trousers was still around his muscular calf.

Laughing with her, Star kicked off the moccasin, watching it sail across the room. Then he swung his legs over the table's edge, straightened his tangled trousers, drew them up both legs, and slid off the table into them. Buttoning the pants up over his flat brown belly, he turned back to face Diane. Up on her knees, she was drawing on the black silk robe. She looked about for the sash, saw it draped over a silver candelabrum atop the buffet.

"Star, will you hand me that—"

"Nope," he said, scooped her off the table, and carried her out of the dining room. He walked through the living room, into the foyer, climbed the marble stairs, went down the long corridor, and stepped inside the one room of the house which Diane had not yet seen.

His bedroom.

"Star," Diane exclaimed when he kicked the door closed behind them, "this is your room?"

Nodding, he said, "Mine. And yours. Ours."

"Darling, it's—it's fabulous." She squirmed, wanting him to lower her to her feet so she could have a look around.

Diane had never seen anything to compare with Star's spacious bedroom. The entire back wall was of gleaming plate glass. Over his shoulder she looked out through the wall of glass at the towering pines and twisted rock formations, silvered by the moonlight. She saw the leaves of the trees trembling in the chill night winds, the clouds drifting across the sky.

"Star, put me down. . . . I want to—"

"Tomorrow, sweetheart," said Star, moving with determined strides across the room.

He reached the oversize bed and continued to hold Diane with one arm. With the other he made short work of peeling the sumptuous fox fur counterpane to the foot of the bed and turning down the beige silk sheets. Still holding her, Star relieved Diane of the black robe, dropped it to the plush beige carpet, then leaned over and gently laid her in the middle of his bed.

When he straightened to unbutton his pants, Diane sat up and looked about, her violet eyes round. She touched the bed's tall headboard, which was plushly padded and upholstered in raw silk of a deep rust hue. The same raw silk covered the walls of the bedroom.

"Star," she said, "I've never seen such a big bed. A half dozen people could sleep in it." She stretched her legs out and rubbed her toes against the soft fur counterpane.

"Not as long as I own the place," Star said in that low, flat voice as he crawled in beside her.

Diane flashed him a bright smile. But when he put a long arm around her to draw her to him, she braced a hand against his chest, and said, "Can't I look around, Star? You know I've never been in this room." They lay on their sides, facing each other.

"Later," he told her, smoothing her hair back off her bare shoulder. "Right now I want to make love to you."

"Darling, you just made love to me." Her violet eyes flashed in the shadowy light.

Star smiled, drew her long, slender leg up over his hip, and said, "No, sweetheart, I don't mean like that. I want to love you properly. To love you the way you should be loved." His hand glided slowly up her thigh and over her hip to the small of her back. "Kiss me. Kiss me, Diane."

His lips touched hers, and Diane opened her mouth to receive his kiss. Star's mouth answered with a slow burning, lingering caress. With his lips on hers, he stroked her back, up and down, with the sensitive tips of his long fingers. Diane sighed deeply, and Star continued kissing her sweetly, tenderly, letting her know they had all the time in the world.

He lovingly stroked her shoulders, her back, her buttocks, until finally his hand slipped between the rounded cheeks of her bottom. Diane squirmed, sighed, and slid her knee higher on Star's body, up to his trim waist. Star moved his hand farther forward, and with slow, infinite tenderness he began intimately caressing her. Diane's mouth left his. She settled back on the pillow and looked into his dark, flashing eyes.

"I love you, Star," she said breathlessly. "You make me so happy."

"I want to make you happy, sweetheart," he said softly, "in bed and out. If you stay with me for a lifetime or leave me tomorrow—"

"I'll never leave you," she breathed, and her eyes slid closed in ecstasy.

Star's fingers were gliding easily now, wet with the hot silkiness flowing from her. He was rigidly erect but firmly resolved not to hurry her or himself, to take plenty of time, to make this a sweet and lasting act of bliss.

After a while Star flexed his hips and surged his pelvis forward, intentionally allowing Diane to feel the rigid hardness of his pulsing erection. He heard her catch her breath.

His caressing hand left her as Diane's arms tightened around him. She turned onto her back and pulled him on top of her. He took her hand in his and drew it down between their naked bodies. His hand fell away. Diane's hand shyly enclosed him. Then her bare body shuddered pleasantly as that hot, hard power involuntarily surged against her loving fingers. Awed, she drew a shallow breath and cautiously guided him into her.

Star made slow, caring love to Diane. Sweetly, gently he took her. He waited for her. Adept now. His studied self-control back in place. Well taught he was. And willing to teach this beautiful woman. Willing as well to learn from her.

Holding back, prolonging their pleasure, Star purposely waited until Diane was so aroused she frantically called his name and bucked her hips, wanting him as deep as he could go. Only then did he give it all to her.

"Sweet love," he murmured, flexing his hips and buttocks, driving rhythmically into her, lifting her to him.

"Star, Star," she screamed, clutching his biceps, her purple eyes wide with shock and wonder.

"Yes, baby. Yes, sweetheart. Oh, yes . . . Diane."

"Staaaaarrrrrrrr," she screamed as love's most pleasurable physical gift was generously given to her by the man she loved.

Diane unselfishly returned the favor, making certain that Star received a like offering. Indeed, he did. Anxiously he accepted the treasured gift of love's extraordinary carnal joy. And Diane experienced a wonderful mixture of feminine pride and tender protectiveness as she clung tightly to Star while he spasmed in total fulfillment, calling her name. And then Star made Diane the happiest woman in all the world.

"I love you, Diane," he said at last, his low, flat voice breaking with emotion. "Sweetheart, I love you. I love you. Oh, God, Diane, honey, I love you!"

Chapter 36

➤➤➤➤ "How would you like to take a hot bath with one tired, dirty Indian?"

It was a half hour later. Star lay sprawled out on his back, totally spent. Diane lay quietly enfolded in his long right arm, snuggled close. When he spoke, she struggled up onto an elbow. She looked at Star's face. His eyes were closed, the long dusky lashes making spiky crescents above the prominent cheekbones. His cruelly sensual lips were relaxed and slightly parted over perfect white teeth. His too-long blue-black hair tumbled errantly over his high forehead and spilled across the beige-cased pillow.

Diane let her gaze leisurely slide down Star's lean frame. The steely length of his limbs was potent even in the relaxed attitude in which he was lying. She smiled dreamily. His superb male body held the same dangerous strength as before, but she was no longer the least bit afraid of all that formidable power.

From a man who looked like Star she had once expected savage cruelty. Instead he'd shown amazing gentleness, and that made him all the more appealing, all the more exciting.

Happy as she'd never been in her life, Diane leaned over and impulsively kissed Star's drum-tight brown belly.

Star's hand lazily lifted, came to rest on her bent head. In that flat, unexcitable voice, he said, "Is that a yes?"

Her lips still on his smooth, warm flesh, Diane replied, "If the tired, dirty Indian is you, then I'm all for it." She kissed his belly again.

Star cocked one dark eye open as his fingers tunneled into her wild mane of raven hair. "You keep that up, Paleface, and there'll be no hot bath."

Smiling, Diane raised her head, looked up at him. "Are you threatening me, Redman?" She laughed gaily. Then screeched loudly, "Starkeeper!" as he cast off his lethargy, yanked her up, pushed her down onto her back, and rolled atop her.

His bare, broad chest crushing down on her breasts, his face inches above her own, Star turned his most menacing expression on her. He had the look of a villain with his dark face and his cruelly sensual lips thinned and stern.

He said, "White girl mighty foolish. Laugh at big, bad warrior."

Diane continued to laugh. And she laughed all the harder when he growled and buried his face in the curve of her neck and shoulder, as if he were the big bad wolf, going to eat her up. She laughed and shrieked and beat on his back while he moved steadily down her body, snorting and biting and blowing on her stomach the way an adult teasingly devils a small child.

Highly ticklish, Diane tossed and squirmed and shouted for him to stop, laughing all the while, loving every minute of it. Ripples of laughter causing her bare body to jerk spasmodically, she grabbed double handfuls of his dark hair and yanked hard, warning him that he'd "better stop it this instant or I'll—"

Star stopped before the sentence was completed. Pressing a wet kiss to her quivering belly, he slid agilely off the bed and stood up. He swiftly pivoted with the natural grace of a dancer, leaned over, encircled Diane's narrow waist, and lifted her to her feet atop the bed. He stood at the bed's edge, knees braced against the mattress, his arms wrapped tightly around Diane's hips, his head thrown back looking up at her.

He said, "Time I take you to magic waters, wash smug smile off pretty white face."

Still laughing, Diane shook her head about, her long, tangled hair swishing around her face and shoulders. "Un—unless you—you plan to —to"—she could hardly speak for giggling—"to . . . wash my mouth . . . out with soap"—she drew a strangled breath, wiped at the tears in her eyes—"I don't think—think you can make me stop laughing."

"Show you I can," he said, promptly tossing her over his shoulder, wrapping a long arm around her thighs, and heading for the bath with her screaming and struggling and kicking.

And laughing.

Star was right. Diane's riotous laughter soon turned to long sighs of quiet contentment as he tenderly kissed her, their lips melded in a soft, liquid movement of unhurried exploration.

They sat in a huge square tub of gleaming black marble with silver fixtures which was filled to the brim with thick, rich suds and hot, steamy water. The giant tub rested along a high-ceilinged wall fashioned entirely of the same black Carrara marble. Directly across the plushly carpeted bath from the black marble tub was a wall of glass, just like the one in the bedroom. A third wall, adjacent to the tub, was solid mirror from floor to ceiling. The fourth was row upon row of black walnut drawers with silver handles, in the center of which was a door leading into a dressing room.

When he'd kissed her into silent submission and total relaxation, Star deftly turned Diane around to sit comfortably between his spread knees. He tied her heavy hair up off her neck with a white leather string, then positioned her so that her back rested against his chest, her head on his left shoulder.

All traces of laughter were gone.

But Diane was smiling foolishly, her eyes closed, as she sat there luxuriating in the steamy chin-deep suds with Star. Sighing softly, she opened her eyes. Through the wall of glass she watched as a chill north wind blew clouds across the Nevada moon. It was magical. Like a wonderful dream from which she never wanted to awaken. Such great fun to be gloriously naked and comfortably warm and at the same time feel as if she were outside in the elements.

"Star?" she said lazily.

His head resting against the tub's padded headrest, Star murmured without opening his eyes, "Yes, sweetheart."

"I like all this glass, but aren't you afraid someone might see us?"

Star's hooded eyes came open. His dark head came up off the tub's rim. He lowered his lips to Diane's slippery shoulder, kissed it, and said, "Sweetheart, this is private property. I own it. Everyone knows I own it. There's not a man in the state of Nevada—white or Indian—who'd be foolish enough to ride onto this property unless he came up the front drive." He turned his face in, brushed his open lips to the side of her neck. "Relax, my love. Our privacy is assured here."

"Our privacy is assured here." Diane softly repeated his statement, liking the sound of it, liking the thought of it. Liking the feel of Star's warm mouth on her wet flesh.

It suddenly dawned on Diane that no one knew where they were. They were naked together in Star's black marble tub at his remote mountain mansion in Nevada and nobody knew it. Nobody! They were safe and alone in their own little private world. How exciting! How grand it would be if they could remain here in sweet seclusion for eternity. Or for at least a few precious days before they contacted anyone.

"Star," she murmured, her hand coming up to tangle in his silver-streaked black hair at his temple. "We do have total privacy here, don't we?"

"Absolute. No one knows we're here," he said, echoing her thoughts. He slowly raised his head. "We're all alone. Just you and me."

Diane turned to look up at him. "Do you know what I'm thinking?" She let her head fall back against his wet shoulder.

"Yes," he said, "but we can't. Tomorrow we are taking the train to meet your family in—"

"Star, let's don't." Interrupting, Diane raised a hand to his chest, trailed her fingers down its center. "Let's stay here."

She turned the rest of the way around to face him, shooting a long, slender leg across his body and bringing it down to sit astride him.

"Sweetheart, we can't. We have to catch that train to San Francisco."

"Why?" She slid her hands around his ribs. "Who'll know the difference?"

Star drew a long breath and gently cupped her face in his hands. All his love in his eyes, he said softly, "Diane, I love you. I want to marry you."

"I want the same thing, Star, but for now I just want to be alone here with you, without the world intruding."

"God, honey, if I had my way, I'd keep you locked up here with me forever. But be sensible." His thumb rubbed back and forth over her soft lips. "I'll have a hard enough time getting your grandfather's permission to marry you."

"I don't need the Colonel's consent," Diane quickly informed him.

"But I do." said Star. "And you do, too, sweetheart. You love me, but if marrying me meant never seeing your grandparents again, you would never be happy as my wife. And I'd be unhappy because you were unhappy." He sighed wearily, closed his eyes, opened them. "Jesus, Diane, don't forget, I kidnapped you. I'm guilty of a very serious crime and one for which I'm sure your grandfather would like to see me hanged."

"The Colonel is guilty of the same crime, darling," Diane reminded him. "You were kidnapped. In chains, dragged down out of the mountains and thrown into a cage."

"Ah, Diane, that was different. Besides, the old Colonel didn't do it. He wasn't—"

"My grandfather is responsible," Diane stated emphatically. "It was the Colonel's show, his employees who brought you in, his decision to hold you against your will." She ran a hand up over Star's slippery chest. "My grandfather did you a terrible wrong, but I love him, so I'll forgive him." She paused, looked into his navy eyes. "And you will forgive him, too, because you love me. Won't you?"

"Yes, of course."

"Well, he'll forgive you for the same reason. He loves me." She flashed Star a brilliant smile and added, "In time he'll learn that you're actually a kind and caring man. You'll learn the same thing about him." She leaned forward, kissed the hard, flat muscles of his chest.

"Maybe you're right," Star said when she raised her head.

"I am. I know I am." Her lovely smile was disarming. "So can we please wait awhile before we go to San Francisco?"

Captivated by her smile, Star asked, "How long?"

"A week!"

He shook his head. "Three days at most."

"Five," she anxiously protested.

"Four. And that's my final offer."

Diane flung her arms around his neck. "Oh, thank you, Star, thank you." She tipped her head back, closed her eyes, and murmured, "Four whole days! Four wonderful days alone here. Four fabulous days with no one on earth knowing where we are—a lovers' holiday."

The idea was as appealing to Star as it was to Diane. He wrapped a hand around the back of her neck, leaned forward, and kissed her. Diane's lips immediately softened, opened. She felt his tongue probing. He drew her closer. She felt his heart beat against hers. She felt his lean frame shudder.

And soon she felt his body changing as his kisses, gentle at first, became more demanding. Her hands slid up to play along the back of his neck. His strong fingertips found the small of her back, pressed her closer. So close she could feel his growing erection pulsing and pressing against the ultra-sensitive flesh between her open legs.

Star reluctantly tore his heated lips from hers. He could tell that Diane was growing aroused, just as he was. He loved to watch her face, the suggestion of sensuality that was always there now heightened by her response to him. The lovely violet eyes had deepened to purple beneath the long, lowering lashes. The earthy, kissable mouth was glistening, the lips full and half parted. Her breathing had changed. It was shallow, short.

Diane *had* become aroused. So aroused she was already wondering if it was possible to make love seated in a tubful of sudsy water. She was also torn. Torn between the desire to close her eyes and keep them tightly closed as if to shut out the rest of the world forever and the desire to open them wide and enjoy these precious moments in this private paradise where the most exciting man she'd ever known was naked and throbbing against her.

In a gesture of sexual intimacy Diane dipped her hands under the water's warm, soapy surface and timidly wrapped them around Star's fully formed erection. Surprised but pleased, he reciprocated, his hands moving under the water, intimately caressing the insides of Diane's pale thighs.

"Sweetheart," he said, swallowing with difficulty, "do you know what you're doing to me?"

"No. Yes. I mean, I'm not totally sure," she admitted frankly. "But I'm curious. Do you mind?"

He shook his head and gritted his teeth when the fingers of her right hand slid slowly, searchingly up to toy with the velvet-smooth head of his throbbing tumescence. Appealingly curious, Diane explored and stroked and acquainted herself with his fascinating male body. She raised her eyes to his face and watched him. His hooded eyes were half closed, and his dark face flushed with heat as her fingertips gently examined the awesome hardness jerking involuntarily from her touch.

"Star, darling?"

"Hmm?" was all he could manage. A vein throbbed on his forehead, and his heart thundered in his chest.

"Is it possible—I can't help wondering—to make love while we're in the water?"

His voice flat but strained, Star said, "Jesus, baby, you have the answer right there in your hands."

"Yes, I guess I do." Then, almost shyly: "Star, will you please make love to me here in your marble tub?"

"If you insist," was his low, clipped answer before he took her fully in his arms.

Diane learned it certainly was possible to make love in the water, and it was quite pleasurable as well. But not half so pleasurable as when, her body a part of his, Star rose to his feet and climbed out of the marble tub. Dripping water and soap suds, he fell to his knees on the plush beige carpet and carefully laid her on her back, following her down.

The lovemaking continued uninterrupted. This was a truly passionate love affair, and both knew that in the other they had finally met their match.

Her eyes opening and closing in erotic pleasure, Diane was rewarded with visual impressions to match the incredible physical sensations.

Outside the gleaming glass wall was a magical wilderness wonderland shimmering in the silvery moonlight. And in the mirrored wall a darkly handsome man making passionate, beautiful love to an eagerly receptive woman who looked remarkably like herself.

The experience was unbelievable.

She was watching the naked pair making uninhibited love in the wild outdoors. At the same time she was warm and comfortable and very much a participant in the intimate act.

In perfect symmetry the pair of lovers in the mirror and the couple making love outdoors moved together, sighed together, even climaxed at exactly the same moment as Star and Diane. But Diane never noticed.

Her purple eyes were tightly closed as she writhed in the deep, shattering throes of ecstasy.

Chapter 37

 Golden days.
Silver nights.
Total perfection.

A brief magical interlude of absolute bliss stolen out of time and place.

Pagans in their own private paradise. Hot-blooded lovers surrendering to desire at any hour of the day or night. Innocent children playing and laughing together. Good friends holding hands and talking quietly at twilight. Close companions, comfortable in their silences, enjoying the peaceful solitude.

They were all these things, Diane and Star, in the following four lovely days, changing roles like a couple of chameleons.

On their very first morning in the mansion Diane awakened at dawn despite the fact that she'd slept for little more than an hour. She stretched lazily, sighed softly, and turned her head to look at the slumbering Star.

Her bare stomach did an immediate flip-flop. Her face pinkened at the vivid recollection of the previous night's wildly ardent lovemaking. Blushing, she squeezed her eyes tightly shut while her full lips curved into an embarrassed smile.

Too happy and excited to attempt falling back to sleep, Diane again opened her eyes. She considered waking Star. She didn't do it. This handsome, gentle man she dearly loved was tired. She'd let him rest. For a while at least.

Very slowly, very carefully Diane disengaged herself from Star's long, imprisoning arms. An inch at a time she scooted over to the huge bed's edge and cautiously sat up.

She rose silently and looked about for something to wear. She spotted—tossed over the back of a chair—the blue collarless pullover shirt that Star had worn on the train. Diane stole quietly across the room, picked up the shirt, and poked her head through the neck opening. She shoved her arms up into the sleeves and pulled the blue shirt down over her body to cover her nakedness. The long-tailed shirt concealed her bare breasts and bottom, but left her pale thighs and long legs uncovered.

A silver-framed door of glass with a gleaming silver knob at one end of the glass wall opened onto an outside balcony fashioned of cedar planks. Diane looked one last time at the sleeping Star, smiled, and slipped out onto the balcony. Barefoot, she crossed the broad cedar gallery to stand at the waist-high railing. Mindless of the early-morning chill, she gripped the smooth rail and stood taking in the marvelous view.

She loved Star's beautiful state of Nevada. She loved his big, comfortable house and its spectacular setting. The landscape spread out before her was nothing short of stunning.

The rocky peaks of Sun Mountain glowing like live coals in the rising September sun. And far, far beyond, the giant redwoods of California's High Sierra, their reigning majesty unchallenged. The lush branches of the towering bristlecone pines quivering in the gentle breeze. Alpine chipmunks scampering over fallen boulders. Pristine white heather growing wild along the mountain's granite ridges.

Diane inhaled deeply.

Here in this place of hushed and intricate beauty, far from the world and its cares, she stood in the chill September dawn glowing with warmth and happiness. It was one of those rare occasions when she fully realized that she was gloriously happy and totally content. Right now. Today. Not last year or five years ago, but now.

Like every other human being who had ever lived, Diane Buchannan had the normal tendency to look back on an occasion or period in her past and fondly recall it as being far, far better than it had actually been, conveniently forgetting any problems or unpleasantness that had existed.

Or else she looked ahead, daydreaming of that bright, yet-to-be-lived day somewhere in the hazy future when everything in her life would be absolutely perfect and she would be totally, everlastingly happy.

Diane was a perceptive and intelligent woman. She well understood that there were precious few times in anyone's life, no matter how successful or satisfying that life might be, when he or she realizes *this* is it. This is the time. This is exactly what I've dreamed of and longed for all my life. Everything to be had on this old earth is mine this very day. This very minute.

Diane knew instinctively that she was as happy at this minute as she would ever be in her life. There might be moments or days just as good in the years that stretched before her, but there would—could—be no better. This was the ultimate, and she was thoroughly enjoying it.

Everything was perfect. From the cool mountain air kissing her face and long, bare legs to the sweet realization that the only man she had ever loved or would ever love was asleep just inside this remote mountain home, a home she hoped to share with him until both were old and gray.

Silently Diane thanked a wise and generous God for giving her Star and the strange, unlikely fates that had brought them together. Grateful to both, Diane savored the moment.

When suddenly she felt that wonderfully new yet familiar tingling of excitement causing the blood to rush through her veins, she knew without looking that Star was near. Very near. His presence was so powerful and exciting her bare knees began to tremble.

Diane drew a shallow breath and turned. She smiled with joy as she watched Star approach, looking sleepy and boyishly handsome. His beautiful dark eyes half hooded, he yawned, raked a tanned hand through his disheveled black hair, and crossed to her. Barefoot, he wore only his tight beige trousers, half buttoned up over his belly. His bronzed torso was naked.

"Good mornin'," he said when he reached her, sliding a lean hand up underneath her long dark hair.

"It sure is now," Diane said, smiling, then encircled Star's trim waist to hug him and stood on tiptoe to kiss him.

It was a warm, sweet, intimate kiss of lovers, and when their lips separated, Star's long fingers were tangled in Diane's heavy hair. He urged her head back as his navy eyes locked with hers.

"Don't," he warned, unsmiling, a hint of the old danger radiating from the depths of his dark eyes, "ever let me wake up again and not find you in my bed."

Diane shivered pleasantly. "I promise you, my love."

Star grinned then, kissed her mouth again, and gently turned her about in his arms. He drew her back against his tall frame and locked his wrists in front of her. For a moment they stood there together, looking out at the mountainous terrain, silently enjoying the beauty and tranquillity.

Star said in a sleep-heavy voice, "How long has it been since I told you I love you?"

Diane smiled and clung to the dark arms around her. "About an hour."

"A whole hour? How thoughtless of me."

"Don't let it happen again."

"I love you," he said, his lips in her hair. "I love you, Miss Buchannan. Very, very much."

Diane's eyes closed with pleasure. "And I love you, Mr. Star. Honest I do."

"You'd better, sweetheart," he said commandingly. Before Diane could reply, he added, "What exactly, I am wondering, are you wearing under my shirt?" Star bent his dark head, harmlessly bit the side of her throat with sharp white teeth, and unlocked his wrists.

He stood close behind her. His hands rubbed across the front of her shirt down to her stomach.

Diane caught her breath. "Would you like to guess?"

"No. I prefer finding out for myself." His hands began sliding downward, his hooded eyes lowering with them.

"Mmm, a wise idea." Diane sighed, as ready to play as he. But a second later she abruptly squirmed away from Star's hands, pointing and shouting excitedly, "Star, look! Look! Did you see it?"

Shaken out of his amorous mood, Star followed her finger. A big black horse was plunging rapidly down the mountainside. Flashing in and out of the trees, neighing and snorting loudly, the huge beast seemed to be headed directly toward the high back fence.

Star grinned. "Yes, baby. I see him."

"A wild stallion!" Diane exclaimed. "A magnificent wild stallion!"

"Plenty of wild horses in Nevada."

"My lord, he's coming right up to the back fence." Diane's violet eyes shone with excitement. "I can't believe it."

Star's grin broadened, but he didn't let Diane see it. From behind her he said, "Want to see the stallion come even closer?"

Diane's head immediately snapped around to look at Star. She saw he was serious. She gave him a mocking smile and shook her head. "Darling, I know what you're thinking, but you're wrong."

"Am I?"

"Yes, you are." Diane's tone was mildly patronizing. "You were able to take that rancher's stallion from the barn without any trouble, so now you suppose you can conquer this black stallion. Isn't that it?"

"I'm in love with a mind reader."

Diane smiled. "Star, that horse you stole was a tame saddle pony." She again shook her head, turned back to admire the neighing stallion prancing nervously back and forth beyond the fence. "I know a little about horses myself. It's doubtful any human will ever get closer to that wild, spirited stallion than we are right now."

"Could be," said Star thoughtfully. Then he added, "But this morning I feel so damned good I'm of a mind that nothing is impossible." He gave her a squeeze, and she nodded and smiled, knowing exactly what he meant. Star said, "If I get that beast to come closer, will you cook our breakfast?"

"Certainly." Diane was quick to agree, comfortable it couldn't be done. "And if—make that when—you don't succeed, you cook."

"It's a bargain, sweetheart."

Diane never saw the teasing smile curving Star's sensual lips or the devilish twinkling of his dark navy eyes. He wet his lips with his tongue, stuck his thumb and index finger into the corners of his mouth, and gave a long, low whistle.

The nervously prancing stallion's ears shot up, quivering forward. He whinnied loudly, his big eyes round. Snorting and blowing, he wheeled about in a semicircle and raced away from the fence. He swiftly charged back up the mountainside, dislodging pebbles and frightening squirrels in his haste to get away. He disappeared into the thick forest of pines.

"There, you see," Diane said. "What did I tell you?"

The words were hardly out of her mouth before the big beast flashed into a clearing high up on the slope. He whipped around and came racing back down at a hard gallop. Diane held her breath when he neared the tall fence enclosing the backyard of the estate. She needn't have. The powerful stallion leaped over that fence as if it weren't there and immediately slowed to a canter.

While Diane watched in openmouthed awe, the gleaming black stallion crossed the yard, coming toward them. Not believing her own eyes, Diane turned to Star. His calm brown face didn't betray a thing. Leaning over the balcony, Diane turned her attention back to the stallion. The big beast was directly below now, shaking his great head and nickering.

Star smiled to himself. He brought both hands down on the cedar railing, enclosing Diane inside in his long arms. Chest pressing against Diane's back, he leaned over her and said to the stallion, "What about it, boy? Can you say good morning?"

The horse's ears shot up, quivering forward to catch his master's familiar voice. He reared up on his hind legs, pawed at the air with his front hooves, and made loud, whistling sounds of salutation. Diane was dumbfounded. And amazed. And impressed.

"Star! That's incredible. I can't believe it . . . it's like he understands and—and—" Suspicion suddenly dawned. Diane stopped speaking. Violet eyes narrowed, she spun about to face Star, caught the traces of a smile and the light flashing in his navy eyes. "So the stallion's wild?" She skeptically lifted a perfectly arched eyebrow. "Never seen him before, huh?"

"Never have." Star laughed then, a deep, rumbling laugh that came from far down inside.

"Why, you big liar!" Diane shoved her elbows into his naked chest to push him away and started hitting him.

Chuckling and half dodging her blows, Star allowed her to punish him for a few seconds before he caught her arms and hugged her tightly to him.

"Well, maybe I've seen the stallion around. Might have spoken to him a time or two."

Playfully Diane bit his bare shoulder. "He's yours, isn't he?" She raised her head, looked at Star.

Star smiled, kissed her haughty nose, and drew her to his side. "Sweetheart, meet Black Star. I've had him since he was a colt." He looked down at the big beast, which was still putting up a racket. "Hey, hold it down, fella. Meet Diane, I've had her only a few precious hours. Beautiful, isn't she?" The stallion whickered and shook his head. "He thinks you're beautiful," Star told Diane.

Her eyes on the black, Diane replied, "And I think he's magnificent. Tell him that."

"He heard you," Star assured her.

Diane smiled. "Naturally I thought he was wild. Darling, is it wise to allow Black Star to run loose while you're away?"

"It's not just while I'm away. It's when I'm here as well," Star said matter-of-factly. "Black Star doesn't like being penned. Concealed beyond the trees, his stable is left open at all times. He comes and goes as he pleases."

"You're not afraid he'll run away? That you might lose him?"

"No. The only way to hold a gem like Black Star is to allow him his freedom. The fence hasn't been built that could hold him if he didn't want to stay." The smile abruptly left Star's face. He looked straight into Diane's eyes. "Diane, I was teasing you earlier when I warned you to never let me wake up without you being in my bed. I didn't mean that."

"You didn't?"

Almost violently Star shook his dark head. "I want you with me, but only as long as that's where you want to be. I would never—"

"Star, I—"

"Let me finish. I kidnapped you. I've held you against your will. That will never happen again. We are equals, you and I. You're free, darling, and always will be." He smiled at her. "This house will never be a prison or cage to keep you inside. I want you to know that." His navy eyes had darkened to black, and his expression had become somber. "If at any time of the day or night you want to leave, you're free to go."

"Star, darling," she said softly, wrapped her arms around his waist, and laid her head on his bare chest, "I'll never leave you. Never."

Chapter 38

"You couldn't run me off if you tried." Diane brushed a kiss to his bare chest, then looked up into his eyes, tightened her arms around him, and added, "So don't ever try."

"In that case," he said, inclining his dark head and pointing inside, "get down those stairs and cook breakfast."

"Come with me?" she asked, her perfectly arched brows lifting hopefully.

A generous smile curved his lips. "Jesus, you really think I'd let you loose in that kitchen by yourself?"

"Coward! Who knows what fantastic cuisine I'd turn out?"

Star chuckled. "Baby, I may feel like a king today, but I have no personal food taster. I'll help with the meal."

"Must I learn to cook, Star?" Diane asked, suddenly serious, pressing closer to him.

"Never," he swiftly replied, his eyes on her full lips.

"Thank goodness," she said with total honesty. "I'm afraid I'm just not cut out for that sort of thing."

"I don't care." Star was as honest as she. "I know something you *are* cut out for," he said as his hands molded the arch of her hips.

"Star, stop it," she scolded, "I'm hungry."

"I know. So am I." His hands slipped up under the blue pullover shirt.

Diane squealed, forcefully pushed him away, and hurried across the cedar balcony. Star watched her sprint toward the door, her raven hair flying wildly, her long, shapely legs churning. Smiling, he followed. Inside, she told him she needed something to wear. He nodded, grabbed her hand, led her into his large dressing room, and told her to take her pick. Diane chose a pair of black twill Levi's and a pale yellow pullover shirt.

She went back into the bedroom while Star yanked a clean white shirt from the rack and shoved his long arms down into the sleeves. Buttoning the shirt up his chest, he walked back into the bedroom. Diane wore the fresh yellow pullover. She was just stepping into the black twill Levi's.

Star grinned appreciatively and dropped down into a chair to observe. Diane pulled the pants up her long, slender legs and over the flare of her hips. The trousers fitted her snugly. They were, in fact, so tight she found she couldn't quite get them buttoned.

Lolling in his easy chair, one long leg draped over its arm, Star watched with amused pleasure as Diane battled with the buttons of the fly, her hair falling into her face, the tip of her tongue caught between her teeth in fierce concentration. He could tell by the faint color rising to her fair, lovely face that she was quickly growing frustrated.

"Need some help?" he asked, grinning, after several seconds had passed.

"No!" Diane whipped her head back and glared at him. "I can manage, thank you."

"As you wish," he said, absently rubbing his chest. She was comical, and she was cute. She was also innocently sexual. The gyrations and wiggling and thrusting of her pelvis made his mouth go dry.

She tussled. She grappled. She wrestled.

She sighed with frustration. She gritted her teeth. She uttered a mild oath under her breath. Still, she couldn't get the tight black trousers buttoned up over her flat belly. When she heard Star's low laughter, Diane irritably whipped her hair back out of her eyes and put her hands on her flaring hips.

"The devil and Tom Walker!" she snapped, looking straight at him. "I can't get these blasted pants buttoned. I must be getting fat!"

Chuckling, Star came to his feet. And to her aid. "No, you're not, sweetheart. You're just about perfect."

He put his hands to her waist, lifted her feet from the floor, and carried her to the rumpled bed. He sat her on the edge of the mattress and knelt before her. He first rolled up the too-long pants legs over her bare feet. While he was about it, he bent his dark head and kissed her right instep.

Then he lifted his head, grinned, and said, "Which is it to be, Miss

Buchannan? The pants buttoned up"—he rubbed his hands along the insides of her knees—"or taken off?"

"Buttoned up," she said after a slight pause, not fully sure that was the choice she really wanted to make. "For now."

"Buttoned up it is," Star said, gently pushed her over onto her back, and got on the bed with her. His weight supported on an elbow, he lay looking down at her while he easily buttoned her Levi's with one hand, his lean, deft fingers grazing the bare flesh of her flat stomach.

"I certainly hope," Diane murmured, smiling up at him, "you're half as good at unbuttoning my trousers as you are at buttoning them."

"My sweet," Star assured her, his navy eyes flashing, "I'm even better."

Diane laughed, leaped up, and cried, "Food! Food! I need food. Please feed me."

Together they went downstairs to the kitchen. After lots of laughter and kisses and bumping into each other, they managed to put a meal of sorts on the table. The bacon Diane fried was burned, and there was enough on the platter to feed a ravenous family of eight. Star made the toast, and it was almost as blackened as the charred bacon.

It didn't matter.

They scraped the burned toast and spread mounds of blackberry jam on it. They broke up the crisp bacon strips, making a contest out of searching for portions that were edible, shouting with gleeful triumph when one or the other found a bite-size piece that wasn't too cremated to eat.

The coffee, too, left something to be desired. Diane was quick to blame it on Star's coffee grinder. The darned grinder hadn't ground the beans to a fine enough powder; that's why the black, hot liquid in their bone china cups was so strong and bitter.

Could it have had anything to do with the fact that she had used too much coffee? Star judiciously inquired. Absolutely not. She quickly set him straight.

Fortunately there was another beverage on the menu that morning, one that couldn't be ruined. Star had squeezed enough oranges to fill a tall crystal pitcher with sweet golden juice so Diane was puzzled when he poured her crystal goblet—and his—only half full. She gave him a questioning look. He winked at her and disappeared into the kitchen. He returned shortly with a bottle of a chilled champagne snagged between his index and middle finger, a stemmed wineglass hooked in his curled thumb, and a white linen towel draped over his left arm.

Grinning, he stepped up beside Diane's chair to show her the label as if she were dining in a fine restaurant and had ordered the bubbly. She immediately took up the game.

With the dismissive wave of her hand and a nod of her head, she said in a cool, brittle voice, "Yes, Pierre, the Piper Heidsieck 'eighty-seven will be quite satisfactory. Quite."

"*Oui,* madame," said Star, bowing grandly from the waist and placing the stemmed glass before her.

Expertly, as he did all things, Star positioned the white linen towel over the top of the bottle, popped the cork, withdrew the towel, and poured a splash of the dry golden champagne into the crystal flute.

Diane lifted the glass, daintily sipped the champagne, held it in her mouth for a few seconds, and swallowed.

"*Bon,*" she murmured, "*bon,* Pierre."

"Ah, *merci, merci.*" He beamed.

Then the pleased waiter laughed and kissed the haughty patron right on the mouth, ending the game. Star dropped back down into his chair and filled their orange juice glasses with the bubbly. They toasted each other and drank.

An hour later they were still at the table, sipping the orange juice-champagne mixture and agreeing, between kisses and laughter, that this drink was indeed *bon.* In time they grew sleepy. Leaving the dishes for later, they went back up for a nice long nap.

It was afternoon when they awakened. Neither felt particularly energetic. Lazily they bathed together, made slow, satisfying love, prepared another not-too-appetizing meal, and sat out on the upstairs balcony to watch the stars come out.

They went to bed late that night and slept in the next morning. Both awoke feeling rested and refreshed. After a noontime breakfast Diane insisted they go outdoors to look for the stallion, Black Star.

So they quit the mansion shortly after noon with Diane carrying several lumps of sugar in hope the magnificent stallion was still somewhere in the vicinity. He was. The black heard the laughter and talking when Star and Diane stepped out onto the broad front porch. The big stallion was there to meet them when they reached the front stone steps, nickering and shaking his head up and down, demanding attention.

Diane laughed and greeted him warmly. She patted his sleek jaw and talked to him in a soft, cooing voice, telling him how beautiful he was and that she hoped he'd allow her to ride him. She also teased him. She devilishly showed him a lump of the sugar, holding it out to him on her palm. Before he could take it, she closed her fist tightly and whipped her hand behind her back.

The stallion wasn't fooled for a second. He whinnied his outrage, took a step forward, stretched his neck, and poked his head around her back, sniffing out the sugar, his velvet muzzle brushing against her closed hand.

"Better give it to him before he bites you," warned Star.

Nodding, Diane brought her hand back in front of her. She petted the big black beast while he gobbled up the sugar cubes, one at a time, from her open palm, chewing rapidly as if he had never had anything that tasted so good.

"Instant friendship," announced Diane proudly. "Black Star likes me. I'm sure he'll gladly allow me to ride him."

"Don't count on it," said Star, taking her hand in his. "Nobody's ever been on his back but me." To the stallion he said, "What about it, boy? Like some oats to go with that sugar?"

Black Star followed the pair as Star led Diane down the front steps and around the house. The backyard was terraced. No flowers or shrubs had ever been planted. Instead nature's own beauty had been utilized and nurtured. Bright orange-pink spurs of wild columbine and rambling rows of ivory heather were showier than any garden-grown cousins could have been. Fragrant cedars lined crisscrossing walks of natural stone. A three-tiered fountain splashed continuously at the center of the yard and comfortable-looking, rust-colored padded lawn furniture was scattered about in clusters.

Beyond the fence, hidden in the trees fifty yards farther up the mountain, were stucco-sided stables and a cedar plank corral. They were empty. The gate stood open.

Black Star snorted, whickered, and followed them into the corral, where his name was spelled out in gleaming silver on the tall crossbars above the gate. Star dropped Diane's hand, ducked into the shaded stable, and brought down a sack of oats.

"See you later, boy," Diane said to the big beast as they left him noisily devouring his oats.

Ready to head back down to the house, Star made the mistake of mentioning he would later show her his favorite place to relax and unwind. A secluded spot higher up on the mountain where he had a hot well, a spring of mineral water he had dug out to make a pool.

Naturally Diane didn't want to wait. She insisted on going there at once. Star squinted up at the heavens. The sky, which had been a deep, cloudless blue when they'd first come outdoors, was now filled with big fluffy white thunderheads. He warned her it was likely to rain.

"At this time of year, sweetheart, it rains in these mountains every afternoon. We'll go up to the hot spring in the morning."

Diane stepped closer, wrapped her arms around his waist. "Please, Star, show me now. I don't mind a few sprinkles. Besides, if we hurry, we can beat the rain."

They didn't beat the rain.

They were about a hundred yards below the spring when the first near flash of lightning streaked across the rapidly darkening sky, followed by a loud crash of thunder.

They looked at each other, smiled, turned, and hurried back down the slope. The cloudburst caught them, pounding them with a fury all the way back down the mountain. They shrieked and shouted and laughed their way home.

By the time they reached the mansion they were soaked to the skin, their hair plastered to their heads. Out of breath, hearts thundering, they ducked in under the slanting porch roof and wordlessly began stripping. When both were naked, they looked at each other, laughed, came together, and kissed. And kissed again.

Leaving their wet clothes in a discarded heap on the front gallery, Star swept Diane up into his arms, carried her inside and straight up the stairs.

The storm worsened as they bathed in the black marble tub, huge raindrops fiercely pelting the glass wall across from them. The sky was as black as midnight, and booming thunder reverberated throughout the house.

After the bath they wrapped themselves in large, thirsty white towels and went into the bedroom. Diane, looking out at the storm, laughed when Star snatched the soft fur counterpane off the bed. He dragged it over and spread it on the floor directly before the wall of glass.

He immediately stretched out on his back, looked up at her with hot dark eyes, and said, "Come here."

They made love on the lush furs while the wind howled through the pines and the rains came in blinding sheets. They stayed there on the bedroom floor through the stormy afternoon, making love and watching the rain. Touching each other. Looking at each other. Star lay on his back. Diane was curled to him, her head resting on his shoulder.

After a long, lazy silence Star said in that low, flat voice, "Diane."

"*You* can call me darling," she murmured.

"Darling," he began again, "assume I know nothing. Tell me everything about you."

Diane felt certain she knew what was on his mind. He was wondering about her and the Cherokee Kid. She leisurely raised up on an elbow, looked down at him. His dark eyes were fixed on the ceiling over their heads.

Without preamble she said bluntly, "Star, the Cherokee Kid was never my lover."

"I know."

"You do?" It wasn't the response she had expected. Diane frowned. "You knew all along that—"

"You've had no lover before me." Star turned his head, looked into her eyes. "Have you, sweetheart?"

"No. No, I haven't," she said, slightly flustered. "And you knew all along?"

"Not all along," he gently corrected. "Since the first time we made love," he said with tenderness, his voice low, soft. Then: "Sweetheart, you are not the only lover I've ever had. There have been many women. Too many. But you're the only one I have ever loved. I'll never touch another, I swear it."

"It's a good thing," Diane replied, her frown disappearing, happiness flooding her. "I have a very jealous nature."

Star laughed softly. "I'll never give you cause to be jealous if you marry me."

"Is this a proposal?"

"Yes. Marry me, Diane. Marry me."

"I thought you'd never ask." She smiled warmly at him. "The answer is yes!"

Star grinned, and Diane leaned over his handsome face and kissed his lips, licking at them, whispering into his mouth, "Yes, oh, yes."

The rain stopped. The sun came out. A colorful rainbow arched across the western sky.

Through the gleaming glass wall the whole world looked fresh and new. Diane laid her cheek on Star's smooth chest and felt his strong arms enclose her. He exhaled, and his breathing became slow and even as he dozed.

Feeling wonderfully safe and secure, Diane sighed with contentment and closed her eyes. The soft pulsing of Star's heart charmed and wooed her to sleep.

Davey Leatherwood walked through the swinging doors of a Lander, Wyoming, saloon and stood behind the Kid.

"The ticket master told us where they're bound."

The Kid didn't move. "Where?"

"Virginia City."

Chapter 39

Day three at Sun Mountain.

➤➤➤➤ Birds chirping sweetly in the lush branches of the bristlecone pines awakened Diane. She smiled even before she opened her eyes. She lazily swept a hand across the wide bed, confident her eager fingers would encounter smooth male flesh stretched tautly over lean muscle and well-structured bone.

Her searching fingertips contacted only the silky beige sheet. Her eyes opened. She turned onto her side, yawned, and looked about. And she smiled again. By the slant of the sunshine streaming through the glass, it was late morning. Perhaps nearing noon. Star had obviously awakened earlier and didn't want to disturb her.

Diane eagerly bounded up, swung her legs over the mattress's edge, and pushed her hair behind her ears. Yawning again, she dug her bare toes into the plush carpet and rubbed at an itchy left eye.

Naked, she crossed the bedroom. From a chair she picked up a discarded white silk robe and drew it on, anxious to get downstairs to Star. She was tying the robe's sash when a rare mountain bluebird glided down to land gently on the balcony's cedar railing. Bright alpine sunlight glinting on its brilliant indigo feathers, the beautiful bluebird was a stunning sight.

Diane was drawn to the exotic little creature. She went out onto the balcony and cautiously tiptoed toward the poised bluebird. She was less than five feet away when the shy little bird cheeped a warning, fluttered its radiant wings, and took flight. Diane made a face as she watched the beautiful bluebird soar through the air out of reach.

She stood a moment more on the balcony, hands resting on the railing, violet eyes watching the bird on wing until it became a tiny blue speck. And then disappeared.

She sighed and was about to go back inside when she heard someone cough. She turned her head to the side and listened. Again the cough.

Diane smiled and shook her head. She'd have to warn Star about those strong black cigars he favored. But first she'd slip down to his library and surprise him.

Diane crept quietly down the long, wide balcony toward Star's upstairs library. The library's tall French doors were thrown open to the fine September morning.

Clamping her teeth down over her bottom lip, Diane sneaked steadily closer. She could hardly keep from giggling when she reached the open doors and saw him. Star was seated behind his large mahogany desk. His back was to her.

She paused in the open doorway. She took a moment to observe the darkly handsome man while he was unaware of her presence. Star drew a sheet of yellow paper out of the middle desk drawer. His long, lean fingers laid a half-smoked cigar in a crystal dish at his elbow. He reached for a writing pen. He began rapidly writing on the yellow paper before him.

Star was so engrossed Diane managed to steal right up behind his chair, silently reach around, and wrap her hands over his eyes.

"Guess who?" she said, laughter bubbling from her lips.

The laughter died in her throat when Star dropped the pen and stripped her fingers from his face with such swift force she felt the jerking pull all the way up to her shoulders. With incredible speed and quiet deadliness, he drew her around his chair.

For one brief frightening moment the man she'd known for the past few days was gone. Before her was a dark, sinister stranger who was ten times more frightening than the untamed Redman had ever been. His navy eyes almost seemed to dance. They had a deadly gleam, a scarily wild look as they clashed with hers. His lips were skinned back over his teeth in a fiercely cruel expression.

Diane trembled involuntarily, totally confused and genuinely frightened.

"Sweetheart," Star said, his face changing instantly, his mean eyes softening as he gently pulled her down onto his lap. His voice had that low, unexcitable tone when he said softly, "Baby girl, you startled me."

Jittery, Diane tried to smile. Couldn't. "I—I'm sorry, I—" Her hand went up to her tight throat. "Star, you scared me half to death. You looked at me like—like—"

"I apologize, honey," he said, his voice soothing as he reached across her. One-handed, Star folded the lined yellow Western Union message form, opened the middle desk drawer, and slipped the paper inside, all the while looking straight into Diane's wide violet eyes. "Am I forgiven?" His smile was warm, winning.

"Yes, of course, but . . . Star, you looked so—so—mean—"

"I'd never be mean to you, sweetheart. Surely you know that." He toyed with the wide lapel of her white silk robe, his thumb and forefinger sliding up and down it. "Kiss me good morning?"

Pulse still beating rapidly, Diane was struck by the unsettling feeling that if she kissed him, she'd be kissing a stranger. A dark, menacing stranger whose kiss would be brutally punishing, without an ounce of warmth. Again she shivered slightly.

"Cold, baby?" asked Star.

"No, I—"

"Kiss me."

Tentatively Diane cupped Star's smoothly shaven jaw in her cold hand, leaned toward him, and cautiously brushed her closed mouth against his lips.

And relaxed immediately.

No stranger's cruelly punishing lips opened under hers, but the warm, seeking mouth of her own true love. Star kissed Diane with a lazy, slow, burning heat that made her softly sigh. The tantalizing tongue that languidly swept along the seam of her closed lips caused them to willingly part. Diane closed her eyes when Star's tongue licked at the fleshy inside of her lower lip, then drummed against her teeth. Her teeth opened to accept fully that pleasure-giving tongue into the sensitive recesses of her mouth.

When the pleasing, prolonged kiss finally ended, Diane lifted her head, smiled dreamily at Star, and said, "Good morning, my love."

"Isn't it?"

He settled her more comfortably on his lap, wrapping a long arm around her waist. His other hand clasped her knees.

"I hope you're not angry with me for interrupting you." Diane draped an arm around his wide shoulders.

"You interrupted nothing, sweetheart," he assured her.

"Yes, I did." She glanced at his desktop. "Weren't you writing out a message? Sending a wire to someone?"

Calmly: "No. I was doing a little figuring. Since you've been here, I've been negligent with my bookkeeping on the mines."

"You're in luck," Diane said sunnily. "I'm a whiz with numbers. I'll help you." She turned a little, pulled open the desk's middle drawer.

Star's hand covered hers. "No, sweetheart, not this morning." He drew her hand up to his lips. Kissing her fingertips, one by one, he said, "No more work today."

"But I'd be glad to help you catch up and—"

"I know you would." He casually raised his knee and with it closed the desk drawer. "It can wait." He lowered her hand from his lips. He pressed it flat against his chest, urged her soft fingers inside his half-open white shirt.

Diane lifted a well-arched eyebrow as she stroked his smooth, warm flesh. "Are you hiding something from me, Starkeeper?"

"I think"—his voice was a caress—"it's the other way around. You're hiding something from me."

"Me? Never. I've nothing to hide."

"I agree, my sweet." Star grinned and tugged the wide lapels of Diane's robe apart. His dark eyes touching the pale bare breasts he'd exposed, he murmured, "Absolutely nothing to hide." He grinned devilishly and lifted his eyes to meet hers.

Her face flushing, Diane pulled the robe together. "You're totally shameless." She laughingly accused him.

"And you're glad I am," said Star. He rose with her in his arms and carried her out of the library, closing the door behind them.

Laughing gaily, Diane completely forgot about the yellow Western Union message paper on which Star had been writing.

In the high-altitude heat of the afternoon the pair trekked up to Star's private hot spring. Diane rode Black Star. Star walked ahead, muttering under his breath.

Diane watched him, smiling. He was annoyed that she had so easily conquered his prized stallion. The big black had allowed her to climb up on his bare back without protest while Star stood there in the sun, arms crossed over his chest, shaking his head and warning her she was courting danger.

When she'd effortlessly settled herself astride the big beast and given Star a triumphant look, Star had frowned, cocked a finger at Black Star, and warned the horse, "Throw her and you'll answer to me."

Now Diane smilingly studied Star as he walked up the trail just ahead. He had the restless way of a cat, a quick, soft step and a wildness like that of a stray bullet. His hair was lifting in the wind, and his shirt collar was open, his chest and throat exposed to the fresh air. The harsh planes of his handsome face were burned dark from the sun.

Diane closed her eyes for a second and shuddered. It was still almost impossible to believe that this complex, exciting, beautiful man belonged to her. Would soon be her husband. She was afraid any second someone would shake her awake and she'd find it had all been a lovely dream.

Not turning, Star called over his shoulder, "Diane, keep a tight rein on him. We're heading into the craggy, creviced terrain where the footing's tricky."

Diane grinned. And typically female, she promptly decided to torment the naturally arrogant, overly protective male. When she was in position, she called to him, "Look, darling, no hands!"

Diane laughed at the worried expression that immediately hardened Star's dark face when he turned to see her standing on the stallion's bare back, her hands casually riding her hips, the long leather reins tucked into her waistband.

"Damn it to hell, Diane"—Star's voice was as hard as his face—"you trying to give me a heart attack? Jesus Christ!"

He snapped his fingers and ordered her to sit down. Still laughing, Diane obeyed. Star then signaled Black Star to halt. The stallion also obeyed. His face set in dark fury, Star approached with sure, determined strides. Diane felt a stirring of unease when he stepped up to the horse, glowered at her, and said, "Okay, Miss Show-off Champion Trick Rider, let's see you perform one more little trick."

"Name it," said Diane with confidence.

"Turn around atop the horse and face backward."

"No sooner said than done." In one swift, fluid movement, Diane made the switch. Facing the wrong direction astride the big mount, she said, "That was easy. Anything else?"

"Yes. Put both hands behind you on Black Star's withers, brace yourself, lean back, and lift your legs straight up into the air."

"Like this?" she said, nimbly lying back and shooting both bare feet up into the air.

"No," said Star, who swung up onto the horse's bare back, parted Diane's legs with his hands, snatched them down, and wrapped them around his waist. He leaned forward, took her by the shoulders, and drew her up into his arms. "Like this, damn you," he said, a muscle clenching in his jaw.

"You mad at me?" Diane asked, looking into those sultry dark eyes and placing her hands on his chest.

"I am," said he coolly. "Better think of something to sweeten my mood."

Diane smiled at him. "I'll do my best."

Staring into those dark, piercing eyes that not only looked but saw, Diane unbuttoned Star's shirt down to his waist and lightly clawed her nails down his naked chest. She bent and slowly kissed the pink welts she had made. When she lifted her head, Star wore that dazzling smile which so easily disarmed and conquered.

"Kiss me," he said, slapping his hand against Black Star's rump to put him back in motion. "Kiss me, you beautiful witch, and don't stop kissing me till we reach the springs."

Diane did just that.

When they reached their destination, they couldn't stop kissing. They slid off the horse, fell to the grass beside the bubbling hot spring, and made hurried, ardent love, tearing off their clothes, murmuring endearments, totally mindless of the big stallion, blowing and snorting above them.

Afterward they romped in the hot spring, purposely losing each other in the thick, vaporous mists just for the fun of the searching for and finding the other. When they were all played out, they lazily relaxed in the bubbling spring.

Star chose a spot to sit where the hot, gurgling water reached the tops of his shoulders. Diane was behind him, her legs around him, feet hooked under his bent knees. She curled herself around Star's back and began to rub his furrowed brow with both hands as they talked again about their lives before they met, learning about each other.

Diane was far more talkative than Star. He listened with a smile as she told how she'd been indulged as a child. Despite the loss of her parents, she'd been cherished and cared for by everyone in the troupe. She'd met so many famous and important people. Had been a guest at the White House, at Buckingham Palace, had mingled with royalty.

"I've been bounced on Victoria's knee—the old queen herself," she told him. Diane fell silent for a minute, then softly said, "Star, we came from two very different worlds, so I hope you'll understand and forgive if—if at times I'm—umm—"

"Spoiled rotten?"

"I am not!" She twisted his left ear.

He chuckled. "You are, sweetheart, but I don't mind. I plan to finish the job myself."

"You already have," said Diane. "I've never known such happiness."

"Same here," said Star, his eyes closed, perspiration trickling down his face.

Diane brushed his silver-streaked hair back and kissed the side of his slick brown throat. Her lips against his flesh, she said, "Darling, tell me. Tell me the truth about that day . . . about your first day at the Colorado School of Mines."

Star's eyes slowly opened. "Are you asking about the white boys cutting off my braids?"

"Yes." She kissed his shoulder. "How did you stand it? I would have run home to Golden Star had I been you."

Star exhaled. "No, if you had been me, you'd have done exactly what I did." He slid farther down into the water, laid his head gently back on her breasts. "That was the turning point in my life, Diane," he said, his elocution slow and deliberate. "I was angry. I was hurt and confused. I had been held up to ridicule for the first time in my life, and I didn't fully understand why."

Diane felt a lump rise to her throat as she listened, picturing the sweet, innocent Star being tortured by a gang of callous white students.

"But I had been taught that a man has to exist in the present moment, to accept what turns up. I learned on that very first day at the university that I was alone. I would have no friends there. I accepted it. How did I actually feel? Lonely," he said with touching honesty, "sad and unutterably lonely."

Tears filled Diane's violet eyes. She tried to swallow the lump growing in her throat. Star waited for her to speak. She said nothing. Slowly he turned to face her.

"You're crying," he said.

"I never cry," Diane said, looking at him through her tears.

"Ah, baby, baby," he said, cupping her chin in his hand, "I shouldn't have told you. Besides, that was a long time ago—and long since healed."

Nodding furiously, tears splashing down her cheeks, she said, "I—I . . . know, but I can't stand the thought of you being hurt."

"Sweetheart, listen to me." Star pointed to a giant sequoia tree on the far distant western horizon. "See that redwood? It's the largest and oldest living thing on earth. The secret of its size and longevity, despite thousands of years of storms and bad weather, is its thick bark. It's fire-resistant and insectproof." He smiled at Diane and added, "It is the same with a human being. He can also have thick bark with which to protect himself. Believe me, my love. And I do have a thick bark. Don't you think?"

Diane nodded, dashed at her tears with the back of her hand, and said with a wide grin, "I think your thick bark's worse than your bite."

Star threw back his head and laughed. Diane looped her arms around his neck and laughed with him.

He hugged her close and said, "That's my girl."

Chapter 40

"Star." Diane pointed languidly toward the flaming western
➤➤➤➤ sky. "An eagle."

Star barely turned his head. Squinting into the brilliant sunset, he
watched the majestic eagle soar gracefully across his line of vision.

"Winged wolves, our Aztec brothers called them."

It was sunset.

Star and Diane were outside on the broad front porch of the mansion.
Diane was sitting at one end of a long, comfortable settee. Star was
sprawled out on his back, his head resting in her lap. Totally relaxed
and lazy from their afternoon at the hot spring, they chose to indulge in
nothing more strenuous or exciting than watching the spectacular Nevada sunset.

They'd said little to each other since they'd settled onto the porch. It
was not a strained silence but a quietness, natural and easy on both
sides. For long moments the only sound was the distant cough of the
mountain lion.

Ten minutes of silence.

Finally: "Tomorrow's our last day."

Diane sighed. "I know. I never knew time could pass so fast." She
sighed again, lifted her hand to Star's face, and touched the tiny white
scar beneath his dark left eyebrow. "How did you get this scar?"

"A fight," he said tonelessly.

Diane made a face. She followed the contours of his less than perfect
nose. "And this?"

"Several fights." He grinned lazily.

Diane traced his sculpted lips with a finger until Star snapped at it, then kissed her hand. "You have a long lifeline," he said, tracking it with his tongue.

Diane took his palm and read it. "So have you."

Star withdrew his hand, hooked an arm around her back, and said, "It's settled. We'll both live a long time. But the fact remains we have only one more day here."

"Must we talk about it?" asked Diane.

Star pressed his face against her ribs. "No, I guess not. But I was thinking we might plan something special for tomorrow since it is—"

"—our last day," she finished for him. "What could be better than this?"

"Nothing. Except perhaps a decent meal."

"Complain, complain," Diane said, shaking her head, "when all I do is slave all day long over a hot stove."

Star chuckled and gave her an affectionate squeeze. "How about tomorrow evening we go into Virginia City, eat in a fancy restaurant, and then make a night of it at Piper's Opera House?"

"Not on your life."

"No?"

"No. I'm not about to share you with anyone else on our last night. So forget it."

"I like your answer." Star grinned broadly. "I've another idea."

"Try me."

"I ride into town tomorrow afternoon, pick up our train tickets to San Francisco, buy you something decent to wear, and have the chef at the Timberline Hotel cater a meal I can bring back here."

"Yes! That's it!" Diane was instantly enthusiastic. "We'll have dinner by candlelight and drink champagne and—and . . . oh, Star, that's a wonderful idea." Her violet eyes were wide and sparkling, her busy brain already making plans for the big evening.

Star's arm slid up her slender back. His hand cupped the back of her neck. "And I'll buy you an expensive, stylish evening gown."

Wide-eyed, Diane looked down at his dark face. "Don't be foolish, darling. I doubt you'll be able to find an expensive, stylish evening gown in Virginia City. And even if you do, how will you fit me? Unless I go along?"

"You," he said, looking up into her eyes, "worry too much. Leave everything to me. I promise that this time tomorrow evening you'll be slipping into a gorgeous gown. And it will fit like a glove."

"I do like pretty clothes," Diane charmingly confessed.

"I do like pretty women," he told her, "in and out of pretty clothes."

She laughed, leaned down, brushed a kiss to his mouth, and started to raise her head. But Star didn't let her. His firm fingers on the nape of her neck urged her face back down to his. He gently bit on her bottom lip and sucked it into his mouth.

And so the kissing began.

Had they not been totally lost in each other, they might have spotted the intruders riding up the mountain. But they were. And they didn't.

Neither Star nor Diane had any idea that they were no longer alone until the crunching of gravel under a heavy bootheel caused Star's eyes to fly open in alarm. He instantly released Diane, leaped to his feet, and crossed the wide porch.

Three men were walking toward him in the fading autumn sunlight. All were huge. All were heavily armed. One was the Cherokee Kid.

"Get inside the house," Star ordered, but Diane refused to go. Her heart in her throat, she defiantly came to stand at Star's side.

"Hands up, Indian!" said the Kid, a rifle pointed directly at Star's chest.

Star lifted his hands.

"You sure that's him, Kid?" Davey Leatherwood asked. "I believe we've got the wrong man here."

The impeccably groomed man looked nothing like the wild-haired, breechclothed creature they'd brought down out of the Rockies that hot summer afternoon. Was it him? the Kid wondered. It had to be. Everyone in Virginia City seemed to know Ben Star. And knew just where to find him. All gave the same directions to this remote Sun Mountain mansion.

"It's him, all right," the Kid replied. "Look at those mean eyes. And that damned silver bracelet."

"I'm the man you're looking for," Star confirmed, as stoically resigned to his own death as a Shoshoni chieftain of old. But not to the death of the woman he loved. "I'm fair game, Kid. But take Miss Buchannan safely back to her family."

"Oh, I'm taking Miss Buchannan," said the Kid, his glance shifting to Diane. "Come on out here, sweetheart. You're safe now."

Diane thought fast. And acted just as fast. Without hesitation, she stepped away from Star's side and crossed to the Kid.

"Kid," she said breathlessly, "thank God you've come for me. I prayed you would." She stood directly in the line of fire between the Kid's raised Winchester and Star.

"Stay out of this, Diane," Star said in a low, commanding voice.

The Kid lowered his rifle. "I'm here now, darlin'," he told Diane.

"And this bastard's going to die." He reached for Diane, drew her to his side, and again raised his rifle.

"Well, then, shoot him and let's get the hell out of here," said Danny Leatherwood. "Want me to kill him?"

"Holster your gun, brother," ordered Davey Leatherwood. "This is between those two."

"Kid, don't shoot him," Diane said to the Kid. "You don't need a gun to kill him." She raised her hands and encircled his bulging biceps with slender fingers. "Do it with your hands."

The idea struck the Leatherwoods as a good one. "Yes! Go get him, Kid!" said Danny.

"Give him hell," urged Davey. "Beat his damned brains out!"

The Kid looked at Diane. "Sure, honey, sure," he said. "I need no weapon."

"Of course, you don't," Diane said, smiled, and slowly reached for his Winchester. But he still didn't trust her quite enough to hand over the rifle. He released her, walked a few yards away, and carefully laid the rifle down. Hoping she'd done the right thing, Diane gave Star a worried, questioning look.

But Star wasn't looking at her.

The minute the Kid laid down his weapon and turned back, Star came after him, navy eyes blazing. His speed was so amazing he caught the Kid off guard. His long arm shot out like a striking serpent, his fist connecting with the Kid's left jaw.

The vicious battle was on.

Diane winced when the Kid's huge fist caught Star's chin and turned his head to the side, staggering him. The two men were evenly matched. They stood toe to toe and traded punishing blows for what seemed an eternity. Finally Star got in an uppercut that felled the Kid. On his back the Kid reached out and grabbed wildly for a rock.

Diane's hands flew to her mouth. She should have known the Kid wouldn't fight fairly.

She held her breath.

The Kid came back up.

Star moved in and threw a left cross. The Kid's right fist shot forward, and he did his best to bash Star's brains out with the rock. Star ducked aside. The rock struck him just above his right ear, a solid blow that knocked him backward to the ground.

He lay there dazed and helpless. Diane was sick with fear. The Kid wiped his mouth on his forearm, spit, and got ready to move in for the kill.

He was starting toward Star when a loud roar made his head snap around in surprise. He looked up to see a huge mountain cat leap agilely upon a close overturned boulder. The lion threw back its great head and roared again.

The Kid's heart pounded wildly.

Recognition swiftly dawned as he spotted the dark diamond patch of fur beneath the lion's raised head. The cat from the Colorado wilds! The same one he had beaten and caged. Dear God, did the cat remember? The answer was not long in coming.

Paralyzed with fear, the Cherokee Kid stood like a stone statue as the mountain lion recoiled and hissed loudly, his tawny fur ruffling.

The big cat snarled, golden eyes narrowed, and showed his flesh-tearing teeth. The Leatherwoods were still fumbling for their pistols when the stalking lion wiggled his haunches, his tail standing straight up. Then shot, hissing, down from the rock.

Coming to himself, Star was as swift and as agile as the cat when he rolled to his feet, shouted a command, and threw up his right hand.

The attack was diverted.

In mid-flight the mighty mountain lion turned his big, limber body and landed softly on his paws directly beside Star.

The Kid knew better than to try to run. The cat would be on him in a flash. He stood perfectly still, shouting to the Leatherwoods, "Shoot him. Shoot the damned lion!"

"I wouldn't advise it," said Star in a cool, controlled voice, and the stunned Leatherwoods didn't dare fire their pistols against the deadly beast or the man with the power to control it.

Star faced the Kid. "I'm in a strangely benevolent mood, Kid. I'm going to let you live." He stepped closer. "If you ever come near me, Diane, or the wild west show again, I'll kill you. No . . . I'll have the cat kill you. Now slowly turn around and walk back down the hill to your horses and ride away."

The Kid eyed Star, and he eyed the big staring cat beside Star. He backed slowly, nervously away, stumbled, and cried out in fear when the lion made a fierce roar. But the big cat stayed where he was, so the Kid turned and walked slowly away.

The Leatherwoods, guns drawn, stood transfixed.

Unchallenged, Star calmly walked over and picked up the Kid's rifle. Diane came to his side.

Star addressed the pair: "Get off my property, or I'll take you in for trespassing. And when you leave, be sure to walk very slowly. This cat of mine is hungry."

The big, frightened brothers, guns frozen in their gun hands, looked at Star, whirled around, and bumped into each other in their haste to obey his command. They crashed to the ground in a tangled heap, Davey's pistol going off, the bullet harmlessly pinging against a large pebble. Danny dropped his gun.

Fearfully they scrambled to their feet and went walking off down the driveway to their waiting horses, shoving each other and breathing hard and stumbling blindly toward safety.

Star and Diane stood in the gathering dusk and laughed as the two big brutes forced themselves to walk slowly down the mountain and finally disappeared from sight.

"Darling"—Diane turned in Star's arms—"are you all right?" When he didn't answer, Diane said softly, "Star?"

"Don't," warned Star, shifting his gaze to Diane, the wide grin still on his dark face, "ever again step between me and a cocked, loaded gun."

"Did I do that?" Diane said, smiling up at him. "Why, I deserve to be punished."

"Perhaps you do." He winked at her. "Let's go upstairs."

Diane laughed softly when he swept her up into his arms and carried her inside.

Chapter 41

➤➤➤ Star tossed the stirrup up over the saddle, pulled the cinch tight under the big black's belly, and threaded the wide leather strap through the silver buckle. Diane patted absently at the stallion's sleek neck and brushed through his long, coarse mane with her fingers, but the main focus of her attention was Star.

Star flipped the stirrup back down into place, plucked a pair of soft black kid gloves from his hip pocket, and drew them on. He lifted, then lowered his black felt Stetson and tugged at the black silk bandanna tied around his neck, adjusting the knot to the right side of his throat.

He looked at Diane and grinned. He reached out, curled a gloved long forefinger down into the open collar of her shirt, and drew her slowly up against him. Continuing to clutch her shirtfront, he lowered his lips to within an inch of hers. And hesitated.

Her hands braced against his hard, muscular chest, Diane raised herself on tiptoe and kissed him, letting him feel the quick fire lick of her tongue against his smooth lips. She immediately went back down on her heels and pulled gently away.

"There's plenty more where that came from," she promised flirtatiously, "so don't be malingering in town."

Star again grinned, nodded, and released her. Diane stepped back. Star turned, gripped the horn, and swung up into the saddle. He lifted his gloved right hand to his black Stetson, touched the stiff brim briefly with thumb and forefinger, and slowly backed the big black away.

Diane stood shading her eyes against the harsh glare of the afternoon sun as he wheeled the mount about and cantered down the graveled drive. Halfway to the entranceway's towering arch of natural stone, he pulled the stallion up. Slowly Black Star turned about in a tight semicircle and stayed there, dancing in place, shaking his great head and nickering. Until his master silently put him into motion.

Diane felt her heartbeat quicken as dark horse and dark rider slowly, surely approached her. The big black pranced as grandly as a well-trained show horse, but her eyes were riveted to the man on his back, hatbrim pulled low over the dark, penetrating eyes. Star's wide shoulders in his snowy white shirt and soft black leather vest moved not at all. His lean body did not bounce or sway or slap up and down. He held himself erect yet easy in the saddle, reins slack in his gloved left hand. His long legs, encased in faded denim Levi's, were loose and relaxed, his booted feet outside the stirrups.

Diane didn't move a muscle as the prancing twelve-hundred-pound creature steadily neared her. She calmly lowered her hands to her sides and waited expectantly. She firmly stood her ground even when the point of the stallion's shoulder brushed against her slender body.

Mounted above, Star pushed the black Stetson back, leaned down from the horse, captured Diane's chin in his gloved hand, and wordlessly kissed her on the lips.

Then he righted himself and was gone.

Diane watched until he was out of sight. Then she raced happily back inside the mansion. She had one million things to do and Star said he'd be gone no more than three or four hours. The warm, sunny afternoon was hers to get herself—and the house—ready for this "very special evening."

The final evening.

In Virginia City Star tied the stallion to the hitch rail and went inside the small storefront Western Union office. He removed his black gloves, stuffed them into his back pocket. From the inside breast pocket of his black leather vest he withdrew two pieces of folded yellow Western Union message paper.

Nodding to the thin, pallid-looking telegrapher behind the caged counter, Star passed him the yellow forms.

"Need to send this wire right away, Mort."

A quarter of an hour later Star stepped back out into the brilliant sunlight, folding the two-page yellow message and shoving it back inside his inner vest pocket.

His next stop was the train depot. He purchased two first-class sleeper tickets to San Francisco, California. The departure date on the bright blue tickets read, "7:00 A.M., Saturday, September 28, 1895." The train tickets went into the pocket of his white shirt.

Star paused on the wooden sidewalk outside the depot, put a long, thin cigar between his lips, and struck a match. He cupped his hands around the tiny flame and puffed the cheroot to life. He leaned for a minute against a lamppost, smoking and considering his next stops.

Minutes later he was standing in the kitchen of the Timberline Hotel, talking with the head chef. The little Frenchman in his white apron and tall white chef's hat was saying passionately that it was impossible! He couldn't possibly prepare the kind of meal Star was requesting in the next two hours. It could not be done! And to expect such a feast to be packed so that it could be taken out and eaten at home?

Impractical! Outrageous! Impossible!

Star calmly listened to the excitable little Frenchman rant and rave and wring his hands. When the tirade ended at last and the flush-faced chef was wadding his tall white hat in his hands, Star smiled easily and walked away.

In the doorway he paused, turned, and said, "I'll be back here at five o'clock. Be sure everything's ready. *Bonjour, Philippe.*"

"Ah, these impatient Americans," said the bristling Philippe to Star's departing back. "Why did I ever leave Paris?"

Next door, at the Timberline Barbershop, the aging barber clipped and cut Star's long raven hair while he sat very still for the next twenty minutes. Star walked back out into the sunshine looking well groomed and feeling half naked. The freshly trimmed black hair barely touched his shirt collar in back. The silver streaks at the temples were brushed straight back.

Two blocks up the street Star turned into Winston's Jewelers. The bell mounted above the store's front door tinkled loudly as he entered. Alan Winston's face shone more brightly than his array of fine jewels when Star chose a particularly expensive piece from the valuable collection.

The small black velvet box tucked in his inside vest pocket, Star mounted his stallion. There was one last important stop before he returned to the Timberline to collect the evening's meal.

Star turned his mount away from the busy street, guided him between two buildings and out the other side. Three blocks north he turned the big black onto a narrow dirt road and started to climb the mountain. Following the winding road up a serpentine path, Star reached a house high above the city, alone and apart from its neighbors.

Star dismounted before the large, handsome yellow and white Victorian house surrounded by a decorative silver-trimmed fence. At the front door Star removed his black Stetson, raked a hand through his hair, then lifted the silver door knocker, and tapped it forcefully several times.

The wide front door opened. A bowing Chinese butler warmly greeted Star, the whites of his slanted eyes disappearing completely as he smiled an effusive welcome.

With a white-gloved hand the friendly Chinese servant motioned Star inside while he turned and called in a surprisingly loud, strong voice, "Missy Rita, you have important visitor. Mr. Ben is here!" He promptly relieved Star of his Stetson.

"Ben?" came a surprised feminine voice from the landing above. "Ben Star?"

"In the flesh," called Star, waiting at the base of the stairs, his booted feet apart, hands at his sides.

A slim, extraordinarily beautiful red-haired woman in a luxurious long dressing gown of shimmering aqua satin came gliding down the carpeted stairs. Her large blue eyes shone with excitement; her full red lips were lifted into a wide smile of pleasure.

Two steps from the bottom, the ecstatically happy redhead threw her arms around Star's neck and kissed him fully on the lips.

"Star, darling," she murmured breathlessly, "I've missed you so!"

A splendid fantasy.

Their last evening in the Nevada mansion was to be a splendid fantasy realized. Diane meant to make sure everything was absolutely perfect.

As soon as Star rode out of sight, she tore back into the house and headed straight for the big dining room. After throwing all the tall French doors open wide to the fresh mountain air, she began clearing the morning's breakfast dishes from the cluttered dining table.

She made a sour face when she carried the plates and coffee cups into the kitchen. Stacks of dirty dishes covered the surface of every countertop as well as the stove and the eating table. The sink was full to overflowing. Sighing, Diane went down on her knees and deposited the latest load on the floor.

She rolled up her shirt sleeves and went to work.

It took more than an hour before the last plate was finally washed, dried, and put away. Diane's pale hands were pink from the prolonged exposure to hot dishwater, and her face was shiny with perspiration, her raven hair limp and sticking hotly to her neck.

She took a short rest on the shaded porch. She dropped down on the steps and shoved her heavy, wilted hair atop her head. She heard a loud, low growl coming from somewhere in the dense pine forest. She smiled, no longer afraid of the big cat. But she did wonder at the cause of his agitation. By the violent sounds he was making, something was certainly disturbing him.

Diane had little time to ponder it.

She hurried back inside, where she meticulously polished the heavy dining-room furniture until the dark wood gleamed. From a drawer of the sideboard she withdrew a claret-colored damask cloth and spread it carefully over the long table. She needlessly polished a pair of ornately carved silver candelabra, placed them strategically on the claret-clothed table and filled both with new tall white candles.

Diane set the table for two with Star's finest. The fragile white bone china with the bordering silver trim. The heavy English sterling. The sparkling, fragile crystal.

She stood back to admire her handiwork, hands on hips. She returned to the table, leaned down, and straightened a soup spoon at Star's place.

She smiled. Then frowned. And snapped her fingers as the idea of flowers on the table struck her. Like an excited child, Diane rushed out into the yard, carrying a straw basket over her arm. She was on her knees gathering bell-shaped blossoms of snowy white heather when she again heard the diamond-throated cat snarling and hissing from some concealed lair farther up the mountain. Diane lifted her head, looked all about, and saw nothing. She shrugged and continued to collect the ivory blooms.

The lovely white wild flowers, painstakingly arranged in a tall crystal vase, added just the right touch to her perfectly set table. Nodding her proud endorsement, Diane backed out of the dining room. In the wide corridor she glanced up at the tall-cased clock.

Already four o'clock!

Diane flew up the stairs, unbuttoning her shirt as she went. The entire time she spent shampooing her raven hair, she could hear the big cat growling and roaring outdoors, sounding as if he was becoming steadily more vexed.

Naked to the waist, wearing only her borrowed black trousers, Diane wandered out onto the upstairs balcony to let the sun dry her hair. She sat down on the side of a long padded chaise and leaned her head over between her knees, brushing and toweling her freshly washed hair.

The loud, close growl of the mountain lion made her head snap up. Diane jumped to her feet, covered her bare breasts with the damp white towel, and moved to the balcony's railing. In plain sight in a small clearing beyond the back fence, the big tawny cat with the dark diamond throat was pacing restlessly back and forth, roaring to the top of his lungs and shaking his great head about.

"Hey," Diane shouted to the big beast, "just what the devil is wrong with you?"

She promptly found out.

The words had hardly left her lips when into the clearing strolled the handsome, lighter-hued female lion. The smaller cat purposely circled the growling, snarling male, hissed loudly at him, then strutted a few yards away, glanced back over her shoulder at him, and lay down.

Diane slowly lowered the white towel to the balcony's railing. She stood there not daring to move, watching. The sleek female cat was taking great delight in teasing and tormenting the excited male.

She rolled; she stretched; she purred low in her throat. The male got up. He cautiously circled the female. Waited until he could stand it no longer and moved swiftly toward her. The female hissed a decisive warning and stung him with a quick, claw-extended paw to the side of his head.

He roared his outrage and jumped back, then foolishly, futilely tried it again with the same maddening results. The female wasn't ready, and until she was, he wouldn't be allowed to get near her.

Diane turned away, her face beginning to flush with embarrassment and heat. She returned to the padded chaise, realizing when she reached it, that she'd left the towel behind.

She didn't go back for it.

Knowing by the intimate sounds and sights she'd witnessed that any second the baiting, goading female would turn sweetly docile and accept the excited male, Diane went back indoors to allow them privacy.

Inside the sunny bedroom she paced restlessly, feeling tightly coiled, mysteriously edgy. Her nerves were raw. Her breath was labored. The nipples of her bare breasts tightened into hard, sensitive buds. Tingles of erotic sensation traveled throughout her body.

Weak-kneed and half light-headed, Diane dropped down into an easy chair. She hooked her knee over an arm and allowed her narrowed gaze to sweep across the room and settle on the big bed. A foolish smile immediately played at her lips.

Pleasantly excited and mildly aroused from innocently observing the intensely sexual drama going on outdoors, Diane eagerly anticipated the heated lovemaking that would take place indoors tonight. As she looked dreamily at the big inviting bed and pictured herself lying there gloriously naked with Star, silence fell outside. Her breath growing shallow, Diane slowly lifted a hand and touched her fingertip to a taut, aching nipple as her eyes slid closed.

She immediately jumped, her eyes opening wide when the brief peaceful stillness suddenly erupted into the scratching, snarling, hissing sounds of the female cat signaling the completion of the mating act.

Diane swallowed and eagerly reached for her discarded shirt. She rose, hastily buttoned the shirt, and went back out to reclaim the white towel from the balcony railing.

Diane smiled when she caught sight of the female cat, lying just where she'd been all along. The well-satisfied lioness yawned lazily and swished her long tail and rolled over onto her back, flexing her unsheathed claws in the air. The big male cautiously eyed her, wisely keeping his distance.

The fabric of her black trousers and loose shirt strangely abrasive against her sensitive flesh, Diane finished drying her hair in the sun and went back downstairs to check on last-minute preparations.

Nothing further to do now but wait anxiously for Star.

Star arrived shortly after six, unsaddled the stallion, and came up to the house, a huge wicker basket over one arm, a large box under the other. He dropped the basket and his Stetson on the kitchen table, shoved the big box behind his back, and started through the house. In the wide corridor he met Diane.

Her first words were, "Star, your hair! You've cut your hair."

"Couldn't go to the big city tomorrow looking like a wild man." He grinned at her. "Now close your eyes and hold out your hands." Diane swiftly obeyed. Star placed the box in her arms. Her eyes opened. "Kiss me and the new gown's all yours," he said.

The box between them, Diane kissed him.

"Don't tell me what it looks like," she warned. "I want it to be a complete surprise."

Star humored her. Nodding, he withdrew the pair of blue railroad tickets from his shirt pocket, showed them to her. "Our tickets to San Francisco." He dropped them in a silver bowl on a low hallway table. "Let's go on upstairs and take a nice long bath and—"

"No." Diane violently shook her head. "I'm going to dress in the guest room. You clean up in our room." She slowly backed away from him. "It'll be more exciting that way. At eight o'clock sharp, we'll meet for dinner."

"Sweetheart," said Star, watching her tenaciously clutch the big box to her breasts, "I will count the minutes."

Chapter 42

She wanted to, but she didn't.

➤➤➤➤ Upstairs in the guest room, Diane made herself wait. She was itching to have a peek inside the big box, but she checked the urge as part of her plan to draw out and enjoy fully the sweet anticipation of their final evening. And so she waited. She didn't allow herself a look until she'd had a long bath and carefully arranged her heavy black hair in glossy curls atop her head.

Then, at last, she tore the lid off the big box, ripped away the white tissue paper, and snatched up the shimmering garment. The beautiful gown of rustling violet taffeta—the exact color of her eyes—was of the very latest European style. The balloon sleeves, puffed to the elbow, were long and fitted at the wrists. The waistline was slender, the neckline round and scandalously low. The gown was extremely tight around her hips and stomach, giving way to a full radiation of stiffly gored skirts.

Smiling with delight, Diane laid the lovely gown across the bed and took from the box violet satin dancing slippers decorated with gold thread, a pair of fancy violet satin and gold garters, and sheer silk stockings.

She struggled for several long, frustrating minutes, then finally managed to get the violet taffeta gown buttoned down her back. She could hardly breathe, it fitted her so snugly. Designed to give the full effects of the popular hourglass figure, the fashionable gown squeezed in her waist, pushed up her breasts, and accentuated her hips.

Diane looked thoughtfully at herself in a freestanding silver-trimmed mirror. She frowned. While the color and cut of the gown were unquestionably becoming, there was one small problem. Her lace-trimmed underpants caused unsightly wrinkles beneath the snug taffeta.

Diane did the only thing she could do. She took off the spoiling underwear and turned back to the mirror. Perfect. The exquisite violet taffeta evening gown looked exactly as it was meant to look. Grinning at herself, Diane felt a little naughty but pleasantly so. Naked beneath the gown save for the sheer silk stockings, satin garters, and dancing slippers, she wondered if Star would suspect.

As regal as a queen, Diane descended the stairs at ten past eight, swept silently across the corridor, and paused in the arched doorway of the drawing room.

Star stood with his back to the cold fireplace, smoking a thin brown cigar. His newly cut raven hair gleamed with blue highlights, the silver wings at the temples brushed straight back above his well-shaped ears. He wore an impeccably cut tuxedo of midnight black gabardine with lapels of shimmering black satin. His shirt was pristine white, the front pleated, the collar stiff, the sleeves' French cuffs set off with shiny silver links. A black bow tie at his throat and neatly arranged in his breast coat pocket a handkerchief of violet silk added a small dramatic touch of color.

Speechless, Diane stared at the tall, compelling Star. Not only was he devastatingly handsome in his well-cut evening clothes, but he was powerfully, intimidatingly male. Dark sensuality and self-assurance radiated from him. A cultured, expensively attired gentleman with gracious manners but with an essence of raw, leashed passion just below the polished surface. A dark, lean god with the devil's own erotic appeal.

Just looking at Star made Diane become vitally aware of her nudity beneath the taffeta gown.

Star sensed her presence, looked up.

And experienced a tremendous shock to his entire nervous system from merely seeing Diane framed in the wide doorway. His knees went weak, his throat dry; his fingers tightened reflexively on his half-smoked cigar.

She was too beautiful to be real. Surely such an ethereal creature would vanish if he reached out to touch her.

Her long, lustrous black hair was dressed attractively atop her head, revealing the sensuous curve of her pale neck and throat. The violet taffeta gown fitted her slender curves as if she had been sewn into it. Never had she been more irresistible. Her high, rounded breasts swelled against the shimmering taffeta bodice to spill appealingly from the daringly low neckline.

So much pale, bare flesh was exposed he was tempted to go to her, bend his head, and kiss her in the dewy shadow between those lovely, tempting breasts. Her waist was nipped in waspishly, and her hips flared provocatively, the shimmering taffeta stretched tightly across her flat stomach.

Star's eyes slowly descended the length of her tall, slim body, then climbed back up to her beautiful face. There was high color in her cheeks, and her violet eyes flashed with purple fire. Her lips were invitingly parted over perfect white teeth.

Star felt totally drained of power.

Hers was a formidable beauty. She appeared to be a pale, unattainable goddess with the flawless face of a pure angel and the bewitching body of a naughty nymph. A seductive, irresistible blend of innocence and wickedness. Oddly she appeared rather demure and modest in the risqué Paris gown yet radiated an earthy, overpowering sensuality which suggested that beneath the shimmering fabric draping the tempting curves, she was naked and warm and willing.

Diane drew a shallow breath as Star snuffed out his cigar in a crystal ashtray and crossed to her. She stood rooted to the spot as a lazy smile curved his sensual lips. He walked slowly, deliberately, around her, touching her with nothing but those dark, sultry eyes. Boldly, hotly he evaluated every angle of her, and Diane could feel the heat of those brazen eyes burning through the shimmering taffeta, singeing the bare, tingling flesh beneath.

Star stopped in back of Diane, so close behind her she could feel the heat of his body. His hands lifted to clasp her bare ivory shoulders gently. He bent his dark head, pressed a warm kiss to the delicate nape of her neck.

Diane trembled.

Star raised his head. His long arms went around her from behind, reaching under her arms and cupping her rounded breasts. He caressed the nipples through the rustling taffeta, stroking them softly as he spoke. "If I should guess exactly what you're wearing under the gown, would you admit it?"

Her eyes half closed, heavy lashes fluttering nervously, Diane murmured, "Yes. Yes, of course." She held her breath.

"Nothing," his low, unexcitable voice calmly stated. "I believe you're naked."

Diane swept his hands away and turned to face him, her violet eyes searching his. "How did you know?"

He smiled, took her hand, and warmly kissed it. "I saw it in your eyes when I looked at you from across the room." He kissed the inside of her wrist. "May I see some proof?"

Her charming girlish laughter filled the air. "Of course, you can." Star's head snapped up, his eyes darkening with interest. "But later," she told him. "Much later."

"Ah, you're a cruel, heartless female," he gently accused. "How you tempt and torture this lowly male."

Diane gave no reply. She again laughed and thought back to the lioness's behavior this afternoon. Recalled how the beautiful feline had driven the big male cat half crazy before she'd accepted him. Suddenly imbued with a heady sense of feminine power, Diane decided to seduce the darkly handsome Star slowly. Devilishly make him wait the way the female cat had made her anxious mate wait. Flirt and tease and tempt him until he was half crazy with wanting her.

Only then would she allow him to take her.

Not one second before.

Diane took Star's offered arm, lifted the skirts of her elegant gown, and went with him to the dining room. He graciously seated Diane, then swiftly lighted the white candles gracing the long claret damask-covered table. The tall French doors were open to the cool evening. A gentle night breeze caused the tiny flames of candles to dance and sway, casting shadows on the walls and on the faces of the two diners.

It was a lengthy, glorious meal. Caviar, lobster, and champagne and too many courses to count. Diane swallowed a bite of the crunchy caviar spread generously on a toasted small triangle of bread, washed it down with a big drink of the champagne, and looked up to see Star closely watching her. The candlelight played on the lines around his blue-black eyes and softened the angularity of his features.

Holding his intense gaze, Diane put out the tip of her tongue, licked her gleaming lips, and said, "I have *such* an appetite this evening. Have you?"

The quick pulse of blood through the vein on his temple was evident in the candlelight. "Yes," he replied. "But not for food. I want you."

As she smiled seductively, Diane's back left her chair. She leaned over the table to give Star a fleeting glimpse of her breasts, the pink-tipped crests appearing and disappearing inside the low-cut bodice.

Star swallowed hard, reached out, and captured her hand. "Sweetheart, let's go upstairs. We'll dine later."

Diane laughed breathlessly. "On the contrary, my love, you should have a healthy portion of veal." She withdrew her hand from his, spread it on her bosom, further calling his attention to the tempting expanse of bare, warm flesh. "You're going to need plenty of energy."

They remained at the dining table for at least another leisurely hour. They sampled the many fine foods but ate little. They drank freely of the fine champagne, and Diane soon began to grow pleasantly tipsy. Star encouraged her, refilling her glass.

"Thank you," she said, stirring her wine with a finger and looking thoughtful for a moment.

She was noticing Star's hands. They were the hands of an artist, a sculptor. She looked at his long, tapered fingers and felt a chill of excitement skip up her spine. "Your hands are beautiful," she said, lifting her eyes to meet his.

"Your body is beautiful," he replied, raising both hands before him. "I want to touch your body with these hands."

Diane shivered deliciously.

"Soon," she promised, draining her glass. She leaned back in her chair, drew a deep, slow breath. The taffeta fabric strained and pulled, accentuating every curve of her body.

"No hurry," said Star, feeling the perspiration dot his hairline. He uncorked a Pommard, poured a glass, and took a drink.

"A drink of your red wine?" Diane asked.

"If you don't mind sharing my glass." Star held the crystal goblet out to her.

"I prefer it that way," Diane replied, smiling at him.

They shared that glass of wine. And the next. And the next.

Soon Diane was no longer seated across from Star. He smoothly coaxed her around the table and onto his lap. Her smile was dazzling when she agreed it seemed a good idea. So she rose, lifted her taffeta skirts, and swept around the candlelit dining table. Holding her skirts daringly high, she sat down on his lap, crossed her legs, and Star caught a glimpse of the inner side of her thighs, soft and as white as ivory.

His vocal cords tied in knots, he said, "There's brandy in the library and a fire burning in the fireplace."

Diane laid her forefinger against his lips. "I like wine."

"You don't like brandy?"

She shook her head. "I don't recall ever tasting brandy."

"You'll love brandy."

"After the brandy we'll dance?"

"If you wish."

"I wish."

Diane clung tightly to Star's arm as they climbed the stairs to the library. She felt a little light-headed but wonderfully relaxed and happy.

The spacious library looked cozy and inviting. A fire burned brightly in the fireplace, the leaping, hypnotic blaze the only light. The French doors were wide open to the balcony. A cold north wind blew the heavy curtains, gusting intermittently, chilling the far reaches of the firelit room. A large square rug of lush black ermine was spread directly before the dancing, warming fire.

Diane released Star's arm and took a seat on the comfortable long sofa. Star remained standing. He tugged loose the black bow tie, slid it free of his white shirt collar, and carelessly draped it over the brass telescope on a stand near the open French doors.

He poured two balloon snifters one-third full of fine Napoleon brandy. He came around the sofa, sat down beside Diane, and handed her one of the snifters.

Smiling into her violet eyes, he watched as she took a sip of the brandy, tilted her head thoughtfully, then nodded her approval. Star drank. Then took her snifter, reached across her, and set both glasses on the end table. He immediately took Diane in his arms and kissed her softly on the mouth. A wise and thorough lover, Star knew that for a woman slow, sure arousal began with kissing.

So between drinks of brandy he kissed her. His lips were warm and smooth and tasted of the brandy. Diane sighed softly and snuggled to him, enjoying tremendously the cozy fire, the aged brandy, the searing kisses.

And making Star wait.

Star felt as if he *had* waited. He wanted her so badly he didn't feel he could wait much longer. So Diane got the full blast of his charm.

Attentive. Complimentary. Affectionate.

Between deep swallows of the brandy and murmured endearments and shocking promises of what was to come, he kissed her again and again with steadily graduating intensity. Then abruptly his heated lips left hers. He swung away and stood up, leaving Diane faint and trembling on the sofa.

Opening the white collar at his throat, Star moved across the room to the hand-cranked phonograph. He cranked the machine, and suddenly mellow music filled the chilly, firelit room. Star returned to Diane. She tipped her head back. He stood there above, looking breathtakingly handsome and appealingly dangerous.

Thrilled by the sexual self-confidence he exuded, Diane took the hand he extended and rose to face him.

His lean fingers lightly gripping hers, he said, "Dance with me?"

"Yes." It was no more than a whisper.

Diane could only nod and swallow convulsively when Star decisively drew her into his arms and said in that low, caressive voice, "And then I'll make love to you."

Chapter 43

❀❀❀❀   His long arm encircling Diane's waist, Star leaned over and picked up his brandy snifter. He offered her a drink. She shook her head. He smiled, lifted the crystal snifter to his lips, and drank as his feet began to move in tempo to the music.

Smiling, Diane put her arm around his neck, spread a hand on his pleated white shirtfront, and moved with him. Effortlessly he led. Easily she followed.

Diane wasn't surprised to find that Star was an expert dancer. Her responsive body sensed every subtle movement of his tall, lean frame well before he made it. She shivered as Star's hard thighs brushed against hers through the layers of their clothing. His hand on her back applied no pressure, yet she was vitally aware of the strong fingers touching her. Undoubtedly he was every woman's dream of the consummate dancing partner. Tall, dark, and graceful.

A sudden flash of jealousy seized Diane as she considered the dozens of beautiful women Star had surely spun around the polished dance floors in mansions of the rich.

Her hand tightened on his neck, fingers grasping at the thick raven hair curling over his white collar. She pressed closer and closed her eyes as they swayed together.

His lips against her temple, Star softly said, "The last time I heard this song I was alone. Chained in the dark." Diane's eyes opened. She tilted her head back to look at him. He continued in that same dispassionate tone. "After the first Denver performance of your grandfather's wild west show. There was a party. A band played "After the Ball." I remember wondering if you were there. If you were dancing. If you were in the arms of the Cherokee Kid."

Diane opened her mouth to respond, but abruptly Star's lips claimed hers in a fiercely possessive kiss that left her weak and breathless and clinging frantically to him.

His blue-black eyes flashing with a heart-stopping blend of fury and desire, he commandingly promised, "You'll never again be in any arms but mine."

"No," she breathlessly assured him, "never. I belong to you, Star."

His hard face immediately softened, and he picked up the steps of the dance. As the sweetly mellow strains of "After the Ball" drifted from the phonograph, Star spun Diane around the shadowy library, calmly undoing her evening gown as they danced.

When the song ended, Diane's violet taffeta gown was open down her back and Star's tanned fingers were brushing her bare, sensitive flesh. The snifter of brandy still held in his other hand, he again offered Diane a drink. She accepted, sighing as she felt the fiery liquid burn its way through her throat and chest and out into her arms.

His spread hand on her bare, slender back, Star pressed Diane closer, tilted his head to one side, and licked the residue of brandy from her glistening lips. Which led to a kiss. To many kisses.

Star began to gradually build the intimacy and excitement. Adept at the art of seduction, he effortlessly managed to peel Diane's violet taffeta gown down her arms and to her waist before she fully realized what was happening. While he dexterously undressed her, he continued to share with her his brandy and his kisses. He kissed her in a dozen different ways and tenderly caressed each inch of ivory flesh he exposed.

When Diane felt the rustling taffeta being eased down over her hips, she pressed closer to Star. Breathlessly she said, "Star, let's go to our room. To our bed."

Gently Star set her back. "Later," he said. "Much later."

And holding her gaze, he urged the full, rustling skirts over the arch of her hips and down her pale, luminous thighs.

"No . . . Star . . ." she breathed, embarrassed, excited.

"Yes, Diane." He bent slightly from the waist, decisively pushed the swirling skirts down until they lay in a shimmering violet pool around her slippered feet.

"Wh-what are . . . you doing?"

"Making love to you," he calmly replied.

Star straightened, lifted a hand, and withdrew the restraints from Diane's fancily dressed hair. He watched appreciatively as the long inky tresses tumbled down around her bare ivory shoulders. A muscle involuntarily danced in his firm jaw, and his eyes darkened with rising passion as he looked at her.

Her hair was a shimmering black cloud around her lovely face, one long, silky strand falling onto her bare left breast. Naked save for the sheer stockings, satin garters, and dancing slippers, her pale, slender body was tinted a soft golden rose in the firelight. Star's eyes were drawn to the triangle of curling raven hair between her firm thighs.

"I want," he said, handing her the brandy snifter, "to dance one more time."

"Dance one more? . . . Star, I'm naked."

"I know, sweetheart. God, I know."

He stepped away from her. Diane trembled and anxiously took a drink of brandy as the chill wind kissed her bare flesh. Star again cranked the phonograph, and the sweetly haunting tune "After the Ball" began to play once more.

Without a word Star lifted Diane free of the discarded taffeta skirts, pulled her into his embrace, and began to dance. Diane didn't question him. She loosely hooked her arm around his neck, the brandy snifter cupped in her palm.

While it seemed shamefully risqué and a bit mad to be dancing naked in the arms of a man fully dressed in evening attire, it was strangely exciting. Powerfully tantalizing.

Diane liked the way Star held her as they danced. So suggestively close. She wasn't sure which was the most arousing: the slick satin of his tuxedo lapels brushing against her taut nipples. Or the rising male flesh pressing insistently against her bare belly through the restraining fabric of his black trousers. Or the bold, artistic hands molding her naked curves to the hard planes of his tall frame. She loved the feel of his dark, warm fingers stroking the nape of her neck, her shoulders and back, the curve of her hips. And finally her bare buttocks.

It was so unconventionally enjoyable Diane was soon straining eagerly against Star, pressing her tingling body intimately closer, anxiously rubbing her pelvis against the hard, sinewy thigh firmly positioned between her legs.

After the first few seconds Diane no longer felt the least bit foolish or awkward. Everything seemed natural and spontaneous. She was glad Star had suggested dancing this way. She naked. He clothed. It was strangely sexy and incredibly stirring.

Star's total lack of inhibitions made for some very creative lovemaking. Which delighted her. She wanted to be just like him. Open and honest and without pretense or shame. Capable of enjoying to the fullest every novel facet of his inventive lovemaking, of their shared physical intimacy.

Star knew what was going through Diane's mind. He could tell by her shallow breathing, by the way she wantonly pressed her tempting naked body to his that she was highly excited and ready for sexual adventure. She'd be agreeable to any kind of loving he dared propose, and that knowledge made his heart pound.

Nature was not to be ignored this night.

He wanted this beautiful woman in any and every way he'd not yet had her. Now was the time. Here was the place. On this final stolen evening in his wind-chilled fire-warmed library, he and this desirable woman would give themselves with equal abandon.

His pulse raging with alcohol and sexual excitement, Star suddenly stopped dancing. While the music played on, he guided Diane down onto the black ermine rug directly before the fire. Sighing, she happily stretched out, resting her weight on an elbow. And was at once vitally aware of the tantalizing tickle of soft ermine next to her bare, awakened flesh. She purred like an aroused lioness.

Star smiled, stretched out close beside her, took the brandy snifter from her hand, and kissed her. The flames of the fire dancing in the depths of his dark eyes, he said in a low, soft voice, "Know what I want to do?"

"Let me guess," Diane murmured, snared by his sultry eyes.

"Everything we've ever done." The leap of her heart made it impossible to reply. His dark hand gently enclosed a pale, bare breast, and he added, "All the things we've *never* done."

"Yes," she managed to say breathlessly, wondering what that could possibly be. "Star, the way you make me feel . . . I never knew."

"I didn't either." He took a small swallow of the brandy, held it in his mouth while he set the snifter aside. He bent to kiss the ivory breast enclosed in his dark hand, painting the pebble-hard nipple with brandy until it glistened wetly. He lifted his head. "I didn't either, sweetheart."

Diane's eyes met his as she drew a ragged breath. She waited anxiously, knowing he meant to lick the liquor from her aching nipple. Longing for him to do it.

Her darkening purple gaze slowly moved down to the pale breast cupped possessively in Star's lean dark fingers. The taut nipple shimmered with the sheen of brandy. And throbbed for the touch of his lips. It seemed to Diane that the very universe was centered there in that aching pink crest.

"Star, please . . ." she murmured weakly.

"Kiss me," he commanded, making her wait. His mouth on hers was fiery hot, and much as Diane reveled in the long, drugging kiss, she couldn't help wishing that his blazing mouth were on her breast.

She exhaled raggedly when Star said against her lips, "What is it, love? What do you want?"

"I want—I want—"

"Say it," he gently prompted. "Tell me, sweetheart."

Diane made a helpless little sound and clasped his tanned face in her hand. She lay flat down on the black ermine rug, pulled him down on her breasts, and nuzzled into the thick silkiness of his blue black hair. And winced with grateful joy as he licked the brandy from her throbbing nipple. She sighed with sweet ecstasy when his mouth warmly enclosed her and he soothingly sucked.

Her head fell back, and she turned to gaze into the leaping flames of the fire. Star's tongue licked at her tight nipples, and his sharp teeth raked back and forth. Her hand clasping the dark hair of his moving head, Diane looked dreamily into the fire and felt as if she were melting in the flames.

She stirred when Star's lips at last deserted her pinkened breasts. With one hand he reached down and removed her slippers. He kissed her hot, flushed face, and placing a hand to the back of her leg, he raised and bent her right knee so that her foot was flat on the ermine rug. With his thumb he hooked the satin garter and slipped it swiftly off, dropping it beside the brandy glass. He then slowly peeled the stocking down her long, slender leg and off over her foot. Diane sighed softly, expecting him to remove the other stocking.

He didn't touch it.

Nor did he toss aside the stocking he'd removed. Holding it loosely in his hand, Star trailed the gauzy silk stocking over Diane's bare body, teasing her with its ticklish, whispery touch. She squirmed and wiggled and grew more excited with each slow pass of stocking over her tingling body.

When Star drew the wispy stocking slowly, surely back up her bare leg until it was directly between her thighs, Diane moaned and rolled over onto her stomach.

Star smiled and began the game anew, starting at the nape of her neck. Not stopping until the silky stocking was drawn gently up into the crevice between her quivering rounded buttocks.

Her hands clawing at the lush black ermine, cheek pressed against it, Diane's eyes closed as the tormenting stocking touched her for a fleeting second and was swiftly withdrawn.

Star tossed the silk stocking aside. He leaned down, pressed his hot dark cheek to her shoulder, then turned her over. His passion-hardened face loomed just above hers, his lips hovering inches from her own. His dark eyes flashed with hot desire as he said hoarsely, "Let me love you, Diane. Give it to me, baby. Give it all to me."

Chapter 44

✦✦✦ Star kissed Diane and began slowly to slide down her body, kissing her chin, her throat, her breasts, her ribs. When his fiery lips reached her flat stomach and continued on their downward path, Diane came anxiously up on her elbows, shaking her head.

"God, don't you dare," she murmured.

But her purple eyes were shining with excitement, and Star could tell the idea thrilled her.

He kissed the small indentation of her navel and said against her flushed, silky skin, "Relax, my love. I'll stop any time you want." With the tip of his tongue he tracked the pale path of fine light hairs from her navel down to the dark, curly triangle between her thighs. "Let me kiss you, sweetheart. Make me happy. Let me make you happy."

"Star . . ." she breathed, overwhelmed with emotion.

"Yes, my own sweet love."

Star lowered his dark face to the raven curls. He nuzzled his mouth and nose in the crisp black coils, opened his lips, and breathed hotly against her. Diane gasped and flung the back of her hand across her mouth. She began to throb and pulsate there between her legs where his hot breath touched her. Star pressed his lips to her. She moaned aloud, and her back arched up off the fur. He touched the tip of his tongue to her. Diane called out his name. Star began eagerly kissing her there, cupping her buttocks with both hands. An involuntary shudder of pure pleasure jolted through Diane.

She came frantically up onto her elbows. Through passion-slitted eyes she looked down and couldn't believe what she was seeing.

The darkly handsome Star fully dressed in black custom-cut tuxedo and white pleated shirt. She totally naked save for one silk stocking and satin garter on her left leg. Star with his face buried in the black curls between her thighs. She lying stretched out wantonly on the ermine rug with her legs widely parted to him.

For an instant the shocking sight seemed disgracefully lewd, and Diane experienced a brief disturbing flash of shame. But the shame swiftly evaporated as Star's heated mouth continued to love her in this heart-stoppingly intimate way. It felt so incredibly good she hoped he would never, never stop. There was nothing appalling about this kind of lovemaking.

It was wonderful.

It was beautiful.

Diane's eyes were no longer partially closed. They were open wide. And she was no longer thinking how shameful the two of them looked. She was thinking she'd never seen anything so powerfully erotic as the sight of Star's dark, handsome face between her legs, kissing her in that most feminine of all spots.

Nor had she ever felt anything more deeply than this sweet pleasure his loving mouth was giving her. The joy steadily increased, spiraled higher and higher. Breathing hard, Diane sagged back down on the soft ermine rug as her heated body began to convulse with the first tiny tremors of impending climax. Her heart racing wildly, the muscles in her thighs jumping involuntarily, she flung her arms up over her head and surged her pelvis up to meet Star's moving, marvelous mouth. She whipped her head to the side and again looked into the fire.

Staring transfixed at the flickering flames, she felt the intense heat of those dancing, leaping flames licking and lashing the throbbing flesh between her legs. She was being devoured by the red-hot fire, completely incinerated in the enveloping blaze.

She gave herself up to the raging inferno. And cried out in shocked ecstasy when her fully ignited body exploded with radiating showers of glorious heat. Star's mouth stayed fused to her as she thrashed and surged and bucked in abandoned rapture. Then went totally limp on the soft fur rug.

Only then did Star lift his head.

Moving quickly up beside her, he kissed her damp temple and held her close in his arms, murmuring endearments until she was calm and lazy and stretching languorously on the lush furs.

Then he rose and hurriedly began stripping. Diane lay lazily below, unashamedly watching as he shrugged out of the tuxedo jacket, jerked the fully buttoned white shirt up over his head and off. He kicked off his black shoes and stockings, unbuttoned his trousers, and sent them to the floor.

Naked, Star lay back down beside Diane, ready to take her again in his arms.

"No, wait," she said, pressing a palm against his smooth bare chest. "Lie down, Star," she softly commanded.

Star nodded and stretched out on his back. Diane rose to her knees and sat back on her heels beside him. Admiring his lean male body, the ridged planes and hollows bathed in the flickering firelight, Diane smiled dreamily.

She said, "Let me love you, Star."

Star swallowed hard. "Yes, baby, sure."

Diane reached out to the brandy snifter Star had placed near the hearth. Purposely snaring and holding his gaze, she lowered all five fingers down into the widemouthed snifter, immersed their tips in the warm brandy, and slowly withdrew them.

Star's belly constricted and became concave when Diane wrapped her free hand around his throbbing, straining erection. Gripping him gently, she placed her brandy-moistened fingertips directly atop the jerking tip. Carefully she painted the velvet smooth flesh with the brandy until it glistened wetly.

Then Diane looked one last time into his wide dark eyes, slowly bent her head, and placed her open lips on him. Star groaned aloud, started to spasm, anxiously reached down, and snatched her up. In preorgasmic excitement and anticipation, he lifted her astride his tensed body, but when he would have melded his hard, straining flesh with her softness, Diane shook her head and stopped him.

"Allow me, my darling," she whispered.

Star's arms fell to his sides, and he held his breath. He watched intently as she took him gently in both hands, rose onto her knees, and lovingly guided him into her yielding flesh.

"Baby, baby," he rasped as Diane slowly, cautiously settled herself fully down onto him.

As Diane had been earlier, Star was thrilled by the sight. She seated astride him, her lovely naked body so soft and pale and perfect against the dark hardness of his own. His gaze lowered to where their bodies were joined, and he felt as if his heart would beat its way out of his heaving chest.

Diane smiled sexily at him, spread her hands on his chest, and began the rolling, erotic movements of her hips.

"Diane, Diane," he murmured in sweet agony.

Star's blue-black eyes slid closed in ecstasy as the woman atop him set the pace, led him, loved him, and brought them to an earth-shattering simultaneous orgasm. His body still a part of hers, Diane sagged down to his chest, her open lips sprinkling kisses on his sleek, perspiring shoulder.

"Star?"

"Yes?"

"Did I love you good?"

Star laughed and hugged her tight. "You loved me good, honey. You loved me real good."

They left their clothes where they'd dropped them. Naked, sated, and sleepy, they staggered down the hall to their room, took a quick bath together, and got tiredly, happily into bed. Their arms wrapped around each other, they fell almost immediately into a deep, dreamless sleep.

Diane was awakened hours later by the bright moonlight streaming through the wall of glass. She slipped silently from the bed. Naked, she wandered over to look out at the full white moon, which was on its morning descent.

Lifting a bare foot to rub her other ankle, she brushed against an item of clothing tossed over the back of a chair. Diane glanced down and saw the soft black leather vest which Star had worn into Virginia City that afternoon.

Smiling, she picked up the black vest. It belonged to the man she loved, so Diane rubbed the soft, supple leather against her cheek and deeply inhaled the unique male scent clinging to it. She blinked curiously when a single piece of folded paper tumbled out of the vest's inside pocket and fluttered to the carpet.

Diane bent and picked it up. She meant to put it back into the pocket, but in the day-bright moonlight she saw to whom the message was addressed. The blood instantly went icy in her veins.

Diane's cold hand shook as she lifted the paper closer and began to read.

September 28, 1895
Pawnee Bill
211 Post—Suite #4
San Francisco, California

The accompanying telegraphic money
order will bind our deal as concerns

your proposed takeover of *Colonel Buck*
Buchannan's Wild West Show.

Blinking in disbelief, Diane read and reread the succinct message. Finally lowering the yellow message paper, she carefully folded it and stuck it back inside the vest pocket. For a long moment Diane stood there trembling in the moonlight, too stunned to move, too astounded to think.

Then into her mind flashed the puzzling incident in Star's library yesterday afternoon. He was writing on a sheet of yellow message paper exactly like the one now folded inside his vest pocket. How strangely he had behaved, violently reacting when she surprised him.

Diane shuddered.

Now she knew the reason. She knew as well his reason for going into town yesterday. The fancy meal had only been his excuse for riding into Virginia City. The real reason had been to send a telegram to her grandfather's oldest enemy, Pawnee Bill!

Diane's first inclination was to shake Star awake, show him the damning telegram, and demand an immediate explanation.

She didn't do it.

No explanation was necessary. The painful truth was right there in the telegram.

Diane was heartsick.

These past four lovely days had meant nothing to Star. *She* meant nothing to Star. His declarations of undying love and marriage proposal were nothing more than a sham. It was all part of a carefully exercised plot. Star was in cahoots with Pawnee Bill. The man who had claimed to love her was only using her. She was nothing more than a pawn.

Revenge!

That was Star's real goal. His only goal. He had coolly planned out his method of revenge and was cleverly executing it. He was paying them back, meting out retribution.

His carefully planned punishment of her had been to make her fall so hopelessly in love with him she'd be miserably unhappy spending the rest of her life without him.

The old Colonel's punishment would be the loss of his beloved wild west show. And with it his will to live.

Her bare legs buckling under her, her stomach constricting in agony, Diane sagged onto her knees. Shivering violently, teeth chattering, she wondered how she could have been such a fool. How could she have let herself believe that this cruel, heartless creature actually cared for her?

Dear God, he hated her!

Hated her so much he had stripped her of all her pride. She had bared and opened not only her body to him but her soul as well. And he had taken everything from her. Everything!

Diane's face burned with shame as she recalled the things they had done just a few short hours ago on the library floor. Her heart squeezed painfully in her naked chest. Tears stung her eyes. She had been skillfully, callously betrayed!

Heartsick and furious, Diane rose from the floor. Holding on to her shaky composure with the obstinacy for which she was well known, she quickly, quietly began getting dressed. She swiftly pulled on the black twill Levi's and yellow pullover shirt, hastily making plans as she dressed.

She had to get away. Now. Before he awakened. In her mind's eye she saw the two long blue rail tickets resting in the silver bowl downstairs in the corridor. She would take one and tear the other up. Then she'd slip silently from the darkened house, hurry up the mountainside, and pray that Black Star was in his stable.

The stallion knew her now. She'd be able to keep him quiet while she bridled and saddled him. She would ride him into Virginia City and hold him there until the sun came up. Then she would turn him loose, send him home. By then it would be too late for Star to get into town before the train's 7:00 A.M. departure for San Francisco.

Slipping her bare feet into the worn leather shoes she'd been wearing on the night Star kidnapped her from the show train, Diane had everything worked out in her mind and was ready to leave.

She was confident that if she could make the westbound train before he caught up with her, Star would not pursue her. Why should he? His revenge was complete. He had no further use for her.

Diane quietly crossed to the open bedroom. She hurried anxiously out into the dim corridor, took a few steps, and stopped.

Her chest aching with pain, her eyes swimming with unshed tears, Diane turned and went back inside the big bedroom. She crossed directly to where the dark, sleeping Star lay sprawled out naked in the moonlight.

Clasping her hand over her mouth to stifle a choking sob, Diane took one last, long look at the lover in whose bed she would never again wake up.

Part Three

Part Three

Chapter 45

Time was running out.

➤➤➤➤ If a staggering sum of money could not be raised before the looming November 1 deadline, the impounded equipment of *Colonel Buck Buchannan's Wild West Show* would belong to the man who had bought off all the creditors and consolidated all the debts: Pawnee Bill.

Unless a miracle occurred, the show would not open come next spring.

Diane Buchannan didn't believe in miracles. She did believe in fighting to the bitter end to save the financially troubled show. She had not yet given up. She refused to admit defeat until any and all possible sources had been exhausted.

So on another dark, rainy October morning in a long string of dark, rainy October mornings, Diane awakened in the Oakland boardinghouse. Groggy with sleep, she painfully recalled the golden mornings she'd opened her eyes to the bright Nevada sunshine wrapped in Star's strong arms.

Diane drew the thin blanket up to her chin. She gritted her teeth against the never-ending ache of loneliness and despair. Four weeks had passed since she'd left him. Now her days, her nights, her weeks were filled with agonies of a kind she'd never expected to experience in this life.

Her first thought each morning was of Star.

Her last thought each night was of Star.

She loved him still. Loved him despite his cruel betrayal. Would love him until she drew her last breath. Loved him enough that she stubbornly refused to press kidnapping charges. Loved him so much she had kept his true identity hidden, refused to tell anyone. The secret would go with her to the grave, along with her hopeless, undying love.

Diane squeezed her eyes shut and shook her head on the thin pillow, vainly attempting to banish her dark, handsome tormenter. Reminding herself one more agonizing time that she meant absolutely nothing to Ben Star. If she had, he would have come for her.

Admittedly she had halfway expected him. Had foolishly hoped he would show up and tell her there'd been a terrible misunderstanding. He loved her, couldn't live without her.

But he hadn't come. Wasn't coming.

Ben Star had tricked her, used her, made her pay with a most humiliating form of revenge. He had made love to her. He had led her to believe that he was in love with her. He had gained her complete trust.

And coldly plotted each time she had apprised him of her grandfather's sad financial state. Again and again she had stupidly told Ben Star that it would break the Colonel's heart if he lost his beloved wild west show to Pawnee Bill. She had to stop thinking of her foolish mistakes. She had to stop thinking of Star. She was where she belonged—with those who loved her.

Diane thought back to the day she had safely arrived in San Francisco. Fondly she recalled the emotional reunion with the Colonel and Granny Buchannan. Their outpouring of love and happiness had been a balm for her aching heart.

And later that evening she'd visited Ancient Eyes at the hospital. His sick black eyes had brightened at the sight of her. She'd squeezed his hand, knowing instinctively that the secret they shared would remain forever between the two of them.

Diane's eyes opened fully on the gloom of her dismal boardinghouse room with its faded yellow and white wallpaper, cracked ceiling, and white iron bedstead.

She sat up and swung her legs to the floor. With the greatest effort of will she forced her mind back to the business at hand. And that business was saving the Colonel's show from Pawnee Bill's clutches!

Dressed and smiling bravely, Diane knocked on her grandparents' door an hour later. Ruth Buchannan let her in, inclining her white head toward the solitary figure slumped in a chair before the room's one window. The aging woman lifted her shoulders in a shrug.

Diane nodded, squared her own slender shoulders, and crossed to her grandfather. He had not yet dressed. He wore a nightshirt and a faded flannel robe. His long white hair had not been brushed. There was a look of deep sadness on his weathered face.

"What's with you, lazybones?" Diane touched his shoulder, leaned down, and pressed a kiss to his tousled white hair. "Time's wasting, Colonel. We need to get across the bay and see if we can—"

"What for?" The Colonel's lifeless blue eyes briefly lifted, touched her, then lowered once more to stare out the window. "I know when I'm beat."

Diane exchanged worried glances with her grandmother, swallowed hard, and went down on her knees beside her grandfather's chair. Pretending a confidence she didn't actually feel, she laid her hand on his wrinkling, age-spotted one and said, "Such nonsense. I refuse to listen to this kind of talk! There's still two days, for heaven's sake, and we've not yet been to every banking institution in San Francisco, so—"

She went on and on about how today their luck could change, told him he couldn't give up, they were not yet defeated. Diane talked and talked, being her most persuasive. But it didn't work. She couldn't reach him. She sighed and fell silent.

"No. It's no use, Diane," said the Colonel. "You're arguing with a Buchannan."

"That's nothing," she said. "So are you!"

The Colonel finally looked into her snapping violet eyes, laughed, and surrendered. "You got me there, child." He shook his white head, still smiling. "Give me half an hour?"

Diane shot to her feet.

"Exactly thirty minutes and no longer." She smiled warmly as the aged man rose from his chair. Pointing a finger in his face, she warned, "And no more defeatist talk, Colonel. I'm not wasting my precious time with a big, overgrown whiner."

She kissed his cheek and was gone.

The dogged pair spent the long, rainy day in San Francisco vainly attempting to find operating capital. They'd been turned down by Crocker and Leland Stanford and the Lick family and Senator George Hearst and all the other powerful moneyed empires and institutions in the city. Desperate, they now went from one small firm to the next.

Heads were shaken at their outlandish proposals. Doors were slammed in their hopeful faces. The purse strings of San Francisco's teeming financial district were pulled tightly shut against Colonel Buck Buchannan's outstretched hand.

At day's end Diane and the Colonel wearily climbed the hill to the

Embarcadero, boarded the ferry in the drizzling rain, and wordlessly crossed the bay back to Oakland.

Inside the dim corridor of the boardinghouse Diane touched her grandfather's shoulder, smiled, and said, "Same time tomorrow, Colonel? I thought we'd try—I—we—" Diane stopped speaking.

The Colonel had started to cry, the tears tumbling out of his pale blue eyes. He sagged against the wall and bowed his weary white head.

Diane had never seen her grandfather cry. She was at a complete loss. This couldn't be. This fearless, legendary old plainsman couldn't be weeping like a frightened child. This big white-haired man who had always been the one she'd turned to, the one all the others turned to as well. The one who unfailingly made everything all right for them all. He couldn't be helpless and afraid.

But he was.

Diane dropped her intrepid pose, put her arms around her grandfather's neck, and hugged him consolingly.

"I'm sorry, Colonel," she said softly, her heart aching for him, "I'm so sorry."

Nodding and patting her back, Colonel Buck Buchannan promptly composed himself. Diane stepped out of his arms as he reached for his handkerchief and dried his eyes.

As if nothing had happened, he said, "Ruth'll be worrying. Let's get on upstairs."

Diane stayed where she was. "You go on, Colonel. Think I'll take a walk before supper."

"It's still raining."

"I know."

He nodded understandingly, exhaled, and slowly climbed the stairs, his lame leg obviously aching from the constant dampness and from walking the streets of San Francisco.

Diane bit her lip, turned, and hurried back outdoors. She stood for a moment on the front steps, deciding in which direction she would walk.

It made no difference. She had no destination. She was fresh out of plans. Where she went was of absolutely no consequence. Either to herself or to anyone else.

Diane slowly descended the wooden steps and turned right. She strolled unhurriedly down the wet board sidewalk. She carried no umbrella; she didn't particularly care if she got wet. She turned her face up to the misting rain, feeling the needles of water sting her face. It felt strangely good.

Fifteen minutes later she was soaked to the skin, her heavy black hair plastered to her head, the long ends clinging damply to her neck and collar. She stood before the huge warehouse where, under lock and key, all the solid assets of *Colonel Buck Buchannan's Wild West Show* were housed.

Rain dripped from the eaves of the big wooden structure. Slow-moving droplets slipped down the rough plank siding. The building looked as if it were weeping.

Diane worked the combination lock and let herself inside the silent warehouse. Blinking in the darkness, she took down a kerosene lantern from a peg beside the door, lit it, and pulled the door closed behind her.

Holding the lantern high, she made her way through the stored props and equipment. Stacks of movable wooden seats. A large, folded tent. Coils of rope, rotting from age. The Colonel's many trophies: the glass-encased medals, dozens of rifles and guns and saddles.

One saddle was missing.

The silver-embossed saddle presented to the Colonel by the queen of England had been sold weeks ago along with other sentimental valuables to pay the boardinghouse bill.

Diane moved on, walking between a mirrored animal coach and the big bell wagon. The chuck wagon was there. The fancy buggy in which Texas Kate rode into the arena. The tribal costumes of the troupe Indians.

Diane abruptly stopped.

On the floor directly in front of her, its colors faded by the sun, lay a large poster advertising the show. Diane reached for it, lifted it up into the lamplight.

Splashed atop the colored poster in bold black letters: "Beauty and the Beast." Beneath the lettering an artist's drawing depicting a naked savage with flowing black hair and wild dark eyes straining against imprisoning chains.

Diane looked pained at the memory. The lamp wavered in her hand. Shadows rippled over the faded poster, giving the eerie appearance of the chained savage moving. Diane's chin began to quiver. Her eyes smarted. Heart pounding painfully, she stared at the likeness of the chained savage.

Her tears spilled over and ran down her cheeks as she read the bold black lettering across the bottom of the poster.

"THE REDMAN OF THE ROCKIES."

Chapter 46

The Redman of the Rockies was not naked. His silver-streaked raven hair was not long and flowing. His navy eyes were not wild. He was not physically restrained in chains.

Benjamin Star was dressed in well-cut dark trousers, a freshly laundered white shirt, and a black vest of soft, supple leather. His hair was shiny clean, neatly trimmed, and carefully brushed. His eyes were dark and brooding.

But he was chained.

In chains he could not cast off no matter how forcefully he strained against them. Chains no silver key could magically unlock. Chains that would never rust or weaken with the passing of the years.

Chains of love.

Brooding alone in his book-filled library, Star sat in his high-backed swivel chair. The chair was turned away from the mahogany desk and tipped back. Star's lean brown hands were folded in his lap. His long legs stretched out in front of him, ankles crossed.

It had begun to snow in the High Sierra, the first gentle flakes tapping on the panes of the tall French doors, then slowly melting to streak down the glass like softly falling tears. The sky was bleak and heavy. A cold autumn wind sighed sadly through the pines.

A deep loneliness was upon Star.

His house was achingly empty. Had been empty since the morning he'd awakened to find the only woman he ever loved was gone. This same mansion which had been so warm and sunny while she was in it was now dark and cold. And empty. Would be forever cold and dark and empty without the raven-haired beauty who had eaten at his table, danced in his library, slept in his bed.

Star exhaled slowly.

And as he had done one thousand times, he relived that last day, that last night, searching for clues he might have missed before. Hoping against hope he'd find some reason, some explanation, other than what he knew in his heart to be the simple, painful truth.

Thinking back, Star could recall nothing she did or said that gave her away. She'd been sweet and loving when he'd kissed her good-bye and rode into Virginia City. Mentally he retraced his steps in town. He'd gone first to the telegraph office to send the wire.

Star reached inside his vest pocket, the same one he'd worn that day. The yellow message paper was still there. He withdrew it, unfolded the pages, and reread the wire he'd sent:

September 28, 1895
Pawnee Bill
211 Post—Suite #4
San Francisco, California

The accompanying telegraphic money
order will bind our deal as concerns
your proposed takeover of *Colonel Buck
Buchannan's Wild West Show.*

Star slid the first page behind the second and read on, his navy eyes narrowing thoughtfully.

page 2
Contracts will be executed at
my San Francisco office. With your
signature on said contracts, your
position is taken out—with agreed
profit—and Stardust Corporation
becomes *Buchannan's Wild West Show*'s sole creditor. STOP

Star stared at the message. Even if Diane had found and read it—and she hadn't—she couldn't have misunderstood its meaning. He was saving the old Colonel's show for him. Buying up all the debt Pawnee Bill had consolidated. Taking Pawnee Bill out of it. Pumping his own money into the troubled show, bailing it out of hock for the Colonel.

Star shrugged, wadded the yellow forms into a ball, and tossed it over his shoulder. What the hell. A deal was a deal. He'd honor the contract —let the old man keep his show—despite Miss Diane Buchannan.

Star again reached inside his vest pocket and brought out a small black velvet box. He popped it open and stared at the perfect blue-white round-cut diamond engagement ring. The diamond looked as dark and lifeless as he felt. There was no light for it to reflect off in the dim, shadowy library.

The hot September day he'd bought the ring for Diane he'd stood out on the sidewalk gazing foolishly at it, grinning. The diamond had sparkled and glittered in the sunlight, its facets almost blinding him with their brilliance. Excited, he'd planned the moment he would give it to her, deciding he'd wait until they were in San Francisco and he'd asked her grandfather for permission to marry her.

Star clenched his even white teeth, clamped the velvet box shut, and shoved it back into his vest pocket. Why torture himself further? It was over and done with. He'd gone in search of her the minute he'd awakened to find her missing. Could it have been made any plainer? He'd stood there ashen-faced as the railroad clerk calmly said, "Sure, the pretty young black-haired woman. She took the seven A.M. train to San Francisco."

A bitter gust of wind from the north rattled the panes of ice-crusted glass in the French doors before him. The chill knifed right through his aching heart. Star leaned forward and rested his elbows on his knees. He stared at the carpet between his shoes.

He shot to his feet. He'd behaved like the lovesick fool long enough. Time to get on with the business at hand. He had a trip to make. An appointment to keep.

Star left the library, strode hurriedly down the long corridor and into his bedroom. He headed straight for his dressing room, reached up to take a brown leather suitcase from an overhead shelf. When he swung the case down, he accidentally snagged a hanging garment on one of the case's silver locks.

A shimmering evening gown rustled to the floor at his feet. A gown whose color reminded him irresistibly of a pair of violet eyes whose power over him he had wished to deny. Star dropped the luggage, crouched down on his heels, and picked up the fallen gown.

Damn her, she was everywhere he turned!

Gently fingering the gown's violet bodice, Star shook his head. To find just the right gown, he'd called on an old lover. The fiery red-haired Rita had been clearly disappointed when he told her he'd fallen in love, planned to marry.

But she'd been one hell of a good sport when he asked where he could purchase an exquisite evening gown for his bride-to-be.

"You won't find what you're looking for in Virginia City," Rita told him. "But you're in luck. I bought dozens of fabulous gowns on my last Paris trip, most of which I've never worn." When he immediately chose the violet taffeta to match Diane's eyes, Rita had tossed her flaming hair and said, "Yes, of course. I picked this gown with you in mind." She laughed and added, "Not exactly the way I'd planned on showing it to you."

Star rose to his feet, lifted the rustling violet gown up to his face, and inhaled deeply. His chest tightened. He opened his hands, let the gown fall to his feet, and kicked it aside.

Diane Buchannan was just what he'd known her to be from the beginning. A spoiled beauty too easily bored. A delectable creature who collected and discarded hearts for the sake of amusement. Another in the long line of pale beauties seeking a forbidden thrill for a short time, then running back to safety when the newness wore off.

The hell with her.

Star jerked up the brown leather suitcase and started packing. He had a train to catch.

Time had run out.

Tomorrow was the first of November. At the stroke of midnight the man who had been buying up all the Colonel's debt would foreclose. Own it all, lock, stock, and barrel.

The hated Pawnee Bill.

Pacing restlessly in her dim boardinghouse room, Diane had never spent a more miserable day in her life. She'd awakened to another bleak, cheerless morning. The early edition of the *San Francisco Chronicle* had been left under her door as usual.

She had yanked it up, just as always, hoping to read something that might spark an idea, bring to mind a possible money source she'd not yet tried. Instead she'd seen—in the society column—an item that added to her sense of despair: ". . . handsome Nevada mining magnate Benjamin Star was spotted quietly checking into the Palace Hotel last evening. . . ."

Dropping the newspaper as if it were hot, trembling with emotion, Diane had told herself she wouldn't think about it. She had enough on her mind. She knew exactly what he was doing in the city! He'd come to join his partner in crime, Pawnee Bill!

Just minutes after that blow the Colonel, acting mysterious, had come to tell her he was going into San Francisco alone. And when she'd announced she was going with him, he refused, put his foot down.

So she'd been left to worry and wonder and walk the floor all day.

Diane was still worrying and wondering and walking the floor when at long last—shortly before four o'clock in the afternoon—the Colonel rapped loudly on her door.

She flew across the room, her questioning eyes on him, her heart in her throat. He sauntered into the room with barely a limp, his shoulders thrown back. His blue eyes held a twinkle that had been missing for weeks. He looked very much like the cat who had just swallowed the canary.

Something had happened, she could tell by his self-satisfied expression. Did she dare hope? Had the deadline been extended? Expectantly she waited for him to speak.

The Colonel unhurriedly crossed the dreary room, lowered himself down into the one chair by the window. Diane anxiously followed.

"Well?" she prompted, hands on hips.

"I've a bit of news," he finally said, and then paused dramatically. Diane, nodding eagerly, was tempted to shake him!

"Yes, go on, go on," she said, tensed, tingling from head to toe.

"Now don't rush me, Diane."

"Nobody's rushing you!" She glared down at him. Still he said nothing. She erupted irritably. "Spit it out, will you, Colonel?"

Unruffled, he gave her a cherubic grin, reached inside his coat pocket, withdrew his spectacles, and carefully put them on, making a big show of adjusting the left earpiece. Then, with great flourish, he withdrew from the coat pocket a folded thick legal-looking document.

He chuckled happily while Diane's violet eyes darkened to purple, snapping with interest and annoyance. Finally he told his impatient granddaughter exactly what had happened in San Francisco.

The Colonel's attorney had been contacted by the attorney of a "show business angel" who desired anonymity. The unnamed patron had bought up all the show's outstanding debts from Pawnee Bill. Had opened a line of credit at the Union Pacific Bank. Had agreed to fund the purchase of needed new rolling stock. The angel had saved the show in the eleventh hour!

Delighted yet skeptical, Diane grilled her grandfather, cross-examining him like a prosecuting attorney. Why had this angel done such a thing? What were his motives? What was the catch? How much of the show did the Colonel have to give away in return for the cash? What percentage? Was he certain Pawnee Bill was not behind the whole scheme? Sure it wasn't some shady deal that in actuality was a ruse to steal the show?

Diane badgered him, but the Colonel had an answer for every question. Save one. He had given up nothing. The show remained solely his. He had only to meet the terms of the contract. He had agreed to pay back the loan—at a fair interest rate—but not until the show was in the black. Quite honestly he was as puzzled as she at this surprising turn of events. The identity of their benefactor was a complete mystery.

"Who knows the reason, Diane?" said the Colonel. "Maybe I actually have a guardian angel and he's—"

"It's time to go, you two." Ruth Buchannan stood in the doorway, adjusting her hat. "We're going to be late if we don't hurry."

"Coming, dear," said the beaming Colonel. He folded the contract, slipped it back inside his breast pocket, patted it happily, and crossed to his wife.

As she followed, Diane's high brow was slightly puckered. "This is all too much. I just can't see why . . . the contracts, Colonel? Whose name is on the contracts?"

"Just the attorney, Diane," he said over his shoulder, "and the title of a corporation."

"What's the corporation called?"

"Stardust."

Chapter 47

"Dearly beloved, we are gathered together in the sight of God to unite this man and this woman in the state of holy matrimony. . . ."

Diane's smile was genuine as she watched the happy pair becoming man and wife. Texas Kate looked amazingly youthful and pretty in a pale peach wedding dress with her brownish gray hair curled tightly around her face and a bridal bouquet of pale purple hothouse orchids clutched in her hands.

Shorty was the shy, nervous bridegroom. Hair slicked back, face shiny clean, he wore a dark western-cut suit, stiff-collared white shirt, and bow tie. His hands were folded before him, and his left leg shook so badly his low-riding trousers rippled visibly.

Diane's fond gaze shifted to the granite-faced best man. Ancient Eyes wore a solemn expression, as befitted the occasion. Wedding ring gripped tightly in his arthritic hand, the aged Ute chieftain appeared to be almost his old powerful self again. Diane was relieved.

He had been so thin and haggard the first time she'd visited him in the Oakland hospital. When she'd walked into his room ahead of the Colonel, she'd read in his black eyes that he had never told what had happened. She'd quickly put her finger perpendicular to her lips and silently signaled "shhh." He blinked in relieved acknowledgment.

". . . And do you, William, take Katherine, to be your lawful wedded wife?"

"I do," Shorty said. His scrubbed-clean face turned beet red, but his voice was firm and clear.

"I now pronounce you man and wife. You may kiss the bride."

Diane, along with all the other well-wishers, threw rice as the laughing pair rushed down the church steps into the foggy afternoon. Her hand raised, she was suddenly struck with a bolt out of the blue.

Stardust.

The Colonel had said the Stardust Corporation had bailed them out! In a flash of vivid remembrance she recalled old Golden Star telling of the mother who'd left her behind when she was a child. Stardust! Golden Star's mother was named Stardust.

Diane's rice-filled hand lowered as her heart began to pound. Was it possible? Had she totally misjudged Star? Had she made the biggest mistake of her life? Had she wrongly accused him of seeking revenge when all he'd ever meant to do was help?

More of Golden Star's words came to her. Clearly, as if the old Indian woman were standing beside her: "If Starkeeper knew someone was sick or in trouble, he would go out and help. He had that in his blood."

"Diane! Diane!" Pulled back to the present, she looked up to see the smiling bride calling her name. "Diane, you ready?" Kate lifted her bridal bouquet. "Here goes. Catch!"

Texas Kate tossed the bouquet directly to Diane. Rice spilled from Diane's hand as she automatically reached up and caught the orchid bouquet. Everyone applauded and whistled.

Texas Kate shouted, "You're all invited to the reception over at the boardinghouse. Let's go cut that wedding cake!"

The eager crowd streamed down the wooden sidewalk behind the bride and groom. Diane anxiously searched out her grandparents.

"There's someplace I have to go, something I have to do," she told them quickly. "Make my apologies to Kate and Shorty."

She gave them no time to reply. The aging pair looked at each other as their independent granddaughter turned and sprinted away, racing toward the waterfront, the bridal bouquet clutched tightly in her hand.

Fog hung like limp gauze over the bare-limbed trees as Diane ran anxiously down to the docks. She made it just as the ferry was starting to back away. Out of breath, heart racing, she lifted her long skirts and leaped onto the moving deck as the ferry's whistle blew a deafening warning.

There were almost no passengers. A few people were scattered around, collars turned up against the chill wind. Diane was oblivious of the cold and fog and damp. She rushed eagerly forward to stand alone up at the bow. Clutching the railing with one hand, the bridal bouquet with the other, she threw back her head and laughed gaily as the steam-driven ferry plowed through the murky waters of the bay.

The winds tossed loose locks of her hair about her head and pressed her clothes against her body. Sprays of salt water stung her face.

Diane didn't care.

Her heart sang with hope. She braced her feet slightly apart and rode the up and down waves of the choppy bay, her shining violet eyes fixed on the lighted city looming ahead through the fog. There in the middle of that big, blazing city was Starkeeper, and she . . .

"I say there, old sport, mind if I join you?" Diane's head turned. A fog-shrouded figure, obviously in his cups, was weaving unsteadily toward her. He wore a silk top hat, a billowing black opera cape, and a lop-sided smile. Managing to maneuver up to the bow's rail, he gripped it and asked, "Do you feel the floor moving? Could it be one of those fearsome quakes one reads about?"

Diane smiled at the drunken Englishman. "No. We're on a ferryboat. That's the turbines. We're moving."

"Ah! Thank goodness," he said, nodding, then asked, "And where, if I may ask, are we bound?"

"San Francisco." Diane chuckled as his look of puzzlement changed to one of delight.

"Splendid. A dynamic city. By Jove, if I'm not mistaken, I know some chaps there. Might just pop in on them." Diane continued to smile. "And you, my dear?" He bobbed his hatted head at the bridal bouquet she held. "Getting married?"

"I hope so," she readily admitted. "I'm not sure."

"Shall we find out?"

"Yes."

"Your young man is in San Francisco?"

"He is."

"Throw the bridal bouquet into the bay. If it floats in toward the Embarcadero, you will be married. If it is carried back to Oakland . . ."

Diane tossed the bouquet into the dark, swirling waters of the bay. She watched with rising despair as the sodden bouquet, riding the ferry's wake, was carried back toward the port of Oakland. The drunken Englishman saw what was happening. He lifted his hands and covered his eyes.

Leaning anxiously over the rail, Diane squinted. The small bouquet was barely visible through the dense fog. Suddenly the trailing winds freshened, and the bridal bouquet was borne steadily in toward the San Francisco docks.

"You can look now!" Diane happily told her companion.

The Englishman's hands came down. He smiled and said in clipped Oxford tones, "I say then, my dear, may I be the first to kiss the bonny bride?"

At the Palace Hotel Diane hurriedly crossed the opulent atrium lobby to the long marble counter. A uniformed employee looked up and smiled.

"Benjamin Star," she casually said, favoring him with a winning smile. "Ben's expecting me. In his usual suite, I presume."

"Yes, miss. Just as always. Corner suite eight-one-four."

In the elevator Diane nervously rehearsed all the things she would say to Star. She stepped into the silent eighth-floor corridor and saw a white-jacketed waiter carrying a covered silver tray. The waiter stopped before the door of suite 814.

"Wait!" Diane called, hurried forward, smiled, and took the tray from the surprised waiter. "I'll take that. I'm going inside."

"But—but—" He reached out for the tray.

"No bother, really." She withheld it. "Thank you, and good evening."

He frowned, shook his head, and walked away.

Releasing a breath, Diane balanced the tray on one spread hand and knocked firmly on the door.

"It's open," came that low, familiar voice from inside, and Diane felt her knees turn to water.

She eased open the tall white door and stepped into the large, lavish suite.

"Just put it there on the table."

Those same low, flat tones, and Diane, nodding foolishly, looked frantically about, searching for the voice's owner. Her breath caught in her throat when at last she caught sight of him. Outdoors on the balcony.

Carefully she placed the tray on a marble-topped table, expecting Star to turn any second and see her. She waited, staring at him, unable to take her eyes off him.

He turned his head slightly and was silhouetted for a moment against the rust-orange glow of the city lights.

"Star." Her lips formed his name, but no sound came.

Suddenly, now that she was in the room with him, all the things she had thought of to say disappeared from her mind.

He was so magnetically attractive, so strikingly handsome standing there with the wind lifting locks of his blue-black hair and billowing his soft silk shirt out from his back. There was still that fierce masculinity about him, and Diane could hardly keep from running, flinging herself into his arms.

"Star." She audibly spoke his name and saw the wide shoulders immediately tense beneath the white silken shirt, the dark head lift.

Slowly he turned to look at her.

An unguarded smile, a brief flicker of recognition in his dark navy eyes, then that forbidding mask fell into place. Animal appeal and cold fury radiated from him. He said nothing. He turned his back on her.

With her pulse pounding in her throat and temples, Diane crossed the spacious sitting room. She stepped out onto the broad balcony. She stood directly behind Star, less than six feet away.

Star felt her presence, knew she was there. He clamped his teeth tightly together, purposely locked his weakened knees, and gripped the balcony railing for support. He vainly wished that his heart would not beat so feverishly. Wished his palms would not perspire. Wished his legs would not experience this awful pins-and-needles sensation.

He wished she would go away.

Diane moved closer.

She gently eased her arms around him, locked her hands in front of him, and laid her cheek on his back. She felt the immediate tensing of his muscles, heard his sharp intake of air.

"If you're ever in my arms again," she said softly, carefully repeating the words he'd once spoken to her, "just one word will do it. The word is *no*. *No.* That's all you have to say. *No.* If you mean it, say it. *No.* And I will stop."

Long seconds passed.

Slowly Star turned in her arms. His dark, tortured eyes met hers. His lean brown hands visibly shook as they lifted to tenderly cup her upturned face. A boyish smile finally lifted the corners of his cruelly sensual mouth.

"Yes," he said, his low voice rough with emotion. "The word is yes. Yes, Diane, my darling. Yes."